March 24, 2016

Pat,
　May this book be a blessing to you as you read and study His word.
　　　　Pastor Scott Payne
　　　　Hebrews 4:12

The Bible 365

Daily Discovering God's Word For Your Life

Dr. Scott Payne

WestBow
Press®
A DIVISION OF THOMAS NELSON
& ZONDERVAN

Copyright © 2016 Dr. Scott Payne.

All rights reserved. No part of this book may be used or reproduced by any means, graphic, electronic, or mechanical, including photocopying, recording, taping or by any information storage retrieval system without the written permission of the author except in the case of brief quotations embodied in critical articles and reviews.

WestBow Press books may be ordered through booksellers or by contacting:

WestBow Press
A Division of Thomas Nelson & Zondervan
1663 Liberty Drive
Bloomington, IN 47403
www.westbowpress.com
1 (866) 928-1240

Because of the dynamic nature of the Internet, any web addresses or links contained in this book may have changed since publication and may no longer be valid. The views expressed in this work are solely those of the author and do not necessarily reflect the views of the publisher, and the publisher hereby disclaims any responsibility for them.

Any people depicted in stock imagery provided by Thinkstock are models, and such images are being used for illustrative purposes only. Certain stock imagery © Thinkstock.

ISBN: 978-1-5127-2942-9 (sc)
ISBN: 978-1-5127-2943-6 (hc)
ISBN: 978-1-5127-2941-2 (e)

Library of Congress Control Number: 2016901886

Print information available on the last page.

WestBow Press rev. date: 02/25/2016

FOREWORD

By Erik Ramsey, Elder and Former Youth Pastor at The Church at Schilling Farms

One of the most challenging things I have ever attempted is to read the Bible in its entirety … consistently and daily. Even during my time as a Staff member and now as an Elder, it has always been extremely difficult to discipline myself to read through the Bible. Time after time I would begin the task determined to complete it. I would schedule the time, the place, prepare a comfortable environment … I even shared with my friends what I was attempting and encouraged them to follow suit. My challenge always seemed doable, but something always seemed to get in the way of me accomplishing my goal. I kept falling into Satan's trap. The last thing Satan wants is for us to read God's Word … for us to allow the Spirit of God to speak to us from the pages of Holy Scripture.

Over the past several years I have become accustomed to being challenged regularly by Pastor Scott. At the end of 2013, he challenged our Church to read through the Bible together, in chronological order, in one year, beginning on January 1, 2014. This time it was different for me. I didn't look at it as a task … just happy to have about 100 people committed to read with me. On day 1, I discovered that Pastor Scott was going to guide us through each day with his perspective on our daily passage of Scripture. Each day he gave us an application of the Scripture in the form of a devotional that also offered thoughts to reflect on and consider in our hearts, and challenges to go deeper with God. That's when I realized that although I was glad so many others were reading with Pastor Scott and me, this time my reading the Bible was truly not a task; it was an opportunity for me to get to know God more. *The Bible 365* was created by God in Pastor Scott's heart, and I was invited, not to accomplish a difficult task, but to feast on God's Word, with the encouragement of a daily devotional that strengthened my spirit, illuminating the Scripture I had read, and using it in my life to help me see God in every aspect of my life.

I glean so much from reading God's Word. Often when I read Scripture I am somehow able to connect the passage to an event or an issue in my life. It's just how I think, or how God created me, but it doesn't come easy with all of the passages of the Bible. I am often left holding the Bible asking, "God what does this have to do with me?" God answers that question, for me and for you, through Pastor Scott's *The Bible 365*. Pastor's devotional correlates to a chronological reading plan of the Bible (included in his book), so we are able to see the historical unfolding of God's Word to His people, along with a thought and prayer provoking devotional guide, which you will be able to use for personal application, as you consider the context, the Truth being conveyed, the Pastor's perspective, the reflections, the keywords, the observations, the questions and, of course, the challenges that God sets in front of us and Holy Spirit makes personal to each of us. Pastor takes the chronological readings of the Bible and helps us see exactly HOW and WHAT it has to do with us.

God reveals so much, corporately and individually, as you read the Scripture each day and follow it up with a short devotion that helps in the understanding of how it might apply to you. One of my favorite Scripture / Devotional combinations in *The Bible 365* is on Day 54. In the book of Numbers Chapter 1 God had instructed Moses to take the first census of the nation of Israel, and gave him the specific way to accomplish the task. Throughout the reading I continually thought that this passage had no personal application for me. I am not going to give it all away, but in 5 short sentences Pastor Scott was able to connect me to what had seemed irrelevant to my life. Part of what I learned from that reading is that I am a part of God's inventory! I have a place of service! And ... I Count! It is important to know that you mean something! This was a typical moment in my *The Bible 365* experience.

Another thing that I absolutely love about Pastor's *The Bible 365* is that it is "to the point" ... No fluff ... Straight to the meaning, the definition and reflection of the Scripture reading for the day. *The Bible 365* never led me; the Bible did that through the Holy Spirit. The devotional got right to the point and challenged me to reflect and think about what I had read. I have heard Pastor Scott say time and time again, "Understand Scripture in light of Scripture." Let the Scripture do the leading. If you want the most out of God's Word, let the Holy Spirit guide you through the meaning of the Scripture. Let *The Bible 365* take your reading to the next level. By reading the Bible in chronological order and by looking to the Holy Spirit for understanding, and considering the reflections and calls to action in *The Bible 365*, you will soon begin to see the connectedness and the continuity of the Bible from chapter to chapter, book to book, and the Old Testament to the New Testament. Then you will be interpreting "Scripture in light of Scripture" and not in light of your life, and wants and desires. You will see Jesus throughout the Bible. You will be excited about reading the Bible and applying the Scripture to yourself, in accordance with God's specific plan for your life.

Now that I have successfully read the entire Bible in chronological order along with Pastor Scott's daily devotions, I can truthfully tell you that nothing gets in the way of my Bible reading time anymore! That is part of God's plan for me and for you. Erik – One; Satan – Zero!

I Challenge You To:
➢ Read the Bible in One Year – Start tomorrow!
➢ Read it Chronologically (Daily Reading Plan included in this book)
➢ Use *The Bible 365* to help you

INTRODUCTION

I didn't intend to write a book. I only meant to lead interested members of my Church and some of their friends into a kind of panoramic Bible Study that would help them understand the completeness and connectedness of the Bible from Genesis to Revelation. I grew up with the mindset that, although, the Old Testament and the New Testament of the Bible were often bound together in one book, they were really separate writings that were able to stand alone. The Old Testament was the history of God and Man before Christ, and the New Testament was like the sequel that told the story of the birth of Christ and the new relationship God built with Man through Christ.

Until the late 1990's, I had never clearly understood that Jesus is present throughout the Old Testament; nor did anyone show me the vital role of the Holy Spirit throughout the entire Bible. I had been leading my Church, according to what other men taught me to do. Strict denominational lines had been drawn, and I wasn't supposed to move outside of them. I finally began to see that to truly understand the depth of God's love and His ongoing compassionate patience with humanity, I had to get to know God from before day one of creation through the present and to the future. It has been an amazing journey discovering that only the Holy Spirit can teach and write on our hearts what man tries to paraphrase and put in a box. I have finally begun to grasp the concept, in a personal and intimate way, that God has always been God and always will be God the Father, God the Son and God the Holy Spirit. I knew the Bible says that God is the same yesterday, today and tomorrow, but for so many years that was something I had been taught by men to teach to others. Recognizing that reading the entire Bible in chronological order, according to the reading plan in this book, would fill in the gaps of knowledge and understanding, which had become increasingly glaring, as I had begun to know the Holy Spirit on a deeper, more personal level and had begun to depend on Him to show me the Truth about the relationship between God and His human creation, I began to sense that God wanted to show me awesome and wonderful things. Embarking on this Spiritual trip from the creation through the end of the age, I began seeing Jesus preparing to come to the earth to "seek and to save that which was lost" (Luke 19:10). When I have read the Bible book by book or one Old Testament book, then one New Testament book, or any other deconstructed reading of God's Word, I could not fully see the beauty and the strength of God's desire to be "our God" and for us to be "His people."

I invited the members of our Church to join me on this journey of discovering and knowing God in a more complete way. On January 1, 2014 about 100 members of our Church and a few of their friends opened their email to find the chronological reading plan, with the passage of Scripture for the first day noted, along with a devotional I had written to help them understand the context of the passage, and to consider, meditate on, and take something personal from the Scripture reading for the day, that could be specifically applied to their lives and grow the level of intimacy they could have with God. Day by day for 365 days, God gave me a word, a thought to reflect on from the reading for that day, and a challenge to consider and apply to my life. I passed this on daily to those who were reading with me. At the end of the year I realized that I had written a book! I am certain God intends this book to be used as a companion, a guide and a help to anyone interested in knowing God more, whether they are just beginning to wonder about God or have been Christians for many years. God Himself has revealed to us Who He is on every page of the Bible, from Genesis to Revelation.

My prayer for you is that, as you begin your journey through the Bible, you will become excited about your growing relationship with God and will stick with your decision to read through the Bible chronologically with this companion devotional book, whether it takes one year, six months or two years. I pray, also, that the words of Jesus, in John 16, will come alive and be made personal for you, as God reveals Himself to you and draws you closer to Himself, and that the Holy Spirit would give understanding of the Scriptures that you have never had before.

"When the Spirit of truth comes, He will guide you into all the truth, for He will not speak on His own authority, but whatever He hears He will speak, and He will declare to you the things that are to come. He will glorify Me, for He will take what is mine and declare it to you. All that the Father has is mine; therefore I said that He will take what is mine and declare it to you." (John 16:13-15)

The Bible 365: Read It! Believe It! Live It! Share It!

ACKNOWLEDGMENTS

To Holy Spirit for giving me understanding!
To my loving wife, Billie, who took this journey with me!
To my family for supporting my life's call!
To my Church and friends that followed the daily reading plan!

May God bless The Word in each of our lives!

365 Daily Chronological Bible Reading Plan

DAY
1 Gen.1-3
2 Gen. 4-7
3 Gen. 8-11
4 Job 1-5
5 Job 6-9
6 Job 10-13
7 Job 14-16
8 Job 17-20
9 Job 21-23
10 Job 24-28
11 Job 29-31
12 Job 32-34
13 Job 35-37
14 Job 38-39
15 Job 40-42
16 Gen. 12-15
17 Gen. 16-18
18 Gen. 19-21
19 Gen. 22-24
20 Gen. 25-26
21 Gen. 27-29
22 Gen. 30-31
23 Gen. 32-34
24 Gen. 35-37
25 Gen. 38-40
26 Gen. 41-42
27 Gen. 43-45

DAY
28 Gen. 46-47
29 Gen. 48-50
30 Exodus 1-3
31 Exodus 4-6
32 Exodus 7-9
33 Exodus 10-12
34 Exodus 13-15
35 Exodus 16-18
36 Exodus 19-21
37 Exodus 22-24
38 Exodus 25-27
39 Exodus 28-29
40 Exodus 30-32
41 Exodus 33-35
42 Exodus 36-38
43 Exodus 39-40
44 Leviticus 1-4
45 Leviticus 5-7
46 Leviticus 8-10
47 Leviticus 11-13
48 Leviticus 14-15
49 Leviticus 16-18
50 Leviticus 19-21
51 Leviticus 22-23
52 Leviticus 24-25
53 Leviticus 26-27
54 Numbers 1-2

DAY
55 Numbers 3-4
56 Numbers 5-6
57 Numbers 7
58 Numbers 8-10
59 Numbers 11-13
60 Numbers 14-15; Ps. 90
61 Numbers 16-17
62 Numbers 18-20
63 Numbers 21-22
64 Numbers 23-25
65 Numbers 26-27
66 Numbers 28-30
67 Numbers 31-32
68 Numbers 33-34
69 Numbers 35-36
70 Deut. 1-2
71 Deut. 3-4
72 Deut. 5-7
73 Deut. 8-10
74 Deut. 11-13
75 Deut. 14-16
76 Deut. 17-20
77 Deut. 21-23
78 Deut. 24-27
79 Deut. 28-29
80 Deut. 30-31
81 Deut. 32-34; Ps.91
82 Joshua 1-4
83 Joshua 5-8
84 Joshua 9-11
85 Joshua 12-15
86 Joshua 16-18
87 Joshua 19-21
88 Joshua 22-24
89 Judges 1-2
90 Judges 3-5
91 Judges 6-7
92 Judges 8-9
93 Judges 10-12

DAY
94 Judges 13-15
95 Judges 16-18
96 Judges 19-21
97 Ruth
98 1 Samuel 1-3
99 1 Samuel 4-8
100 1 Samuel 9-12
101 1 Samuel 13-14
102 1 Samuel 15-17
103 1 Samuel 18-20; Ps.11, 59
104 1 Samuel 21-24
105 Ps. 7, 27, 31, 34, 52
106 Ps. 56, 120, 140-142
107 1 Samuel 25-27
108 Ps. 17, 35, 54, 63
109 1 Samuel 28-31, Ps. 18
110 Ps. 121, 123-125, 128-130
111 2 Samuel 1-4
112 Ps. 6, 8-10, 14, 16, 19, 21
113 1 Chron. 1-2
114 Ps. 43-45, 49, 84-85, 87
115 1 Chron. 3-5
116 Ps. 73, 77-78
117 1 Chron. 6
118 Ps. 81, 88, 92-93
119 1 Chron. 7-10
120 Ps. 102-104
121 2 Sam.5; 1 Chron.11-12
122 Psalm 133
123 Psalm 106-107
124 1 Chron. 13-16
125 Ps. 1-2, 15, 22-24, 47, 68
126 Ps. 89, 96, 100-101, 105, 132
127 2 Sam. 6-7; 1 Chron. 17
128 Ps. 25, 29, 33, 36, 39
129 2 Sam. 8-9; 1 Chron. 18
130 Ps. 50, 53, 60, 75
131 2 Sam. 10; 1 Chron.19; Ps. 20
132 Psalm 65-67, 69-70

DAY
133 2 Sam. 11-12; 1 Chron. 20
134 Psalm 32, 51, 86, 122
135 2 Samuel 13-15
136 Ps. 3-4, 12-13, 28, 55
137 2 Samuel 16-18
138 Psalm 26, 40, 58, 61-62, 64
139 2 Samuel 19-21
140 Psalm 5, 38, 41-42
141 2 Sam. 22-23; Ps. 57
142 Psalm 95, 97-99
143 2 Sam. 24; 1 Chron. 21-22; Ps. 30
144 Psalm 108-110
145 1 Chron. 23-25
146 Ps. 131, 138-139, 143-145
147 1 Chron. 26-29; Ps. 127
148 Psalm 111-118
149 1 Kings 1-2; Ps. 37,71, 94
150 Psalm 119
151 1 Kings 3-4
152 2 Chron. 1; Ps. 72
153 Song of Solomon
154 Proverbs 1-3
155 Proverbs 4-6
156 Proverbs 7-9
157 Proverbs 10-12
158 Proverbs 13-15
159 Proverbs 16-18
160 Proverbs 19-21
161 Proverbs 22-24
162 1 Kings 5-6; 2 Chron. 2-3
163 1 Kings 7; 2 Chron. 4
164 1 Kings 8; 2 Chron. 5
165 2 Chron. 6-7; Ps. 136
166 Psalm 134, 146-150
167 1 Kings 9; 2 Chron. 8
168 Proverbs 25-26
169 Proverbs 27-29
170 Ecclesiastes 1-6
171 Ecclesiastes 7-12

DAY
172 1 Kings10-11; 2 Chron. 9
173 Proverbs 30-31
174 1 Kings 12-14
175 2 Chron. 10-12
176 1 Kings 15; 2 Chron. 13-16
177 1 Kings 16; 2 Chron. 17
178 1 Kings 17-19
179 1 Kings 20-21
180 1 Kings 22; 2 Chron.18
181 2 Chron. 19-23
182 Obadiah; Ps. 82-83
183 2 Kings 1-4
184 2 Kings 5-8
185 2 Kings 9-11
186 2 Kings 12-13; 2 Chron.24
187 2 Kings 14; 2 Chron. 25
188 Jonah
189 2 Kings 15; 2 Chron. 26
190 Isaiah 1-4
191 Isaiah 5-8
192 Amos 1-5
193 Amos 6-9
194 2 Chron. 27; Isaiah 9-12
195 Micah
196 2 Chron. 28; 2 Kings 16-17
197 Isaiah 13-17
198 Isaiah 18-22
199 Isaiah 23-27
200 2 Kings 18; 2 Chron. 29-31 Ps. 48
201 Hosea 1-7
202 Hosea 8-14
203 Isaiah 28-30
204 Isaiah 31-34
205 Isaiah 35-36
206 Isaiah 37-39; Psalm 76
207 Isaiah 40-43
208 Isaiah 44-48
209 2 Kings 19; Psalm 46, 80, 135
210 Isaiah 49-53

DAY	DAY
211 Isaiah 54-58	250 Ezekiel 34-36
212 Isaiah 59-63	251 Ezekiel 37-39
213 Isaiah 64-66	252 Ezekiel 40-42
214 2 Kings 20-21	253 Ezekiel 43-45
215 2 Chronicles 32-33	254 Ezekiel 46-48
216 Nahum	255 Joel
217 2 Kings 22-23; 2 Chron. 34-35	256 Daniel 1-3
218 Zephaniah	257 Daniel 4-6
219 Jeremiah 1-3	258 Daniel 7-9
220 Jeremiah 4-6	259 Daniel 10-12
221 Jeremiah 7-9	260 Ezra 1-3
222 Jeremiah 10-13	261 Ezra 4-6; Psalm 137
223 Jeremiah 14-17	262 Haggai
224 Jeremiah 18-22	263 Zechariah 1-4
225 Jeremiah 23-25	264 Zechariah 5-9
226 Jeremiah 26-29	265 Zechariah 10-14
227 Jeremiah 30-31	266 Esther 1-5
228 Jeremiah 32-34	267 Esther 6-10
229 Jeremiah 35-37	268 Ezra 7-10
230 Jer. 38-40; Ps. 74, 79	269 Nehemiah 1-5
231 2 Kings 24-25; 2 Chron.36	270 Nehemiah 6-7
232 Habakkuk	271 Nehemiah 8-10
233 Jeremiah 41-45	272 Nehemiah 11-13; Ps. 126
234 Jeremiah 46-48	273 Malachi
235 Jeremiah 49-50	274 Luke 1; John 1
236 Jeremiah 51-52	275 Matthew 1; Luke 2
237 Lamentations 1-2	276 Matthew 2
238 Lamentations 3-5	277 Matt. 3; Mark 1; Luke 3
239 Ezekiel 1-4	278 Matthew 4; Luke 4-5
240 Ezekiel 5-8	279 John 2-4
241 Ezekiel 9-12	280 Matthew 8; Mark 2
242 Ezekiel 13-15	281 John 5
243 Ezekiel 16-17	282 Matt.12; Mark 3; Luke 6
244 Ezekiel 18-20	283 Matthew 5-7
245 Ezekiel 21-22	284 Matthew 9; Luke 7
246 Ezekiel 23-24	285 Matthew 11
247 Ezekiel 25-27	286 Luke 11
248 Ezekiel 28-30	287 Matthew 13; Luke 8
249 Ezekiel 31-33	288 Mark 4-5

DAY
289 Matthew 10
290 Matt. 14; Mark 6; Luke 9
291 John 6
292 Matthew 15; Mark 7
293 Matthew 16; Mark 8
294 Matthew 17; Mark 9
295 Matthew 18
296 John 7-8
297 John 9-10
298 Luke 10
299 Luke 12-13
300 Luke 14-15
301 Luke 16-17
302 John 11
303 Luke 18
304 Matthew 19; Mark 10
305 Matthew 20-21
306 Luke 19
307 Mark 11; John 12
308 Matthew 22 Mark 12
309 Matthew 23; Luke 20-21
310 Mark 13
311 Matthew 24
312 Matthew 25
313 Matthew 26; Mark 14
314 Luke 22; John 13
315 John 14-17
316 Matthew 27; Mark 15
317 Luke 23; John 18-19
318 Matthew 28; Mark 16
319 Luke 24; John 20-21
320 Acts 1-3
321 Acts 4-6
322 Acts 7-8
323 Acts 9-10
324 Acts 11-12
325 Acts 13-14
326 James
327 Acts 15-16

DAY
328 Galatians 1-3
329 Galatians 4-6
330 Acts 17
331 1 & 2 Thessalonians
332 Acts 18-19
333 1 Corinthians 1-4
334 1 Corinthians 5-8
335 1 Corinthians 9-11
336 1 Corinthians 12-14
337 1 Corinthians 15-16
338 2 Corinthians 1-4
339 2 Corinthians 5-9
340 2 Corinthians 10-13
341 Romans 1-3
342 Romans 4-7
343 Romans 8-10
344 Romans 11-13
345 Romans 14-16
346 Acts 20-23
347 Acts 24-26
348 Acts 27-28
349 Colossians, Philemon
350 Ephesians
351 Philippians
352 1 Timothy
353 Titus
354 1 Peter
355 Hebrews 1-6
356 Hebrews 7-10
357 Hebrews 11-13
358 2 Timothy
359 2 Peter; Jude
360 1 John
361 2, 3 John
362 Revelation 1-5
363 Revelation 6-11
364 Revelation 12-18
365 Revelation 19-22

The Bible 365

Day One
The Pastor's Perspective: Your word for the day!

inbreathing – *(noun)* ***infusion***
in-bree*th*-ing

Reading Plan: Genesis 1-3

Genesis opens with God bursting on the scene actively involved in creation. God created everything for His pleasure. The only part of creation that received His divine **inbreathing** (2:7) was the human dimension expressed in Adam and Eve. God made Adam and Eve, and gave them the choice whether or not to trust Him to provide for their present and eternal needs. This relationship was the beginning of God's divine plan for mankind. The temptation and failure of Adam and Eve to resist sin fractured their connection with God.

Reflect on these thoughts:
- God created you for a relationship with Him.
- Because of your sins, you must receive His free gift of a recreated and eternal relationship with Him, through the shed blood of His Son Jesus Christ.
- You may walk in the power of His indwelling Spirit!

Take it to the next level: Are you acknowledging you are a creation of God willing to receive His Holy Spirit into your life?

inbreathing: say it, believe it, live it!

This is my perspective for today, Pastor Scott

4-6-16

Dr. Scott Payne

Day Two
The Pastor's Perspective: Your word for the day!

inchoation – *(noun)* ***start or starting point***
in-koh-**ey**-sh*uh* n

Reading Plan: Genesis 4-7

The biblical record indicates an **inchoation** for family, murder, mercy, and worship. Adam and Eve were to procreate the earth and influence their children to know God. But sin had become a part of human DNA. Their children would have the same choices they had been challenged with; trust God and reject sin, or reject God and experience sin. Cain would choose poorly and take the life of his brother because of the sin of jealousy. Even though early generations had long life (many 800+ years) allowing for a population explosion, sin was growing as well. God would judge evil with a great flood, but would rescue anyone who followed Him by faith.

Reflect on these thoughts:
- Your actions have an effect on others.
- Jealousy is a deadly sin.
- God desires to show mercy.
- Worship is a response to God.

Take it to the next level: God continues to offer you a new beginning. Confess your need for Him, and your desire to discover His forgiving grace and mercy. Worship the Creator!

inchoation: say it, believe it, live it!

This is my perspective for today, Pastor Scott

The Bible 365

Day Three
The Pastor's Perspective: Your word for the day!

degenerated – *(verb)* ***declined; deteriorated*** **degenerate** - *(adjective)* ***degraded; deteriorated***
dih-**jen**-uh-reyt-ed   dih-**jen**-uh-reyt

Reading Plan: Genesis 8-11

The activities of humans have **degenerated** to new lows within 1,600 years of creation. The world has turned its back on their Creator, but God still believes in His creation. God sees a man (Noah) and his family who He can pass over with His judgment, and with whom He can begin a new relationship.

God uses this experience of judgment to enter into a covenant with Noah and the human race. Using the rainbow as a sign, God promises to never destroy His creation with water again. The human heart remains wicked, but the Holy Creator offers the wisdom of a second chance to those who will faith Him.

Know these things during evil days:
- God is looking for a righteous man or woman who will listen to Him, not the voices of others.
- You must never let your guard down.
- Be on watch for any **degenerate** thought or behavior.
- Do not partner with unbelievers.
- And, God loves and will bless obedience.

Meditate on this thought: God regenerates the heart of anyone who will seek Him and live out His ways. The **degenerate** heart will face God's ultimate judgment on His terms.

degenerated: say it, believe it exists, avoid it!

This is my perspective for today, Pastor Scott

Dr. Scott Payne

Day Four
The Pastor's Perspective: Your word for the day!

syllogism – *(noun)* ***logical argument that does not end in finding truth***

sil-uh-jiz-uh m

Reading Plan: Job 1-5

There is a large school of thought **(syllogism)** that says, "God punishes sin; suffering is the result of sin; therefore, if a person suffers he must be a sinner." This is man's simple attempt to understand why God would allow people to suffer, but it misses the mark of biblical truth. God uses the life experiences of Job to answer the question of suffering in this manner: He does not act in response to human events without purpose or cause, nor does He declare all suffering a result of sin. Suffering is often used by God to teach lessons and to strengthen a person.

Observations:
- Satan is the accuser of God's people.
- God is actively involved in the lives of His people.
- God's people will trust Him through the good and the bad.

Make this personal: The struggles and sufferings of this life can serve you well if you deny Satan and faith God!

syllogism: remember, trusting God is better than trying to figure Him out.

This is my perspective for today, Pastor Scott

Day Five
The Pastor's Perspective: Your word for the day!

probity – *(noun)* ***righteousness; truthfulness***
proh-bi-tee

Reading Plan: Job 6-9

Probity is a major characteristic of a person who is dependent on God. When his friends approach Job, his honesty contradicts their assumptions about his plight. Job doesn't understand the suffering life is dealing him, but he refuses to abandon his trust in God.

Considerations:
- It's tempting to find someone or something to blame for your despair.
- It's acceptable that friends will let you down, but God never will.
- It's reasonable to expect hardships in your life.
- It's important that you have an advocate in order to approach God. (Read again Job 9:32-35)

Make this personal: When life is hard, don't fall prey to the blame-game. Refuse to turn your back on God! Take an honest look at yourself, and then confess that God is your only hope!

probity: say it, believe it, live it!

This is my perspective for today, Pastor Scott

Dr. Scott Payne

Day Six
The Pastor's Perspective: Your word for the day!

ascendant – *(adjective)* ***prevailing; dominant***
uh-**sen**-duh nt

Reading Plan: Job 10-13

God holds the **ascendant** position among all rivals. Nothing can compete with His power, wisdom, or judgment. Even though Job's three friends challenge his integrity, and point to his sin problem, Job is more interested in God's opinion. Job realizes man's answers to life's pressing issues are inadequate. It's important to value God's verdict on his actions versus what others think.

Reflections:
- Misery looks for company (12:4-6). Remember that as you evaluate the thoughts of others.
- God permits suffering, but He accomplishes His will on the final results of all life experiences.
- Your life is better off in God's hands rather than yours.

Make this personal: Listen to the thoughts of others, but value the views of God.

ascendant: say it, believe it, live it!

This is my perspective for today, Pastor Scott

Day Seven
The Pastor's Perspective: Your word for the day!

bamboozled – *(verb)* ***tricked; deceived***
bam-**boo**-*zuh* ld

Reading Plan: Job 14 -16

Satan has **bamboozled** humanity into believing God is against His creations; those that buy into this lie of Satan are used by him to testify against God, and they seek to discourage men and women of faith. Job refuses to listen to his "so called friends" as they seek to blame him for the painful experiences in his life. He cries out to God for the understanding that he needs to endure.

Considerations for the walk of every believer:
- Satan says there's no life after death; God says there is hope of a resurrected life.
- Satan says don't listen to God; God says His truth will set you free.
- Satan says God doesn't trust man; God says He believes in man.
- Satan says there's no one that can speak to God on your behalf; God says you have an advocate.

Take this personally: Stop listening to the voice of Satan and the noise of his followers (don't be **bamboozled**); instead, tune in to God's voice and His followers.

bamboozled: say it, believe it, avoid it!

This is my perspective for today, Pastor Scott

Dr. Scott Payne

Day Eight
The Pastor's Perspective: Your word for the day!

judicial – *(adjective)* ***judgmental; critical***
joo-**dish**-uh l

Reading Plan: Job 17-20

Job is convinced that fair-minded, God-seeking people will not possess a **judicial** spirit. He pleads with his friends not to judge him as a sinner just because he is going through a difficult season in his life. That is a great temptation for you to guard against. You must realize that God is the only righteous and ultimate judge. True friends will correct but never condemn another.

Remember:
- Your words should bring a person closer to God.
- You will stand before God and give an answer for the way you lived your life.
- Satan wants to drive a wedge between you and God.
- Your suffering will produce God's results in your life.

Be watchful and consider this: God uses all things and people to draw you closer to Him. You know it, now share that truth with others.

judicial: say it, believe it, and leave it to God!

This is my perspective for today, Pastor Scott

Day Nine
The Pastor's Perspective: Your word for the day!

omniscient – *(adjective)* ***all-knowing***
om-**nish**-*uh* nt

Reading Plan: Job 21-23

Job is becoming more convinced that God is the **omniscient** One ("all-knowing One") and that his "so-called friends," while they might mean well, are totally misinformed. They believe God is judging Job because they only see the external circumstances which point to failure in Job's life. Job, on the other hand, believes God sees through the externals of life and can view a person's heart (motives). Job is confident that, if he could stand in God's presence and plead his case, God would declare him innocent. He arrives at that conclusion because he knows God would not forsake him. He and God had a love/trust relationship.

Let these thoughts reverberate through your heart and soul:
- Avoid evaluating God's approval of your life based on the externals. Allow God to convict or affirm you.
- Avoid viewing death as a punishment. Allow God to eliminate your fear with faith in the promise of abundant life.
- Avoid the judgmental voices of Satan and others. Allow God to be on display in your life by following His way, keeping His commandments, and treasuring your relationship with Him.

Take this to another level: God knows all, sees all, and understands all! He is the **omniscient** One. You can trust Him through all.

omniscient: say it, believe it, live it!

This is my perspective for today, Pastor Scott

Dr. Scott Payne

Day Ten
The Pastor's Perspective: Your word for the day!

veracious – *(adjective)* **truthful; accurate**
vuh-**rey**-shuh s

Reading Plan: Job 24-28

Job continues to make a **veracious** declaration about his life and the God he serves. Even in the midst of a lack of clarity on his plight, he knows the truth about God and life; therefore, he rejects the tenets of the wicked. He refuses to denounce his faith in God's favor on the righteous and the ultimate judgment that the wicked will face. An appearance of success in this life is not a guarantee that the final judgment will deliver a positive verdict.

Three power thoughts:
- Words reflect your heart. Your words are a witness of what and who you value.
- Wicked people will reap a guilty verdict in the afterlife. God's people will be vindicated.
- Wisdom is the possession of God, and He only dispenses it to those who sincerely seek it.

Make this a personal matter: Walk your life out with integrity before God and others. A personal relationship with Him will produce a **veracious** testimony to the world that God is faithful!

veracious: say it, believe it, live it!

This is my perspective for today, Pastor Scott

Day Eleven
The Pastor's Perspective: Your word for the day!

evince – *(verb) **make known; prove***
ih-**vins**

Reading Plan: Job 29-31

Job reminisces about what his life was like before tragedy befell him. Before the outbreak of bad things he was a well-respected man. Job is able to **evince** his actions and motives in his human relationships. He spends time recounting how he lived and how he helped others. After a thorough inventory of his past, he remains confident that God would approve of him but remains perplexed by God's silence and the difficulties life continues to hurl at him.

Reflect on these questions:
- Are you fair in all your dealings with others?
- Do you avoid feeling superior over others who fail to live up to your standards?
- Are you expecting anything in return for your generosity?

Take this to the next level: Make sure your activities declare a faithful relationship with God and others.

evince: say it, believe it, live it!

This is my perspective for today, Pastor Scott

Dr. Scott Payne

Day Twelve
The Pastor's Perspective: Your word for the day!

inculpate – *(verb)* ***blame; incriminate***
in-**kuhl**-peyt

Reading Plan: Job 32-24

A fourth person, a young man by the name of Elihu, verbally assaults Job. Elihu tries to **inculpate** Job with a different set of accusations. He is convinced that Job is less than honest about his lack of repentance and personal sin. You should be cautious about people who judgmentally point out your failures.

Consider these applications:
- Misunderstanding God's truth is no respecter of age; the old and young do it.
- It's not difficult to twist God's Word and make it mean what you desire.
- Never cheapen God's grace with false repentance, and avoid people who expect that of you.

Take this to the next level: Seek to live a life beyond repute, and be slow to judge others.

inculpate: say it, believe it, and be leery of it!

This is my perspective for today, Pastor Scott

Day Thirteen
The Pastor's Perspective: Your word for the day!

theophany – *(noun) **deity manifestation***
thee-of-uh-nee

Reading Plan: Job 35-37

Elihu continues his discourse on why Job lacked a **theophany** in the midst of his circumstances. Elihu remains confident that the problem lies within Job and that God is so far beyond His creation there can be no answers to the hard issues of life. This is true of the cynic that sees God so far removed from humans that He can't relate to them. Elihu can only consider the possibility that God would use the hardships of life to draw the wayward sinner (which Job must be) back to Him. Elihu portrays God's awesome creative work in a beautiful poetic theme, but fails to recognize God's loving relationship with His creative work.

Take a moment to consider:
- You can seek the favor of a just and perfect God.
- Your love relationship with God is the basis for your service and good works.
- God wants a relationship with His rebellious creation.
- God is the dominant One in the relationship. He is God and you are not!

Take this to the next level: God has an offer you shouldn't refuse; respond to Him in faith, and He will work all things for good and His purpose in your life.

theophany: say it, believe it, expect it!

This is my perspective for today, Pastor Scott

Dr. Scott Payne

Day Fourteen
The Pastor's Perspective: Your word for the day!

vindicated – *(verb)* ***absolved; freed from blame***
vin-di-keyt-ed

Reading Plan: Job 38-39

Now it's God's turn! Through the process of God questioning Job you discover there is something more than an intellectual answer to the mystery of innocent suffering. You learn that not only is Job **vindicated**, but God's trust in him was **vindicated** as well. God's line of questioning is not designed to humiliate but to instruct. Job is coming to grips with his limited knowledge and the greatness of God!

Observe:
- God comes to Job in the midst of the storm.
- Job discovers that God is not his enemy.
- Job realizes he must accept God by faith as his Creator, Sustainer, and Friend.

Take this to the next level: A child of God does not have to defend himself. If there is a relationship with your Creator he will **vindicate** you! Are you ready to surrender and accept God as Creator? He will never leave you or forsake you.

vindicated: say it, believe it, experience it!

This is my perspective for today, Pastor Scott

Day Fifteen
The Pastor's Perspective: Your word for the day!

penitent – *(adjective)* ***remorseful; repentant***
pen-i-t*uh* nt

Reading Plan: Job 40-42

God brings the Q & A with Job to a close by comparing the fear humans have for many created things on Earth. If man fears these things how can he question the power and purpose of the One who created all things? Job concludes that only God can handle and do all things, therefore he must submit to God. A **penitent** Job confesses he has challenged God without consideration of the awesome greatness of the Creator. He repents of his sins and seeks God's forgiveness. God rewards his humility and rebukes those that have given Job a false impression of His character.

Reflect on these statements:
- God will challenge our misconceptions of His character.
- The wonder of God is indisputable.
- The wicked will experience judgment.
- Suffering may not be a result of sin.
- God may not give you the answers to your questions, but He will show grace and mercy.
- God will respond positively to any repentant heart.
- God goes beyond your expectations when He restores your future.

Take this to the next level: It's better to be close to God than bitter and distant from God.

penitent: say it, believe it, experience it!

This is my perspective for today, Pastor Scott

Dr. Scott Payne

Day Sixteen
The Pastor's Perspective: Your word for the day!

certitude – *(noun)* ***conviction; certainty***
sur-ti-tood (tyood)

Reading Plan: Genesis 12-15

God shows His grace on Abram and blesses him beyond all measure. Abram's journey begins with obedience but takes a quick turn to self-dependency. Finally, Abram comes to a place of **certitude** when he discovers he cannot provide for himself. Acknowledging God is able to meet his needs beyond his expectations, Abram marks the important experiences of life by worship and sacrifice. Children and the lands of Canaan become an inheritance, and the world will be forever changed by the covenant of the Creator with one man.

Considerations:
- God is looking for obedience.
- Your failure is not final if your faith causes you to seek God.
- God's ways are better than yours.
- God will accomplish great things when you trust Him.

Take this to the next level: Do you see yourself letting God actively take control of your life?

certitude: say it, believe it, experience it!

This is my perspective for today, Pastor Scott

The Bible 365

Day Seventeen
The Pastor's Perspective: Your word for the day!

emulation – *(noun)* ***rivalry; contention***
em-yuh-**ley**-sh*uh* n

Reading Plan: Genesis 16-18

This reading portrays several sharp contrasts. These contrasts were products of the **emulation** that existed between: the natural and the supernatural, Sarai and Hagar, Ishmael and Abram's son yet to be born, disbelief and belief, your way and God's way.

You can easily relate to similar **emulations** you experience today. These conflicts should serve as opportunities to seek God's ways rather than yours.

Consider these thoughts:
- Remember, you can't serve two masters. You will love one and hate the other (Luke 16:13).
- Your life's journey is a spiritual (supernatural) journey. God is spirit and those who know Him and follow Him must do so in spirit and truth (John 4:24).
- When you live by your plans rather than God's, pride will get you in trouble every time! Pride comes before the fall (Proverbs 16:18).
- Disbelief is a symptom of a lack of trust. Nothing is impossible with God (Matthew 19:26).
- There's a way that seems right to man, but it leads to destruction (Proverbs 14:12).

Think this through: There can be no rivalries with God!

emulation: say it, believe it, avoid it!

This is my perspective for today, Pastor Scott

Dr. Scott Payne

Day Eighteen
The Pastor's Perspective: Your word for the day!

prevarication – *(noun) **lie; misrepresentation***
pri-var-i-**key**-sh*uh* n

Reading Plan: Genesis 19-21

The life of Abraham is framed in the **prevarications** that call his faith in God into question. His earlier deceptive behavior with Pharaoh apparently had taught him little about God's protective hand. Once again, he resorts to a time of **prevarication** when encountering Abimelek. Despite many outstanding qualities, Abraham appears to struggle with deception - reminding us that even great men and women of faith can fall prey to sin.

You can still take encouragement from the fact that while there is bad in the best of mankind, there is good in the worst! For Abraham, his journey of faith will continue to mature as he faces greater challenges. The faithfulness of God will serve to instruct Abraham in how to become a faithful father and follower.

Considerations for your walk of faith:
- Expect visits from God in unexpected ways.
- Always be on guard for challenges that come to strengthen your faith.
- Know that God will judge the unrighteous.
- Understand that God will accomplish what He starts.

Meditate on this thought: God is growing your faith in ways you least expect.

prevarication: say it, believe it, avoid it!

This is my perspective for today, Pastor Scott

Day Nineteen
The Pastor's Perspective: Your word for the day!

cede – *(verb)* ***give up; surrender***
seed

Reading Plan: Genesis 22-24

You must be ready to **cede** any area of your life that God wants to change. This is a driving theme in your reading today. Abraham must be willing to **cede** his son Isaac. Then a wife and mother must be **ceded** to God. Rebekah must **cede** to God's will in order to find the man she will call husband. This is what God requires. You must give all you have to be used for God's purposes, honor and glory!

Take into account these thoughts:
- Your relationship with God is one based on who's in control.
- God provides everything you need to be successful when you're willing to surrender.
- The Lord gives and the Lord takes away, blessed be the name of the Lord (Job 1:21).
- A superior life is the joy of those who surrender their life to God.

Meditate on this thought: You can trust God with anything!

cede: say it, believe it, live it!

This is my perspective for today, Pastor Scott

Dr. Scott Payne

Day Twenty
The Pastor's Perspective: Your word for the day!

vying – *(verb)* ***contending***
vahy-ing

Reading Plan: Genesis 25-26

God has made it very clear there will always be opposition to Him and His people. The scriptures identify the **vying** for God's approval by two sets of brothers. Ishmael has a very difficult challenge in relating to his brother Isaac. They will mend their relationship after the death of their father, Abraham, but their relatives will have an ongoing rivalry. Esau and Jacob also become adversaries in their quest for significance.

Focus on these observations:
- Bad choices will lead you down the wrong path.
- Avoid repeating the sins of your forefathers.
- A careless life reaps a bad harvest.
- God keeps His promises.

Meditate on this thought: You are responsible for living a God-centered life!

vying: say it, believe it, avoid it!

This is my perspective for today, Pastor Scott

Day Twenty-One
The Pastor's Perspective: Your word for the day!

shenanigan – *(noun) **mischievous deception***
sh*uh*-**nan**-i-g*uh* n

Reading Plan: Genesis 27-29

It would appear the **shenanigans** of Jacob come full circle on him! With his mother's assistance he deceives his father into giving him the family blessing. Normally the elder son would receive the blessing. Esau is enraged by his brother's actions: first taking his birthright, and now tricking their father into giving him the family blessing. For Jacob these actions will come back to haunt him when he arrives at his uncle Laban's house, and must marry Leah before he can have Rachel as the wife he had asked for. But God has promised Jacob He will continue His covenant through him and his children.

Thoughts to reflect on:
- Avoid the trap of lazy behavior. It will always cost you.
- God will accomplish His purposes in spite of your actions. Correction will be painful, and repentance comes with rewards.
- Sacrifices typically partner with success.

Meditate on this thought: Destination is not the issue, how you get there is!

shenanigan: say it, believe it, avoid it!

This is my perspective for today, Pastor Scott

Dr. Scott Payne

Day Twenty-Two
The Pastor's Perspective: Your word for the day! s

surreptitious – *(adjective)* ***secretive; underhanded***
sur-*uh* p-**tish**-*uh* s

Reading Plan: Genesis 30-31

Most of the characters in this section of your reading possess a **surreptitious** motive that drives their decisions. Laban is concerned about the loss of value he will see if Jacob leaves the family. Therefore, he tricks Jacob into staying. Jacob refuses to leave without a profit. He devises a scheme to stay longer but takes more possessions when he does depart. Rachel leaves as though her father has disowned her and she has lost her inheritance. She will take the family gods and deny the theft later. The **surreptitious** behavior of each one of them is an unworthy action and reflects poorly on them and their potential. But God works through their failures, bringing peace and resolution to a dysfunctional family.

Take a moment and probe these points:
- Children are a blessing: Jacob's children will become a nation of people!
- What goes around typically comes around.
- Never operate in the dark (secret), keep your life and actions in the light (open).
- An attempt at peace is better than making war.

Meditate on this thought: Look in the mirror before you begin any criticism of others!

surreptitious: say it, believe it, avoid it!

This is my perspective for today, Pastor Scott

Day Twenty-Three
The Pastor's Perspective: Your word for the day!

skirmish – *(noun) scuffle; fight*
skur-mish

Reading Plan: Genesis 32-34

The central figure in your reading today is Jacob. He must deal with a potential **skirmish** with his brother (Esau) and actually gets involved in a **skirmish** with God, a wrestling match he will never forget! Throw in the conflict Jacob's sons had with the men of Shechem, conflict seems to be the theme of the day. God remains faithful to His promise and sees Jacob and his family through each ordeal with a measure of success. Many times the conflict or encounter is unavoidable, but walking in the light of God's presence and power is a must.

Ponder these points:
- Most of your fears related to any situation are exaggerated! Jacob's fears about Esau are unfounded.
- A repentant heart usually receives forgiveness. Esau forgave Jacob; it would seem Jacob's approach to Esau prepared the way.
- If you sincerely want God's blessing — then go for it! Jacob refused to retreat from his struggle with God until he had received a blessing.
- Be careful with whom you partner. Jacob's alliance with the men of Shechem has an unholy consequence.

Meditate on this thought: You can grow through the struggles in life, but you must acknowledge God is your Help!

skirmish: say it, believe it, honor God through it!

This is my perspective for today, Pastor Scott

Dr. Scott Payne

Day Twenty-Four
The Pastor's Perspective: Your word for the day!

vicissitude – *(noun)* ***change; alternation***
vi-**sis**-i-tood, tyood

Reading Plan: Genesis 35-37

The winds of **vicissitude** are blowing strongly during the formation of the nation of Israel. The chosen people of God will find their identity in one of Isaac's sons, Jacob (renamed Israel).

Radical changes occur among the descendants of Abraham: Jacob's new name, the birth of the last son to Jacob (Benjamin), the death of Rachel, Isaac's death, the record of Esau's (Edom's) family and, how through him, the birth of a hostile nation towards Israel (the Edomites) is given rise, and finally the jealous actions of Joseph's brothers. These events serve to strengthen the birth of new nations, and clarify the intentions and motives of the people involved.

Ponder these points:
- Encounters with God will produce change. Jacob's meeting with God results in the changing of his name.
- Obedience to God is marked by worship and sacrifice. Jacob and those who follow after him will always offer sacrifices of praise to God.
- The oppositions to God's purpose and His people are real. The record given to the genealogy of Esau's (Edom's) line demonstrates the size and scope of the conflict to come.
- God always provides for His people. Joseph is being positioned to save a family and a nation.

Meditate on this thought: If you stay close to God during the seasons of change you will become better not bitter.

vicissitude: say it, believe it, honor God through it!

This is my perspective for today, Pastor Scott

Day Twenty-Five
The Pastor's Perspective: Your word for the day!

bulwark – *(noun) safeguard; protection*
boo l-werk, -wawrk, **buhl**-

Reading Plan: Genesis 38-40

God was a **bulwark** in the lives of Tamar and Joseph. Both do more than survive during challenging times because of God's faithfulness.

The story of Tamar has a difficult context to understand in our culture, but one thing is undeniable, she becomes a very important part of the lineage of Jesus Christ. The genealogy of Christ will be traced back to one of Tamar's sons, Perez. God chooses to show His favor on her.

Joseph's life goes from bad to worse, but God remains his source of strength and protection. Even in the midst of false accusations and imprisonment, Joseph will advance to a powerful position of influence. In all situations, he refuses to compromise his faith and integrity. God will complete the work He has started in Joseph.

Ponder these points:
- You should avoid taking matters into your own hands. Be a person of your word, and wait on God to order your steps. You can't afford to proceed without God's guidance!
- When truth calls your intentions into question, submit to truth and confess your wrongdoing. You are a better person when you have the wisdom to admit your faults!
- Flee sin and the temptation that would draw you towards sin. You can say no to sin!
- Listen to God, and place your confidence in Him. You should speak His truth!
- God delivers you in His perfect timing for His greater purposes. You can trust Him!

Meditate on this thought: Nothing is too hard for God! He's got your back!

bulwark: say it, believe it, live it!

This is my perspective for today, Pastor Scott

Dr. Scott Payne

Day Twenty-Six
The Pastor's Perspective: Your word for the day!

kudos – *(noun) accolades; tributes*
koo-dohz, dohs, -dos, **kyoo**-

Reading Plan: Genesis 41-42

It's hard to get your mind around the fact that God can use the difficulties of life to accomplish great things! You can see this fact clearly in the life of Joseph. In the reading for today one man goes from a prison to a palace, from managing criminals to managing a country!

Giving God **kudos**, Joseph acknowledges that only God can produce positive results from negative circumstances. If you want to understand what the future holds, then listen to the One that holds the future.

Ponder these points:
- Never give up on God's promises.
- Guard the integrity of your life with good choices.
- Always seek God for answers during challenging times.
- Hold people accountable for their actions.
- Know your character will always be tested.

Meditate on this thought: Joseph understands God is the BIG answer for larger than life questions!

kudos: say it, believe it, give it to God!

This is my perspective for today, Pastor Scott

Day Twenty-Seven
The Pastor's Perspective: Your word for the day!

divulge – *(verb)* ***make known; disclose***
dih-**vuhlj**, dahy-

Reading Plan: Genesis 43-45

Through a series of events Joseph sets his brothers up to go home and return to Egypt with their brother Benjamin. Their father is very reluctant to allow his sons to return with Benjamin, but has little choice with the drought that is occurring.

Once the brothers return with Benjamin, Joseph becomes deeply moved with love and compassion for his family. Joseph **divulges** his identity and embraces his brothers with a forgiving spirit. With Pharaoh's blessing, the members of Joseph's family are invited to live close to Joseph and find all the provisions they'll need to prosper during the next five years of drought. Their father, Israel, could not have been more blessed.

Hold nothing back! Make others aware of your faith walk and trust in God.

Ponder these points:
- Let God teach the lessons you believe others should learn.
- Honesty will always reap a joyful harvest.
- There's nothing better than a family reunion.
- A parent's greatest joy is seeing his kids grow in faith.

Meditate on this thought: Love your family while you still have them!

divulge: say it, believe it, share it!

This is my perspective for today, Pastor Scott

Dr. Scott Payne

Day Twenty-Eight
The Pastor's Perspective: Your word for the day!

perspicacity – *(noun)* ***perceptiveness; insightfulness***
pur-spi-**kas**-i-tee

Reading Plan: Genesis 46-47

The **perspicacity** of Joseph served himself and others well. God called him out for a great time of need. His ability to navigate those difficult times would bring survival and blessings to him, his family, and others. This is something you need to ask of God; wisdom and understanding is a gift God freely gives to those who ask.

Ponder these points:
- God always seems to speak to those who make true sacrifices to Him.
- Obedience bears fruit in the life of any believer.
- God may use a Pharaoh to bless His people.
- For what are you willing to die?

Meditate on this thought: Desperate times may call for desperate measures! The best action you can take at all times is to trust in God.

perspicacity: say it, believe it, ask for it, live it!

This is my perspective for today, Pastor Scott

Day Twenty-Nine
The Pastor's Perspective: Your word for the day!

providence – *(noun)* ***divine foresight and care***
prov-i-d*uh*-ns

Reading Plan: Genesis 48-50

The **providence** of God could not be more evident than in the lives of Jacob and Joseph. In spite of their failing human behavior God continues to accomplish His great promises made to them and their forefathers. You can take courage and hope that God will complete something good in your life. Just as these two men illustrate great failure, they also demonstrate great faith. The divine is ready to work in the lives of imperfect humans who will confess God and seek His ways.

Ponder these points:
- Your life will leave a pronouncement on your family and may bless their future.
- What you say to your children may become a self-fulfilling prophecy.
- Invest in your family and believe the best for them.
- God will complete what He starts. Listen to Him and not the voices that oppose Him.

Meditate on this thought: Allow God to take what might have been used for harm to bless you.

providence: say it, believe it, live it!

This is my perspective for today, Pastor Scott

Dr. Scott Payne

Day Thirty
The Pastor's Perspective: Your word for the day!

extricate – *(verb) **rescue; disentangle***
ek-stri-keyt

Reading Plan: Exodus 1-3

Today you have started the journey through the book of Exodus. The descendants of Israel have spent 400 years in Egypt, and their stay has moved from choice to captivity. The new ruling Pharaoh decides to turn up the heat on a growing threat! He will intensify his persecution of the Hebrews and diminish their numbers and the foreboding sense he has of their power and influence. In this context another spiritual leader emerges (much like Abraham) who will serve as an intermediary between God and His people. Moses ascends to this position. He is to **extricate** God's people from the pagan influence of a Pharaoh that opposes the mighty hand of God.

Ponder these points:
- Opponents of God will persecute God's people.
- God delivers His people who call out to Him.
- When you see a burning bush go check it out.
- Trust God to order your steps and reveal His plans.

Meditate on this thought: God has called you to set captives free.

extricate: say it, believe it, practice it!

This is my perspective for today, Pastor Scott

Day Thirty-One
The Pastor's Perspective: Your word for the day!

intermediary – *(noun) **go-between***
in-ter-**mee**-dee-er-ee

Reading Plan: Exodus 4-6

The stage is set for the classic showdown between God and man. Pharaoh, a pagan king, has never been confronted with opposition like he will face with the living God of Creation. Moses will be the **intermediary** God uses to faceoff against Pharaoh. This conflict will serve God's purposes, and usher in a new connection with the Hebrews who have forsaken their call to be His people.

Ponder these points:
- Many times God provides partners to accomplish the mission He gives you.
- The opposition to God and your call as a follower is relentless.
- Never doubt the mighty hand of God.
- Don't grow weary in doing what God has placed in your heart.
- You can be the **intermediary** for others that brings connection with God rather than conflict.

Meditate on this thought: God hears the cries of His people and will send deliverance.

intermediary: say it, believe it, live it!

This is my perspective for today, Pastor Scott

Dr. Scott Payne

Day Thirty-Two
The Pastor's Perspective: Your word for the day!

contumacy – *(noun) rebelliousness; disobedience*
kon-too-m*uh*-see, ty*oo*

Reading Plan: Exodus 7-9

Contumacy defines the attitude and actions of Pharaoh. It's hard to believe that an individual can neglect the appeals of God, and abort all reason in order to stand defiantly before the Creator. The actions of God and the reactions of Pharaoh serve to remind you to tread carefully as you live before the Almighty God. Defying God is a slippery slope that extracts a great premium from the rebellious.

Reflect on these key observations:
- God will reassure His faithful and obedient follower.
- God demonstrates (displays) His power while His opponent can only deceive with imitation.
- A rebellious attitude can be addictive and deadly.
- Pride contributes to a hardening heart towards God and others.

Meditate on this thought: Die to your way and live; live your way and die.

contumacy: say it, believe it, avoid it!

This is my perspective for today, Pastor Scott

Day Thirty-Three
The Pastor's Perspective: Your word for the day!

Pesach – *(noun)* ***Passover***
pe-sahkh

Reading Plan: Exodus 10-12

After Pharaoh's repeated lack of response to God's insistence to let His people go, drastic measures are just around the corner. **Pesach** was established by God to remind the Israelites of their deliverance from Egypt. It was initiated by the final plague that caused Pharaoh to let God's people leave Egypt. God sent the death angel to kill the first born of the Egyptians, but the angel would pass over the Hebrews that had placed blood on the doorposts of their dwellings. They were directed to celebrate a meal in connection with the evening of **Pesach**.

Consider several conclusions:
- When God offers you an option to avoid judgment, take it.
- Following God's directions gives life; disobedience to His commands brings death.
- Tell of God's faithfulness to upcoming generations.
- Worship God with your first fruits.

Meditate on this thought: God will make a way out.

Pesach: say it, believe it, celebrate it!

This is my perspective for today, Pastor Scott

Dr. Scott Payne

Day Thirty-Four
The Pastor's Perspective: Your word for the day!

protagonist – *(noun)* ***main character***
proh-**tag**-*uh*-nist

Reading Plan: Exodus 13-15

Moses has become the **protagonist** of a nation finding its way out of bondage into freedom. The senior leader of the Israelites enjoys the highs and lows of serving his people. Moses acknowledges his strength to lead is grounded in God's authority and purpose. Through his humility he seeks to point his people to God's love, care and promises to bless them and provide for them. This is the promise God makes to all those who trust Him and follow His ways.

Some obvious observations:
- God expects you to show your dependency on Him by committing the first returns of your work and life to Him.
- God will lead you at all times whether times are good or bad, light or dark.
- God will stand between you and the enemy.
- Your life is more blessed when you trust God rather than complain to God.

Meditate on this thought: God may use you to make a difference in the lives of others.

protagonist: say it, believe it, live it!

This is my perspective for today, Pastor Scott

Day Thirty-Five
The Pastor's Perspective: Your word for the day!

expostulate – *(verb) **strongly disagree***
ik-**spos**-ch*uh*-leyt

Reading Plan: Exodus 16-18

The children of Israel continue **expostulating** with Moses about the mistakes of leaving Egypt. They long for Egypt because of their lack of food and water. God hears their grumbling and provides what they need, but it's done conditionally. They must receive their provisions God's way. This requires total obedience to God and a strong trust-factor in Him to meet their needs.

Moses will receive counsel from his father-in-law (Jethro) as to how to manage the administrative concerns of the Israelites. A judiciary is established to settle disputes without having to go directly to Moses every time. Moses will hear only serious cases.

A few notable mentions:
- There is a difference in murmuring and in requesting.
- God may only provide what you need daily in order for you to remain dependent on Him.
- It's healthy to journal or save items that help you remember God's faithfulness.
- God will deal with your enemies.
- One person can't do it all. God typically uses a plurality of leaders to provide direction.

Meditate on this thought: How you appeal to a person makes all the difference in the world.

expostulate: say it, believe it, watch how you do it!

This is my perspective for today, Pastor Scott

Dr. Scott Payne

Day Thirty-Six
The Pastor's Perspective: Your word for the day!

lustrate – *(verb) **ceremonially purify***
luhs-treyt

Reading Plan: Exodus 19-21

God required His people to **lustrate** themselves before they came before Him. He is a perfect and Holy Creator, and those who approach Him must do so on His terms. God started His covenant relationship through one man (Abraham), and now He is ready to covenant with a people (Israel). Just as with Abraham it will require the Israelites to purify themselves by making inward and outward preparation for their divine appointment. Even after a time of offering and washing they are too afraid to hear directly from God so they plead with Moses to speak to them on behalf of God. They need an intermediary. This is a foreshadowing of your need for an intermediary also, and yours is Jesus Christ. You must **lustrate** yourself before coming into the presence of God, but it is Jesus Christ that qualifies your appearance.

A few thoughts for your consideration:
- God invites you into His sanctuary.
- You must prepare yourself daily to walk with God by following His directions.
- A healthy fear of God is good.
- God's family takes relationships seriously.

Meditate on this thought: When you hear from God your life will never be the same!

lustrate: say it, believe it, obey it!

This is my perspective for today, Pastor Scott

Day Thirty-Seven
The Pastor's Perspective: Your word for the day!

amicable – *(adjective) friendly; congenial*
am-i-k*uh*-buh l

Reading Plan: Exodus 22-24

The covenant relationship God has with His people will influence the way they relate to one another. Their relationships will be **amicable**, and when difficulties arise there will be a fair way to reconcile the issues.

As God gives them the new land, they are to avoid any contact with pagan people or other gods. The Israelites are to be a set apart people. They will recognize their commitment to God with three annual feasts: the Feast of Unleavened Bread, the Feast of Harvest, and the Feast of Ingathering.

The people will affirm and reaffirm their loyalty to God!

Reflect on these thoughts:
- You are personally responsible for your life and possessions.
- Treat others and their property fairly.
- A good moral life is a reflection of God's character.
- God expects you to honor Him with the stewardship of your possessions.
- Giving your word is a serious matter. Let your yes be yes and your no be no.

Meditate on this thought: How you treat others reveals the relationship you have with God!

amicable: say it, believe it, live it!

This is my perspective for today, Pastor Scott

Dr. Scott Payne

Day Thirty-Eight
The Pastor's Perspective: Your word for the day!

tabernacle – *(noun)* ***tent; sanctuary; dwelling place***
tab-er-nak-*uh* l

Reading Plan: Exodus 25-27

Your reading today focuses on the importance God placed on the establishment of the **tabernacle**. He gives Moses specific instructions on how to construct the **tabernacle** and its contents. God promises His presence will remain in the **tabernacle**, and His people are to make sacrifices and experience special ceremonies there.

This is a foreshadowing of the Christ follower becoming the dwelling place of His Holy Spirit.

Reflect on these thoughts:
- God has special expectations for His presence among His people.
- God wants a dedicated place that invites His presence.
- Personal sacrifice is an expected response when approaching God.
- Only a priest is allowed to enter the most holy place.

Meditate on this thought: God offers you the opportunity to experience His presence. God with you!

tabernacle: say it, believe it, experience it!

This is my perspective for today, Pastor Scott

Day Thirty-Nine
The Pastor's Perspective: Your word for the day!

expiation – *(noun) **means of atonement***
ek-spee-**ey**-shuh n

Reading Plan: Exodus 28-29

God instructs Moses to inform his brother Aaron, his sons, and his descendants that they will serve Him and the people as priests. The priests are assigned a special wardrobe and given specific responsibilities that relate to the offerings and sacrifices the people are to present God. The Old Testament teaches that God required a sacrifice (the blood of an animal) for sin. The New Testament declares Jesus Christ (the pure divine blood of Messiah) made the **expiation** of your sin.

Reflect on these thoughts:
- A priest should have a distinctive appearance.
- Sin must collect a price.
- The priest would receive a special anointing.
- According to the Bible Christians are a priestly people.

Meditate on this thought: But you are a chosen race, a royal priesthood, a holy nation, a people for his own possession, that you may proclaim the excellencies of Him who called you out of darkness into His marvelous light. (I Peter 2:9)

expiation: say it, believe it, be grateful for it!

This is my perspective for today, Pastor Scott

Dr. Scott Payne

Day Forty
The Pastor's Perspective: Your word for the day!

impetuous – *(adjective)* ***impulsive; reckless***
im-**pech**-oo-*uh* s

Reading Plan: Exodus 30-32

It's hard to miss the importance God places on details and His expectations for His people's obedience to His commands. He has determined that some distance must be kept between Him and His creation. The priests will stand in the gap to connect God and His chosen nation.

While Moses is meeting with God, on the mountain, the Israelites become an **impetuous** people and fall prey to a vacuum in leadership. They entice Aaron into forsaking God and constructing a false god for their focus of worship. This backfires on them once Moses arrives back to the camp, and they are judged for their rebellion.

Reflect on these thoughts:
- You must approach God on His terms not yours.
- God uses His servant leaders to influence His people.
- You tend to blame others for your mistakes.
- There are consequences for your sins.

Take this to the next level: Wait on the Lord for a sense of His truth and direction for your life.

impetuous: say it, believe it, avoid becoming it!

This is my perspective for today, Pastor Scott

Day Forty-One
The Pastor's Perspective: Your word for the day!

descry – *(verb) discern; ascertain*
dih-**skrahy**

Reading Plan: Exodus 33-35

Moses would **descry** God! It was his desire and request made to his Creator, that he might **descry** the glory of God. Moved by the appeal God invited Moses to catch a glimpse of His back.

The time Moses spends with God is clearly evidenced by the glow on his face. His face is so radiant that he wears a veil when he stands before the people.

Construction of the Tabernacle becomes a national project and will require a willing sacrifice from the people. It's not just what's given but how it's given (the attitude of the giver) that qualifies the outcome.

Reflect on these thoughts:
- God loves a repentant heart.
- People will detect your time spent with God.
- You must avoid relationships that are not God honoring.
- God expects His people to take care of His dwelling place among them.

Take this to the next level: Seek God and you will find Him.

descry: say it, believe it, seek it!

This is my perspective for today, Pastor Scott

Dr. Scott Payne

Day Forty-Two
The Pastor's Perspective: Your word for the day!

exorbitant – *(adjective)* ***excessive; extravagant***
ig-**zawr**-bi-t*uh* nt

Reading Plan: Exodus 36-38

The Israelites were encouraged to bring their free-will offerings to Moses in order that the Tabernacle might be constructed. Gifts came in daily and before too long the report came to Moses that the people were giving an **exorbitant** amount and collections were far exceeding the needs.

These valuables and materials were then passed on to the skilled workers to construct the Tabernacle. And in time, the dwelling place of God among His people is completed.

Reflect on these thoughts:
- It is a blessing to give to God's work.
- May your generosity be as great as the Israelites.
- Use your skills for God's purposes and glory.
- It's rewarding to finish what you start.

Take this to the next level: Oh, that you might be a cheerful giver because you love God and others.

exorbitant: say it, believe it, be it!

This is my perspective for today, Pastor Scott

Day Forty-Three
The Pastor's Perspective: Your word for the day!

behest – *(noun)* ***directive; command***
bih-hest

Reading Plan: Exodus 39-40

God's **behest** for Moses to establish the Tabernacle and the Priesthood would include the Israelites response as well. The nation had to stand in agreement with the **behest** of God and walk out their agreement through their actions.

The priestly garments were completed, the Tabernacle erected, and a final anointing of the priests was followed by God's consuming presence in the Tabernacle. True obedience opened a tremendous door of blessing as "they did as the Lord commanded."

Reflect on these thoughts:
- Doing God's work is very fulfilling.
- You love hearing "job well done."
- What are you doing with what God has given you?
- God's anointing in your life will produce a God-size result.

Take this to the next level: God loves obedience more than sacrifice. (I Samuel 15:22)

behest: say it, believe it, do it!

This is my perspective for today, Pastor Scott

Dr. Scott Payne

Day Forty-Four
The Pastor's Perspective: Your word for the day!

reparation – *(noun) **amends; restitution***
rep-uh-**rey**-shuh n

Reading Plan: Leviticus 1-4

Reparation for the sins committed by God's people had to be made by the sacrifice of an animal. The blood of the sacrificed animal was used symbolically to cover the sins of the individual. The Israelites were required to participate in a system of sacrifices (offerings), because God wanted His people to confess their sins. Hand in hand, that confession was made with an animal sacrifice.

Reflect on these thoughts:
- The giving of offerings and sacrifices were made through the priests.
- There was a cost to be paid for sin knowingly or unknowingly committed.
- A portion of the offerings went to the priests.
- Obedience to God through the offerings for sins was a perpetual action.

Take this to the next level: The sacrifice of Jesus Christ pays in full the **reparation** for your sins.

reparation: say it, believe it, do it!

This is my perspective for today, Pastor Scott

Day Forty-Five
The Pastor's Perspective: Your word for the day!

fiat – *(noun)* ***decree; mandate***
fee-aht; **fahy**-*uh*-t, -at

Reading Plan: Leviticus 5-7

God gave Moses a **fiat** related to the offerings He will require from the people. The Israelites were being called to a holy existence before a Holy God, and their offerings served to prepare them to become a holy nation. Their confession of sin and God's acceptance of their sacrifices for those confessed sins paved the way for their cleansing with the priests being the go-between in the sacrificial process.

Reflect on these thoughts:
- Every person is given something to present to God.
- God makes the rules because He is the authority.
- God provides for His servants through the gifts of His people.
- Leaders must listen to and obey God's instructions.

Take this to the next level: The road to holiness is paved with acts of obedience.

fiat: say it, believe it, obey it!

This is my perspective for today, Pastor Scott

Dr. Scott Payne

Day Forty-Six
The Pastor's Perspective: Your word for the day!

impious – *(adjective)* ***ungodly; irreverent***
im-pee-*uh* s, im-**pahy**-

Reading Plan: Leviticus 8-10

Your reading focuses on the dedication of Aaron and his sons to serve as priests between the people and God. The priestly preparation for their mission among the people required very specific sacrifice and anointing. Then and only then, were the priests ready to make sacrifices on behalf of the people. In response to their obedience, God astounded the people with the fire of His glory. However, two of Aaron's sons (Nadab and Abihu) died because of their **impious** behavior.

Reflect on these thoughts:
- Every person needs forgiveness of sins.
- God requires a remedy for all sins.
- God is holy.
- You must be holy before approaching God.
- God's presence will consume the unrighteous.

Take this to the next level: Never approach God with impure motives or a lack of respect.

impious: say it, believe it, avoid it!

This is my perspective for today, Pastor Scott

Day Forty-Seven
The Pastor's Perspective: Your word for the day!

verboten – *(adjective)* ***forbidden; not allowed***
ver-**boht**-n

Reading Plan: Leviticus 11-13

God spells out the things that are **verboten** for the children of Israel. There are nutritional and physical issues that are addressed in your reading: things that could be eaten and things that could not be; the cleansing of a new mother required seven days for a son and two weeks for a daughter; sores that will heal and sores that will reveal an unclean position. In addition, a critical principal is discovered and mandated — any contact with the unclean must be presented to the priests.

Reflect on these thoughts:
- God's children must follow His prescribed diet.
- Don't eat or touch what is unclean.
- A mother's health is restored by God's perfect plan.
- A skin disease must be taken seriously.
- Don't question what God forbids, obey His decrees.

Take this to the next level: Jesus has become your perfect priest to provide your perfect healing!

verboten: say it, believe it, obey it!

This is my perspective for today, Pastor Scott

Dr. Scott Payne

Day Forty-Eight
The Pastor's Perspective: Your word for the day!

salubrious – *(adjective)* ***healthy; wholesome***
s*uh*-**loo**-bree-*uh* s

Reading Plan: Leviticus 14-15

God is interested in the **salubrious** life of His people. One reason God established the priestly role among the Israelites was to care for their physical and spiritual needs. God laid out His process for healing and restoring a person with a skin disease or a blood issue. The person must be reconnected to the healthy community only after their healing by approaching the priest to present an offering of sacrifice. Even the poor had sacrifices that were acceptable before God.

Reflect on these thoughts:
- God commands the ill be quarantined.
- Illness can be a result of sin or it can be the consequence of a fallen world.
- When God heals a person they must give God a sacrificial offering.
- Everyone has something they can offer God.

Take this to the next level: Make sure you always give God the praise for your healing.

salubrious: say it, believe it, claim it!

This is my perspective for today, Pastor Scott

Day Forty-Nine
The Pastor's Perspective: Your word for the day!

flagitious – *(adjective)* ***wicked; heinous***
fl*uh*-**jish**-*uh* s

Reading Plan: Leviticus 16-18

Everyone has sin and sin must be confessed and forgiven. That was true for the priests as well. God gave Moses strict counsel for Aaron and his sons as related to their sin sacrifice that must precede the people's sacrifices. The Day of Atonement would become the annual Israelite sacrifice made for the sins of God's people. Moses also informed Aaron that God's people are to avoid the eating of blood.

Laws related to sexual relationships were made clear to the people. They were to disavow themselves from the **flagitious** practices of pagan nations that freely had sex with any member of their family. God also forbade same sex and animal relationships. Once again the people were to be a holy nation set aside for God's glory and purpose.

Reflect on these thoughts:
- God requires that you deal with all sin regardless who you are.
- You are not to consume the blood of an animal.
- You must subject your sexual relationships to God's command.
- God expects your complete loyalty (no other gods in your life).

Take this to the next level: Keep God first in your life, and He will direct your choices.

flagitious: say it, believe it, deny it!

This is my perspective for today, Pastor Scott

Dr. Scott Payne

Day Fifty
The Pastor's Perspective: Your word for the day!

scrupulous – *(adjective)* ***principled; conscientious***
skroo-pyuh-luh s

Reading Plan: Leviticus 19-21

It became abundantly clear that God's people were to be **scrupulous** in all their dealings. God said that He expects all humans to be treated equally and with respect. Fairness should be based on God's standards not man's standards. The foundation of all relationships and choices must be God's ordinances.

God used a priestly order to proclaim His law and commands which defined divine and human relationships. Furthermore, He established clear standards for His priests.

Reflect on these thoughts:
- Justice must be blind.
- You must see Jesus as the Priest you go to for God's Truth.
- Jesus is the only perfect High Priest.
- God does not negotiate Truth with His creation.

Take this to the next level: God's laws are designed to promote your welfare and not harm you.

scrupulous: say it, believe it, live it!

This is my perspective for today, Pastor Scott

Day Fifty-One
The Pastor's Perspective: Your word for the day!

fete – *(noun) **holiday; celebration***
feyt, fet

Reading Plan: Leviticus 22-23

Your reading begins with the restatement of what is an acceptable offering to God. Clean is the key thought. The one sacrificing, and that which is sacrificed, must be clean before God. God will accept only the holy offerings - anything else is profane to Him.

God instructed Moses on the significance and importance of the Feasts. These **fetes** were special times when the people were to remember God's presence with them and were to make offerings to Him. By keeping the Feasts the people were declaring that "I am the Lord your God!"

Reflect on these thoughts:
- Consider carefully what you dedicate to God.
- God is not interested in a defective offering.
- Remember the remarkable times in your life God has been with you.

Take this to the next level: What does it take to make your life acceptable before God?

fete: say it, believe it, practice it!

This is my perspective for today, Pastor Scott

Dr. Scott Payne

Day Fifty-Two
The Pastor's Perspective: Your word for the day!

impartial – *(adjective)* ***unbiased; neutral***
im-**pahr**-sh*uh* l

Reading Plan: Leviticus 24-25

God was establishing His "fairness doctrine" among His people. God's expectation of His people: be **impartial** in your treatment of one another. Judgment for one's actions had to be equitable in all matters.

There were very specific rules related to forgiving debts and restoring possessions. These were periods of Jubilee for the nation, and He reminded the people that they were stewards of their possessions, not owners. God owned everything!

Reflect on these thoughts:
- Be careful how you use the name of the Lord.
- God expects you to treat others with respect and equality.
- A Sabbath is to represent rest for God's people.
- God promises He will provide what you need when you obey His Sabbath.
- You should be benevolent and caring for the poor among you.

Take this to the next level: If you've experienced forgiveness you must be ready to forgive!

impartial: say it, believe it, live it!

This is my perspective for today, Pastor Scott

Day Fifty-Three
The Pastor's Perspective: Your word for the day!

approbation – *(adjective)* ***praise; approval***
ap-r*uh*-**bey**-sh*uh* n

Reading Plan: Leviticus 26-27

God's people were to look for His **approbation** as it related to their obedience to His commands. The failure to walk faithfully before God would invite the judgment of God. God took disobedience seriously, and the Israelites were told they should understand walking away from their commitment to God would be a costly decision.

The people were given a full range of choices to honor their gifts and sacrifices to God. They even had a plan by which they could redeem their offerings (pledges, gifts in kind, other assets). For example they could pledge the house they were living in and eventually release the house from the pledge by giving the value pledged plus 20%. This system of dedication allowed everyone to participate in giving to the Creator.

Reflect on these thoughts:
- You can give your life to God (none too small, too insignificant, too poor, or too useless).
- God responds by giving you blessings when you love and obey Him.
- Your disobedience to God's commands invites His judgment.
- God's ears are always listening and ready to receive a penitent person.
- Everyone is expected to give to God, and He provides the way for any willing heart.

Take this to the next level: Stay faithful and obedient to God, and be a cheerful giver!

approbation: say it, believe it, seek it!

This is my perspective for today, Pastor Scott

Dr. Scott Payne

Day Fifty-Four
The Pastor's Perspective: Your word for the day!

computation – *(noun) calculation*
kom-pyoo-**tey**-sh*uh* n

Reading Plan: Numbers 1-2

God instructed Moses to appoint leaders from each of the twelve tribes to assist in the first census of the nation of Israel. The **computation** was based on men twenty years old and above—all who were able to go to war. The total count was six hundred and three thousand, five hundred and fifty.

The tribe of Levi was not included in the count. They were appointed Levites over the tabernacle and would tend to its needs and camp around the tabernacle in order there be no wrath on the congregation of the children of Israel. The rest of the tribes would assume position on all four sides of the tabernacle.

Reflect on these thoughts:
- When God says take inventory, then take an inventory.
- Do the work God commands, no more-no less.
- God's House needs no protection, but you must guard your position to God.
- Your battle should not be on holy ground, it should be in the world.
- All of God's people count and have a place of service.

Take this to the next level: Make sure you are in the count of God's people!

computation: say it, believe it, participate in it!

This is my perspective for today, Pastor Scott

Day Fifty-Five
The Pastor's Perspective: Your word for the day!

ministration – *(noun)* ***assistance; care***
min-*uh*-**strey**-sh*uh* n

Reading Plan: Numbers 3-4

Instructions were given to Moses and Aaron concerning the care of the Tabernacle. There were special preparations that must be made each time before moving the dwelling place of God (Tabernacle). The **ministration** of the Tabernacle was given to several clans of the Levites. Each time the Tabernacle was moved, it had to be disassembled by Aaron and his sons, and then carried by the clans assigned to move it. If the Levites touched the holy things of the Tabernacle they would surely die.

Reflect on these thoughts:
- God assigns the care of His holy things to those He chooses.
- There is honor to accepting the assignments God gives you.
- Execute the assignments God gives you the way He tells you to do them.
- Everyone has a purpose and assignment from God.

Take this to the next level: The presence of God must be experienced on His terms.

ministration: say it, believe it, participate in it!

This is my perspective for today, Pastor Scott

Dr. Scott Payne

Day Fifty-Six
The Pastor's Perspective: Your word for the day!

vow – *(noun)* ***promise; pledge***
vou

Reading Plan: Numbers 5-6

God took a **vow** seriously. Today's reading focuses on two key relationships that required a **vow**; marriage and the Nazirite. You should be very careful before making a pledge to another person or to God. God expects you to follow through with your commitments. There are consequences you face if you break your oath.

Reflect on these thoughts:
- A pure God expects His people to be pure.
- Be sure your sins will find you out.
- God provides a way for sin to be forgiven.
- God is ready to bless you. Receive it!

Take this to the next level: Be a person on integrity and character.

vow: say it, believe it, live in it!

This is my perspective for today, Pastor Scott

Day Fifty-Seven
The Pastor's Perspective: Your word for the day!

benefaction – *(noun)* ***support; contribution***
ben-*uh*-fak-sh*uh* n

Reading Plan: Numbers 7

Your reading plan focuses on the **benefaction** of the leaders of Israel. They made gifts of carts that would be used by the servants of the tabernacle. For twelve straight days the leaders of the tribes brought identical gifts to support the work of the priests and the function of the tabernacle. Their free will gifts were pleasing to God!

Reflect on these thoughts:
- Leaders should set the example of giving before the people.
- Your gifts will meet the needs of God's purposes.
- The people of God should support the plans of God.
- God will show up when His servant leaders lead out!

Take this to the next level: You are a servant leader if you are supporting the work of God.

benefaction: say it, believe it, live in it!

This is my perspective for today, Pastor Scott

Dr. Scott Payne

Day Fifty-Eight
The Pastor's Perspective: Your word for the day!

supervene – *(verb) interrupt; develop unexpectedly*
soo-per-**veen**

Reading Plan: Numbers 8-10

God would **supervene** with the Israelites through the priests, the cloud, the fire, and the Holy of Holies. His presence with them would make all the difference in their live. Their faithfulness to stay loyal to Him would bring blessings upon them and curses upon their enemies.

The Levites were to take the place of the first born of Israel to be the Lord's servants in the tabernacle. They assumed their roles in the tabernacle as they served the people and God.

The Passover had to be experienced annually by the Israelites and even the strangers that may have dwelled among them. This reminder brought back to them God's deliverance while in Egypt.

The nation followed God by staying close to the tabernacle. When it moved, they moved. When it remained in one place, the people remained there as well. They had success by staying close to the tabernacle. Any signal to move, meet or maintain their position would be identified by the sounds of trumpets.

Reflect on these thoughts:
- Stay close to God and know His power and provision.
- There are always signs of God's presence. If you're looking for them you'll see them.
- Remembering God's faithfulness is encouraging.
- God leads in a number of different ways!

Take this to the next level: How do you sense God's presence in your life?

supervene: say it, believe it, live in it!

This is my perspective for today, Pastor Scott

Day Fifty-Nine
The Pastor's Perspective: Your word for the day!

bellyache – *(verb) **complain; gripe***
bel-ee-eyk

Reading Plan: Numbers 11-13

Didn't take long before the children of Israel were unsatisfied with God's provisions. They began to **bellyache** because of a lack of meat. God heard their wailing and gave them more than they bargained for - meat for a whole month.

God spoke to Moses about sharing the responsibilities of leading the people. Moses was commanded to select seventy elders from among the people to serve alongside him. These men were given some of the power of the Spirit Moses possessed.

A brief challenge to Moses' authority would come from Miriam and Aaron, but God ended that quickly by giving Miriam a seven-day case of leprosy.

Twelve spies were sent out to scout the Promise Land. Upon their return, ten of the men reported that it would be impossible to take the land. Caleb disputed their claim and challenged the people to possess the land God had given them.

Reflect on these thoughts:
- Protect your heart from a lack of gratitude before God.
- You are not designed to go it alone.
- You must live and serve by the power of the Holy Spirit.
- With God all things are possible!

Take this to the next level: Complaining rarely changes a thing; trusting God always makes the difference!

bellyache: say it, believe it, avoid it!

This is my perspective for today, Pastor Scott

Dr. Scott Payne

Day Sixty
The Pastor's Perspective: Your word for the day!

meander – *(verb)* ***amble; wander***
mee-**an**-der

Reading Plan: Numbers 14-15, Psalm 90

The Israelites continued to rebel against God and Moses, even to the point of wanting to replace Moses as their leader. Because of their continued disobedience, God declared two judgments on them: they would not be allowed to enter the Promise Land (current generation less Joshua and Caleb), and they would **meander** in the wilderness for forty years.

God warned the people they would not be successful if they tried to go it alone. Their victory could only be secured if they stayed obedient and close to Him! They had to continue with the sacrificial system He had given them and wear tassels on the corners of their garments to remind them to keep the commandments of the Lord.

The Psalmist remembered a prayer of Moses declaring the beauty of the Lord and the frailty of His creation. This was good counsel for the children of Israel as they would become a chosen nation.

Reflect on these thoughts:
- Listen to God and obey Him or He will move to someone else.
- It's futile to live without God's presence in your life.
- Sin can be forgiven and sacrificing to God should be a joy!
- Place markers in your life to encourage you to stay faithful to God.
- Remember God is eternal and your eternity depends on your relationship with Him.

Take this to the next level: Take a moment and meditate on the beauty of the Lord!

meander: say it, believe it, avoid it!

This is my perspective for today, Pastor Scott

Day Sixty-One
The Pastor's Perspective: Your word for the day!

apostasy – *(noun) a falling away from a stated belief*
uh-**pos**-tuh-see

Reading Plan: Numbers 16-17

It's difficult to understand why servant leaders would turn against the spiritual leaders that God had placed over them. Rebellion was not over-looked by God. The **apostasy** of Korah and those partnered with him in the rebellion against Moses and Aaron would cost them their lives. Sins of the rebellious leaders spread to the rank and file, and many of the Israelites paid the supreme price for their identity with Korah. God confirmed Aaron's spiritual role among the people by causing his rod to bud while the other tribal leaders rods failed to bud.

Reflect on these thoughts:
- Make sure you are hearing from God before you challenge His leader or plan.
- Be careful who you spend time with, and who you allow to influence you.
- It's best not to question God's ways.
- God marks His chosen people.

Take this to the next level: Pray God will give you wisdom in picking your friends!

apostasy: say it, believe it, avoid it!

This is my perspective for today, Pastor Scott

Dr. Scott Payne

Day Sixty-Two
The Pastor's Perspective: Your word for the day!

blunder – *(noun)* ***mistake;***
bluhn-der

Reading Plan: Numbers 18-20

Once again the significant role of the priesthood was confirmed and some of the expectations related to their service and giving were considered.

The animosity between the descendants of Jacob (Israel) and Esau (Edom) continued to fulfill prophecy as the Edomites refused to let the Israelites pass through their land on their march to Canaan.

The **blunder** Moses and Aaron made would cost them their dream of seeing the Promise Land. They were told to take the rod with them but to speak to the rock, and it would bring forth water. Moses struck the rock with the rod, and thus brought the judgment of God on him and his brother.

Reflect on these thoughts:
- You should expect the priest to serve God and His people.
- God's servants do receive gifts from God through His people.
- The road to success is rarely straight or easy.
- Never assume God's ways and guard your heart towards God and others.

Take this to the next level: Make sure you know God's way before you begin your day!

blunder: say it, believe it, avoid it!

This is my perspective for today, Pastor Scott

Day Sixty-Three
The Pastor's Perspective: Your word for the day!

espy – *(verb)* ***notice; detect from a distance***
ih-**spahy**

Reading Plan: Numbers 21-22

The Israelites once again found themselves at odds with God over their complaining ways. Faced with God's judgment for this sin, fiery serpents began inflicting death on the people. They confessed their sin to Moses and asked him to pray the Lord would remove the serpents. They would find their deliverance by looking at a bronze serpent placed on a pole.

King Balak of Moab sent a request to Balaam to place a curse on the Israelites. Balaam sought God for wisdom on this matter. God said no! On Balaam's trip to meet with Balak, his donkey **espied** the Lord in a narrow pass on the road. The donkey told Balaam he should see the angel of the Lord standing in the pass and to stop beating him for not proceeding.

Reflect on these thoughts:
- Only God can forgive your sin.
- You can't strike a deal with the enemy.
- Only spiritual eyes can detect spiritual things.
- If God can cause a donkey to talk, He can give you sight to see.

Take this to the next level: Will you ask God to reveal what's on the road ahead of you?

espy: say it, believe it, experience it!

This is my perspective for today, Pastor Scott

Dr. Scott Payne

Day Sixty-Four
The Pastor's Perspective: Your word for the day!

authenticity – *(noun)* ***genuineness; validity***
aw-then-**tis**-i-tee, aw-thuh n

Reading Plan: Numbers 23-25

The **authenticity** of Balaam's service before Balak is noteworthy. He did not waiver in his commitment to communicate God's word concerning the nation of Israel. Balak wanted to hear a curse pronounced on Israel but Balaam could only bless God's people.

It's hard to believe that the people God protected could turn their backs on Him and embrace false gods. Their betrayal would bring God's wrath on the people, but it is short lived because of the zealous pursuit of Phinehas and Aaron for God's favor.

Reflect on these thoughts:
- You need God's blessing not man's.
- You must speak God's truth and not what people want to hear.
- You can't handle a relationship with those who serve false gods.
- God will judge sin.

Take this to the next level: Go all in with your love for God, and He'll go before you and bless you.

authenticity: say it, believe it, live it!

This is my perspective for today, Pastor Scott

Day Sixty-Five
The Pastor's Perspective: Your word for the day!

amplitude – *(noun)* ***bigness; largeness***
am-pli-tood, -tyood

Reading Plan: Numbers 26-27

God commanded Moses to take a second census. It had been almost 40 years since the first census was taken. This action served to prepare the people to enter the land of Canaan and also provided the basis for dividing the land once they occupied it. The **amplitude** of the inheritance would be based on the size of each tribe.

Concerned for his imminent death, Moses sought God's direction for a new leader. Joshua became God's new spokesman, and his assignment was witnessed before the people of Israel and in the presence of Eleazar the priest.

Reflect on these thoughts:
- You should take a periodic inventory of your assets.
- You should deal equitably with people.
- Women have equal value in God's sight and should in your dealings as well.
- God is always preparing someone else to assume your role.

Take this to the next level: God owns everything, and He will give and take as He pleases.

amplitude: say it, believe it, accept it!

This is my perspective for today, Pastor Scott

Dr. Scott Payne

Day Sixty-Six
The Pastor's Perspective: Your word for the day!

stigma – *(noun)* ***stain; blemish***
stig-m*uh*

Reading Plan: Numbers 28-30

God had Moses reinforce His expectations of the required offerings from the Israelites. The offerings were numerous, and God insisted that no **stigma** be found on the sacrifices. These sacrificial and offertorial obligations pointed to the enormous expectations a perfect and holy God had for those He called to be His. It also foreshadows the coming of the One who would fulfill all these requirements like no nation or person could do.

God demanded that a person's vow or pledge be taken seriously. Your yes should be yes and your no should be no (Matthew 5:37). However, there was a way in which a father could overrule his children or a husband could overrule his wife.

Reflect on these thoughts:
- Giving to God reflects your attitude towards your possessions and your Provider.
- Messiah (Jesus Christ) demonstrated the greatest life of sacrifice and offering.
- You should respect your spiritual leaders (Hebrews 13:17).
- Consider your words before you speak them. Honor your commitments!

Take this to the next level: Do you consistently keep your word?

stigma: say it, believe it, avoid it!

This is my perspective for today, Pastor Scott

Day Sixty-Seven
The Pastor's Perspective: Your word for the day!

requital – *(noun)* ***payback; retaliation***
ri-kwahyt-l

Reading Plan: Numbers 31-32

The Lord told Moses that **requital** on the Midianites was the next command for the Israelites. The campaign would see the total destruction of Midian: it's kings, warriors, men, women (unless they had never known a man), and boy children. The plunder would be divided among those that went to war and the congregation and both groups were required to give a portion of that plunder to the priests.

Two of the twelve tribes (Reuben and Gad) requested they be given property on the east side of the Jordan, but promised they would enter Canaan with the other ten tribes to conquer the land with their men of war. But once the Promise Land was secured, their men of war would return to their families on the east side.

Reflect on these thoughts:
- God will defeat His enemies.
- Never keep anything in your life that will threaten God being first in your life.
- Make your requests known to God and others.
- Fulfill your commitments to family!

Take this to the next level: Do you live your life in community with other believers?

requital: say it, believe it, do it God's way!

This is my perspective for today, Pastor Scott

Dr. Scott Payne

Day Sixty-Eight
The Pastor's Perspective: Your word for the day!

recapitulate – *(verb) review; summarize*
ree-k*uh*-**pich**-*uh*-leyt

Reading Plan: Numbers 33-34

Moses wanted to **recapitulate** the forty-year exodus of the Israelites from Egypt to Canaan. He recorded their moves from place to place until they eventually arrived at the plains of Moab by the Jordan at Jericho. God gave Moses a strict command for the people before they crossed the Jordan and entered the land of Canaan; they were to drive out all the inhabitants and destroy the false gods. If they failed to do this, it would be an act of sin.

Before entering the Promise Land, God gave Moses the boundaries of their new land and identified the tribal leaders that would divide the inheritance for the people.

Reflect on these thoughts:
- It's important to journal the experiences of your past.
- When you look back in your journey of life you will see the hand of God at work.
- Never make friends with the devil or those who live like him!
- Remove evil from your presence.
- Don't be afraid to take hold of what God has given you.

Take this to the next level: Review your past, and embrace your future for God's glory and your joy!

recapitulate: say it, believe it, do it!

This is my perspective for today, Pastor Scott

Day Sixty-Nine
The Pastor's Perspective: Your word for the day!

asylum – *(noun)* ***sanctuary; refuge***
uh-**sahy**-*luh* m

Reading Plan: Numbers 35-36

The Lord commanded the Israelites to provide cities for their priests. Six cities were to become places of **asylum** for anyone accused of killing another person. Once again you can see God's perfect plan working out in His selection of the priests' cities becoming host to those in great need.

God ensured that the inheritance of a family stayed in the tribe in which it originated. If an inheritance of a father was passed down to a daughter, and she remarried, she was required to marry within her own tribe. This would insure the inheritance remained in the tribe of the father's clan.

Reflect on these thoughts:
- The people are to provide for those who care for their spiritual provision.
- The punishment must fit the crime.
- God will guarantee the stability of the tribes of Israel.

Take this to the next level: God provides a safe place for you!

asylum: say it, believe it, trust it!

This is my perspective for today, Pastor Scott

Dr. Scott Payne

Day Seventy
The Pastor's Perspective: Your word for the day!

preceptor - *(noun) teacher; adviser*
pri-**sep**-ter, **pree**-sep-

Reading Plan: Deuteronomy 1-2

The book of Deuteronomy represents the final record of Moses' leadership among his people. This is the written account of God's instructions to the people as they prepared to enter the Promise Land.

Today's reading begins a recounting of the decisions made thirty-nine years earlier that prevented the people from possessing Canaan. The record revisited becomes a **preceptor** to the new generation that disobeying God's directions only leads to wandering in a wilderness. Disobedience to God not only cost the older generation their place in the inheritance of the lands given them, but when they followed God's ways they were always successful.

Reflect on these thoughts:
- Don't waste your time trying to better God's ways.
- Remind yourself that the Lord goes before you and will fight for you.
- You can learn things during your wilderness times.
- God will reward the faithful even if they are in the minority.
- The enemies of God are set up for defeat.
- Your great teacher (**preceptor**) is Holy Spirit *(John 14:26)*.

Take this to the next level: Rid yourself of any reason that would hinder your obedience to God!

preceptor: say it, believe it, trust Him!

This is my perspective for today, Pastor Scott

Day Seventy-One
The Pastor's Perspective: Your word for the day!

disentitle – *(verb) invalidate; disqualify*
dis-en-**tahyt**-l

Reading Plan: Deuteronomy 3-4

As the nation listened to God and obeyed Him, they continued to experience victory. Beautiful lands and assets were obtained before crossing the Jordan and taking the Promise Land. Two and one half of the twelve tribes took possession of their land on the east side of the Jordan; the other nine and one half tribes possessed their land on the Transjordan side.

Moses gave the people a clear review of the results of disobedience. Even his lack of obedience to God **disentitled** him from entering the Promise Land. He cautioned those crossing the Jordan to avoid repeating the failures of their fathers. Moses encouraged them to stay faithful to God, obey His voice, teach God's ways to their children and avoid false gods.

Reflect on these thoughts:
- It never ends well for God's enemies.
- Celebrate God's provisions in your life.
- Even the most faithful can misstep and fall into disobedience. Guard your heart!
- It is your responsibility to heed and teach God's ways.
- You can avoid false gods by staying true to the One and only God.

Take this to the next level: Don't give up your right to an abundant life in the here and now!

disentitle: say it, believe it, avoid it!

This is my perspective for today, Pastor Scott

Dr. Scott Payne

Day Seventy-Two
The Pastor's Perspective: Your word for the day!

mitzvah – *(noun) **good deed (or command to do a good deed)***
meets-**vah**, **mits**-v*uh*

Reading Plan: Deuteronomy 5-7

God expected the nation of Israel to set a high standard for the world's moral code. For the Jew it would center on the development of the **mitzvah**. Knowing God's commands and keeping them were paramount to His blessings and the faithful witness of the Israelites to the nations.

Reflect on these thoughts:
- Your obedience to God will determine the joy in your life.
- God's law simply stated is to love Him and teach His ways to your children.
- God has initiated His love towards you based on His character not your worthiness.
- You must avoid sin and seek God's favor by being a faithful child.

Take this to the next level: God loves obedience more than sacrifice!

mitzvah: say it, believe it, live it!

This is my perspective for today, Pastor Scott

Day Seventy-Three
The Pastor's Perspective: Your word for the day!

fiasco – *(noun)* ***debacle; failure***
fee-**as**-koh

Reading Plan: Deuteronomy 8-10

Even though His Word had not been followed, God was ready to forgive and bless His chosen people. Moses cautioned this young nation (Israel) not to become prideful once they entered into the Promise Land and settled there. Moses recounted the numerous times the Israelites had turned from God. The **fiasco** created by God's people had brought much disappointment to all, and it was time to learn from these mistakes and completely trust God and obey His commandments. God loved them and would go before them providing everything they needed for success. They had to allow God to lead!

Reflect on these thoughts:
- Past failures do not have to define your future.
- God wants to bless you.
- It may serve you well to inventory the times people have stood in the gap and prayed for you.
- Living for God is as much for your good as it is for others.

Take this to the next level: Celebrate the affections God has for you and that you are a part of His forever family!

fiasco: say it, believe it, avoid it!

This is my perspective for today, Pastor Scott

Dr. Scott Payne

Day Seventy-Four
The Pastor's Perspective: Your word for the day!

devoir – *(noun)* ***duty; responsibility***
duh-**vwahr**

Reading Plan: Deuteronomy 11-13

The commands of God were an important part of every Israelite's **devoir**, and each person's faithfulness to God would determine the success they experienced in their new home. The blessings God promised Israel in the Promise Land were contingent on their obedience.

The children of God would possess the lands in Canaan, but they would be expected to seek the place the Lord assigned them to make their offerings and sacrifices. They were also told to completely destroy the foreign places of worship and the symbols of the foreigner's false gods. They were to make no place for the influence of false gods or false ways of worship.

Reflect on these thoughts:
- Loyalty is your natural response to those you love. Do you love God?
- God provides for His children. Do you sense the blessings of God in your life?
- God will not share His glory with another. Do you place anything or anyone ahead of God?
- God expects you to gather in corporate worship. Do you consistently bring your offerings and sacrifices of praise to God's House?

Take this to the next level: Live your life in such a way to honor your Heavenly Father and compliment members of your forever family!

devoir: say it, believe it, live it!

This is my perspective for today, Pastor Scott

Day Seventy-Five
The Pastor's Perspective: Your word for the day!

triumvirate – *(noun) trio; threesome*
trahy-**uhm**-ver-it

Reading Plan: Deuteronomy 14-16

God established principles by which His people must do life. He spoke to the improper way to mourn, meats that were acceptable versus unacceptable, and giving patterns.

Every seven years God's people were to cancel all debts. Also, they were to express generosity to the poor and bring an offering to the priests every three years for the use of ministry.

If a slave served an Israelite for six years, then in the seventh year that slave must be set free. If the slave desired to stay, then his or her ear would be pierced.

There was a **triumvirate** of festivals that must be celebrated every year by all the men of Israel. The Feast of First Fruits, Feast of Weeks, and Feast of Tabernacles were reviewed and patterns of observation remembered.

Reflect on these thoughts:
- Giving to God is an expression of your priorities and gratitude towards God.
- You should support the work of God's church and the special needs of others.
- You should remember God's blessings and provisions in your life.
- Sets of three should remind you of The Father, The Son, and The Holy Spirit!

Take this to the next level: Your life finds its completeness in the experience of God as three!

triumvirate: say it, believe it, appropriate it!

This is my perspective for today, Pastor Scott

Dr. Scott Payne

Day Seventy-Six
The Pastor's Perspective: Your word for the day!

presage – *(noun)* ***sign; warning; foreshadowing***
pres-ij

Reading Plan: Deuteronomy 17-20

God was willing to allow His people to be led by a king, just as other nations were, but God Himself wanted to appoint the king. This God-appointed king would be answerable to God for the way he served and led the people.

In addition, the Israelites were to provide for their priests and practice their faith in God with purity. The **presage** of a new Prophet similar to Moses is foretold.

God spoke to several issues concerning Israel's new land: cities of refuge for the innocent, a person's guilt as witnessed by at least two or three people, and the proper principles for waging war.

Reflect on these thoughts:
- Be careful what you ask for.
- Respond to God's faithfulness by being faithful.
- Look to God's ministers to help influence your life.
- Avoid the wicked and give evil no place in your life!

Take this to the next level: Allow nothing to threaten a healthy relationship with God!

presage: say it, believe it, expect God's best!

This is my perspective for today, Pastor Scott

Day Seventy-Seven
The Pastor's Perspective: Your word for the day!

defiance – *(noun)* ***bold disobedience; insolence***
dih-**fahy**-*uh* ns

Reading Plan: Deuteronomy 21-23

Any act of **defiance** by God's people would not be tolerated. Specific laws were given as it related to avoiding responsibility for the blood of an innocent man, relationships with captive women, rights of the firstborn, rebellious children, dealing with lost things, sexual immorality, keeping the camp grounds clean, and how to lend things to a member of God's family and the outsider. Disobedience came at a high price, even death itself at times.

Reflect on these thoughts:
- You must take your relationships with others seriously.
- You should always treat your parents with respect.
- Marital fidelity is an important issue for God's people.
- Your relationships with others should be defined by your relationship with God!

Take this to the next level: A rebellious attitude before God is not an option!

defiance: say it, believe it, avoid it!

This is my perspective for today, Pastor Scott

Dr. Scott Payne

Day Seventy-Eight
The Pastor's Perspective: Your word for the day!

amen – *(interjection)* ***agreed; truly***
ey-men, ah-men

Reading Plan: Deuteronomy 24-27

As the Israelites were making their final preparations to cross the Jordan and enter the Promise Land, they were reminded once again of their special place as God's people. Israel would be a holy people that honored God's commands and faithfully followed His leading. As they passed through the valley between Mount Gerizim and Mount Ebal, they heard the voices of the Levites pronouncing God's curses on sin and then each curse followed by all the people saying **Amen**!

Reflect on these thoughts:
- Taking care of your family is a family matter.
- You should always give God the first of any returns you receive.
- You are special because God loves you.
- You must avoid the things that God has cursed.

Take this to the next level: Your best position in life is to be in agreement with God.

amen: say it, believe it, live it!

This is my perspective for today, Pastor Scott

Day Seventy-Nine
The Pastor's Perspective: Your word for the day!

esoteric – *(adjective)* ***secret; mysterious***
es-*uh*-**ter**-ik

Reading Plan: Deuteronomy 28-29

God gave His people some of the **esoteric** meanings of His words. They were beginning to understand the reasons behind the commands of God, and the blessings or curses that followed. There would be no room for prideful disobedience within the nation of Israel. Disobedience to God meant His total abandonment to their sinful failures and the placing of plagues on them that exceeded those seen in Egypt. However, if they lived in obedience to Him their lives would flourish!

Reflect on these thoughts:
- Your life can always get better when your obedience to God is growing.
- You haven't seen the worst as long as you continue acts of disobedience towards God.
- God is ready to reveal the hidden things of His word to you.

Take this to the next level: The secret things belong to God!

esoteric: say it, believe it, embrace it!

This is my perspective for today, Pastor Scott

Dr. Scott Payne

Day Eighty
The Pastor's Perspective: Your word for the day!

attest – *(verb)* ***confirm; substantiate***
uh-**test**

Reading Plan: Deuteronomy 30-31

Heaven and earth would **attest** to the faithfulness or disobedience of God's people. Long life and blessings would follow the children of Israel that kept the laws of God.

Moses and the people would also **attest** to the transition in leadership from Moses to Joshua.

The law of God became a permanent foundation in the nation of Israel as Moses commanded it be read to the entire nation every seven years. He also gave them a song that they were to teach their children that would **attest** to God's faithfulness and their rebellion.

Reflect on these thoughts:
- Return to God with a repentant heart and God will renew His covenant with you.
- Stay close to the Word of God so that you may keep it.
- You must be ready to pass on the responsibilities of serving God and others to those who come after you.
- Use songs to teach your children about the ways of God!

Take this to the next level: Love and obey God because you have a personal relationship with Him not because someone else expects you to!

attest: say it, believe it, live it!

This is my perspective for today, Pastor Scott

Day Eighty-One
The Pastor's Perspective: Your word for the day!

benison – *(noun)* ***benediction; blessing***
ben-*uh-zuh* n, -shu n

Reading Plan: Deuteronomy 32-34; Psalm 91

Moses has reached the age of one hundred and twenty years. God has told him he will not enter the Promise Land, and the time has come for him to enter into his eternal rest. Before the final **benison** was pronounced on his life, he blessed the people of Israel. Then he went up on Mount Nebo, and God allowed him to view the land the people would soon inherit. He died on Mount Nebo and the Israelites mourned his death for thirty days. God's chosen man, Joshua, assumed the role of leader.

The psalmist speaks of the incredible love God has for those who find their refuge in Him. The people of God found their satisfaction and salvation in the Lord!

Reflect on these thoughts:
- Remember the days of your past and celebrate God's faithfulness.
- You should bless those you love while you are still able.
- No one compares to your God.
- God's work will continue!
- God will guard you with His awesome presence and power!

Take this to the next level: Commit yourself to finish life well!

benison: say it, believe it, celebrate it!

This is my perspective for today, Pastor Scott

Dr. Scott Payne

Day Eighty-Two
The Pastor's Perspective: Your word for the day!

sanctify – *(verb) **consecrate; set apart***
sangk-t*uh*-fahy

Reading Plan: Joshua 1-4

The time had come! God's people were ready for a major transition in their lives: moving from receiving the Law through their wilderness journey to newfound victories in the Promise Land.

Joshua assumed the leadership role of the Israelites and God's word came directly to him as it did to Moses. He commanded the people to **sanctify** themselves in order to allow God to do great wonders among them.

The nation crossed the Jordan and camped at Gilgal. A stone altar placed at Gilgal marked the momentous crossing.

Reflect on these thoughts:
- Your faith must believe the Bible.
- Your faith will count the cost.
- Your faith will move you to new places.
- Your faith will strengthen your resolve to stand firm for God!

Take this to the next level: Get yourself free from sin that God might do great things with you!

sanctify: say it, believe it, live it!

This is my perspective for today, Pastor Scott

Day Eighty-Three
The Pastor's Perspective: Your word for the day!

knavish – *(adjective)* ***deceitful; dishonest***
ney-vish

Reading Plan: Joshua 5-8

Things seemed to have started well for Israel as they began their campaign to possess the Promise Land. Before the dramatic defeat of Jericho the males of Israel experienced circumcision (a mark of God's covenant relationship with His chosen people).

The **knavish** behavior of Achan cost him his life, the lives of his family and the defeat of his nation at the battle of Ai. After the penalty of Achan's failure is executed, God delivered Ai and the benefits of her spoils to His people.

Reflect on these thoughts:
- Do you carry the sign of a relationship with God?
- Do you follow God's voice even if it doesn't make sense?
- You can't possess the forbidden things.
- You must never forget victory is impossible without God!

Take this to the next level: What God will give you is far better than what you can take for yourself!

knavish: say it, believe it, avoid it!

This is my perspective for today, Pastor Scott

Dr. Scott Payne

Day Eighty-Four
The Pastor's Perspective: Your word for the day!

stratagem – *(noun)* ***scheme; ploy***
strat-*uh*-juh m

Reading Plan: Joshua 9-11

After the initial invasion of Canaan, the Israelites focused on two major campaigns: battles waged on the southern kings and then on the northern kings. The exception was with the Gibeonites who cleverly devised a **stratagem** for their enemy. Joshua and his leadership believed their scheme, and made an ill-advised treaty with them.

The battle against the southern kings of Jerusalem, Hebron, Jarmuth, Lachish and Eglon produced God-sized support. At the request of Joshua, God caused a destructive hailstorm to fall on the enemy and prolonged the day so that the Israelites were able to pursue the enemy and completely destroy them.

The northern kings of Hazor, Madon, Shimron and Akshaph responded to the threat of Israel by creating a confederation. They were utterly defeated.

Reflect on these thoughts:
- Ungodly alliances produce Godly judgment.
- Deception is a dangerous strategy.
- No army (regardless of its size) can defeat God's purpose.

Take this to the next level: When you're in the center of God's will look for the miraculous!

stratagem: say it, believe it, avoid it!

This is my perspective for today, Pastor Scott

Day Eighty-Five
The Pastor's Perspective: Your word for the day!

ardent – *(adjective)* ***zealous; passionate***
ahr-dnt

Reading Plan: Joshua 12-15

In today's reading, reference was made to the kings defeated by Moses versus the kings defeated by Joshua. The battles won on the east side of the Jordan would become the lands possessed by the Reubenites, the Gadites and the half-tribe of Manasseh. The other nine and a half tribes would possess the lands to the west of the Jordan.

Caleb, now eighty-five years old, quickly approached Joshua and requested the hill country of Hebron. Because Caleb was an **ardent** follower of God, Joshua granted his wish.

The tribe of Judah received the land portion assigned to them.

Reflect on these thoughts:
- God's people fought on both sides of the Jordan in order to possess the land. You are to serve something greater than your self-interests - serve the Lord!
- The Israelites received their reward for obedience to God (some on the east and some on the west side of the Jordan). Your obedience to God will produce results regardless of the place or the time.
- Faithfulness always has a payday. What was true for Caleb will be true for you!
- A fully devoted follower will patiently wait on God's reward.

Take this to the next level: There are still great things left for you to accomplish regardless of your age!

ardent: say it, believe it, live it for God!

This is my perspective for today, Pastor Scott

Dr. Scott Payne

Day Eighty-Six
The Pastor's Perspective: Your word for the day!

venerate – *(verb) esteem; revere*
ven-*uh*-reyt

Reading Plan: Joshua 16-18

The process of dividing the land to each of the twelve tribes continued with Joseph, Ephraim, the other half tribe of Manasseh, and Benjamin. They received their inheritance as assigned by Joshua. The tribe of Joseph requested more land because of their population, and they were given the hill country in addition to their allotment. Because this tribe would have to deal with the threat of the Canaanites, they expected help from Ephraim and Manasseh.

During the declaration of the inheritance to the other half tribe of Manasseh, several women who had lost their husbands appealed to Joshua for a portion of the land. Joshua **venerated** God when he kept the commitment Moses had made to the women of Manasseh and gave them their inheritance.

Reflect on these thoughts:
- You honor God by keeping your commitments to Him and others.
- You understand that to whom much is given, much is required.
- You never stop working to obtain and retain your inheritance.
- You are to honor boundaries God establishes.

Take this to the next level: Be careful what you ask for.

venerate: say it, believe it, live it!

This is my perspective for today, Pastor Scott

Day Eighty-Seven
The Pastor's Perspective: Your word for the day!

plenary – *(adjective)* ***complete; comprehensive***
plee-n*uh*-ree

Reading Plan: Joshua 19-21

After the disposition of the lands to the tribes of Israel, the **plenary** promises of God were experienced. The nation possessed its land, and the cities were appointed and given to the priests for their service. The cities of refuge were identified and the people were ready to do life in their new lands.

Reflect on these thoughts:
- You should see God as your place of refuge in times of trouble.
- You can seek out the help of God through His ministers.
- God will always finish what He starts.

Take this to the next level: Know the promises of God because He will complete them.

plenary: say it, believe it, expect it!

This is my perspective for today, Pastor Scott

Dr. Scott Payne

Day Eighty-Eight
The Pastor's Perspective: Your word for the day!

consonance – *(noun)* ***harmony; unity***
kon-suh-nuh ns

Reading Plan: Joshua 22-24

Joshua was coming to the end of his life. He challenged the nation to stand in **consonance** with their love for God and His law. The two and one half tribes of Israel that crossed the Jordan to conquer Canaan were released to return home. Joshua exhorted them to stay faithful to their faithful God. The tribes that remained on the east side of the Jordan were addressed directly by Joshua as well. They were to remain committed to wholly follow the Lord God.

The people of Israel said goodbye to two key spiritual leaders in the history of God's nation: Joshua and Eleazar.

Reflect on these thoughts:
- God-size leaders will challenge your faith walk.
- It's good to place reminders in your life that encourage you to stay faithful to God.
- You should expect tests to your claims to faith in God.
- Respect those who serve you.

Take this to the next level: Do you stand in agreement with those that love the Lord God?

consonance: say it, believe it, live it!

This is my perspective for today, Pastor Scott

Day Eighty-Nine
The Pastor's Perspective: Your word for the day!

tergiversate – *(verb) flip-flop; abandon belief*
tur-**ji**-ver-seyt

Reading Plan: Judges 1-2

Joshua had died and now judges led God's people. Even though the land had been given as an inheritance, there were still territories that must be conquered and subdued. The Israelites continued to **tergiversate** their relationship with God and pay a high cost for their unfaithfulness.

Failure was the experience of battle after battle because of Israel's lack of success in totally routing their enemies. They took a territory but failed to remove the entire enemy and the false gods of the land. Slowly the enemy-people and false gods would influence the Israelites to abandon the true God. God would place a judge in leadership to call the people back to Him, but when the judge died, the failures of the people would be repeated again. God then would put another judge in place. This would go on for over 300 years.

Reflect on these thoughts:
- Claiming God's promise is a process not an event.
- You must remove the evil people or evil thing from your life. Completely remove!
- Partial obedience may be considered disobedience.

Take this to the next level: What areas of your life are not completely surrendered to God?

tergiversate: say it, believe it, avoid it!

This is my perspective for today, Pastor Scott

Dr. Scott Payne

Day Ninety
The Pastor's Perspective: Your word for the day!

gallantry – *(noun)* ***valor; courage***
gal-uh n-tree

Reading Plan: Judges 3-5

Israel failed their first test after settling in the Promise Land. They quickly settled down with the Canaanites, Hittites, Amorites, Perizzites, Hivites and Jebusites. They married their children and served their gods. God heard the cries of His people for help, and rose up men and women of **gallantry** to deliver them. The people would follow God's leader, but once the leader died they returned to their sinful past, serving the false gods of other nations.

Reflect on these thoughts:
- God is looking for those who will serve His purpose.
- God will use your enemies to draw you back to Him.
- God is no respecter of persons. He will use anyone that is willing to obey Him.
- God will deliver you from your enemies if you will call on His name.

Take this to the next level: May the music of your heart be an expression of your love and devotion to God.

gallantry: say it, believe it, live it!

This is my perspective for today, Pastor Scott

Day Ninety-One
The Pastor's Perspective: Your word for the day!

annihilate – *(verb)* ***defeat; destroy; crush***
uh-**nahy**-*uh*-leyt

Reading Plan: Judges 6-7

Once again the Israelites had disconnected from God and were struggling with the oppressiveness of the Midianites. God calls out a new judge to lead the people. Gideon was told to **annihilate** the altar to Baal and cut down the Asherah pole. The place of false worship was replaced with an altar to sacrifice to the true God. Gideon could be fearless in his leadership because God assured him that he would be victorious over the enemy. God was superior over the enemy by using a small force of Israelites to defeat a much large army.

Reflect on these thoughts:
- Many times God will call the unlikely to serve His purposes.
- God calls the surrendered not the strong.
- God loves honesty from those that follow Him.
- You can count on God to fight your enemies and give you the victory.

Take this to the next level: Don't hesitate to ask God for a sign.

annihilate: say it, believe it, practice it with what doesn't honor God!

This is my perspective for today, Pastor Scott

Dr. Scott Payne

Day Ninety-Two
The Pastor's Perspective: Your word for the day!

procure – *(verb)* ***obtain; acquire unscrupulously***
proh-**kyoo** r

Reading Plan: Judges 8-9

Gideon had defeated much of the Midianite army. However, the remaining men and their two kings were on the run. Gideon and his band of three hundred men were fast after them. The small army of Israel was denied provisions, by the cities of Sukkoth and Peniel, during their pursuit of the Midianite kings. Gideon promised they would be repaid upon his return from battle. The two kings were caught and killed by Gideon. He then turned his attention on Sukkoth and Peniel bringing judgment on their lack of help for his men during the chase of the Midianite kings.

Abimelek, the son of Gideon, by way of one of his concubines, would **procure** the title of king. One way he accomplished this was by killing sixty-nine brothers (only one of seventy escapes, Jotham). Abimelek's sin would come full-circle, as he would die by the sword of his armor-bearer.

Reflect on these thoughts:
- You must follow God with your whole heart. Gideon never waivered in his affection towards God.
- You've been told, be sure your sin will find you out. Jotham shouted out the pending judgment of God on the sins of the people from a tree on top of Mt. Gerizim.
- Sin must be punished. All who failed to wholly follow the Lord paid for their sin.
- God can use anything or anyone to levy His judgment. A woman from Thebez cost Abimelek his life.

Take this to the next level: God detests sin and so should you!

procure: say it, believe it, avoid it!

This is my perspective for today, Pastor Scott

Day Ninety-Three
The Pastor's Perspective: Your word for the day!

green-eyed monster – *(noun)* ***envy; jealousy***

Reading Plan: Judges 10-12

Much of the narrative of your scripture reading deals with the leadership of one of the six judges in Israel. The oppression of the Ammonites has taken a toll on the Israelites. The Israelites repent from their worship of Baal, and God has responded by calling forth a new judge, Jephthah, to lead the people. After seeking God's blessing to war with the Ammonites, Jephthah made a regrettable error and pledged to sacrifice the first thing he saw when returning from his victory over the Ammonites. He defeated the Ammonites and found his only child, a daughter, waiting to greet him when he arrived home. Tragically he sacrificed her a few months later. The **green-eyed monster** influenced the Ephraimites and an intertribal conflict was birthed with the Gileadites. This cost the tribe of Ephraim 42,000 men!

Reflect on these thoughts:
- Don't place yourself in an oppressive situation because of sin.
- God is your only help in time of need.
- Your words reveal your relationships.
- Be careful what you pledge to God.

Take this to the next level: Know your enemy!

Green-eyed monster: say it, believe it, avoid it!

This is my perspective for today, Pastor Scott

Dr. Scott Payne

Day Ninety-Four
The Pastor's Perspective: Your word for the day!

exploit – *(noun)* ***achievement; accomplishment***
ek-sploit

Reading Plan: Judges 13-15

Samson was a unique choice for judge of Israel. He would not need an army to have victory over the Philistines. He would become an unlikely deliverer of the people because of his **exploits,** both personal and as a warrior-judge, against the enemy of God's people.

Reflect on these thoughts:
- Raise your children as God commands.
- Make sure what you ask for has God's blessing.
- There are some things better left to silence.
- You will always find your strength in the Lord.

Take this to the next level: Only God can quench your thirst!

exploit: say it, believe it, make sure God leads it!

This is my perspective for today, Pastor Scott

Day Ninety-Five
The Pastor's Perspective: Your word for the day!

deviation – *(noun)* ***irregularity; abnormality***
dee-vee-**ey**-shuh n

Reading Plan: Judges 16-18

Deviation from God's expected principles cost one man's life and influenced a tribal failure. Samson totally lost his spiritual focus and allowed pride and sinful appetites to damage his ability to fulfill God's purpose. From prison to a position of repentance between two temple pillars he regained his power and destroyed his enemy. The tribe of Dan stole the idols of Micah, and carried off Micah's personal priest. The priest and the idols would separate the tribe from God's presence.

Reflect on these thoughts:
- You can't allow pride to drive your decisions.
- Ask God to shape your appetite.
- Your failures are never final.
- You can't shape God; you must allow God to shape you.
- You need God's wisdom, not man's blessing.

Take this to the next level: Let God determine the direction for your life!

deviation: say it, believe it, avoid it!

This is my perspective for today, Pastor Scott

Dr. Scott Payne

Day Ninety-Six
The Pastor's Perspective: Your word for the day!

repugnant – *(adjective)* ***repulsive; disgusting***
ri-**puhg**-nunt

Reading Plan: Judges 19-21

The **repugnant** actions of the tribe of Benjamin demanded a response from the other tribes of Israel. It's hard to believe that family members would have committed sinful acts towards their own, but the moral offenses committed by the Benjamites towards the Levites were unconscionable. The Israelites went up against their own people, and, after almost destroying the entire tribe of Benjamin, they relented with the desire to restore the fractured tribe. The Israelites committed a sin as they found a way out of a vow they had made in order to assist the Benjamites in repopulating. This season brought a sad epitaph, "Israel had no king; everyone did as they saw fit."

Reflect on these thoughts:
- You must constantly check your moral compass.
- You don't respond to an evil request with an evil option.
- Do you grieve for those that have sinful deeds?
- Pay attention to how you get to where you're going!

Take this to the next level: Life must be lived with a high moral code.

repugnant: say it, believe it, avoid it!

This is my perspective for today, Pastor Scott

Day Ninety-Seven
The Pastor's Perspective: Your word for the day!

ardor – *(noun) zeal; fervor*
ahr-der

Reading Plan: Ruth

When Ruth's husband died she (a Gentile) chose to stay with Naomi, her mother-in-law (a Jew). Ruth had great **ardor** for Naomi and refused to leave her side. The two women left Moab and returned to the land of Judah. Returning to Naomi's home Ruth went to the field of Boaz to gather leftover grain. She found favor in the sight of Boaz and eventually became his wife. She gave Boaz a son, and the boy became the grandfather to King David. A Gentile woman who remained faithful to her Hebrew mother-in-law found herself in the genealogy of a King!

Reflect on these thoughts:
- It's your responsibility to take care of your family.
- Protect your character.
- God will reward your faithfulness.
- You are a part of God's love story.

Take this to the next level: Are you passionate about your love relationship with God?

ardor: say it, believe it, live it!

This is my perspective for today, Pastor Scott

Dr. Scott Payne

Day Ninety-Eight
The Pastor's Perspective: Your word for the day!

scarce – *(adjective)* ***rare; deficient***
skairs

Reading Plan: I Samuel 1-3

The Israelites had experienced a time when the word of the Lord was **scarce,** and few forms of communication between God and the people existed. Samuel would become the last of Israel's judges. He came on the scene by way of a God-blessed pregnancy of a barren woman named Hannah. Hannah vowed before the Lord that if He would grant her request for a son, she would dedicate him to the Lord's service. God granted her prayer and Samuel was given to the priest, Eli, for the Lord's use. God's judgment on the house of Eli for the wickedness of his sons would prepare the way for Samuel to become a prophet.

Reflect on these thoughts:
- Never let your circumstances keep you from seeking God's help.
- Keep your vows to the Lord.
- You can't permit evil to reside in your home.
- You must listen to the voice of God.

Take this to the next level: Never be satisfied with a season when you can't hear from God!

scarce: say it, believe it, avoid it!

This is my perspective for today, Pastor Scott

Day Ninety-Nine
The Pastor's Perspective: Your word for the day!

regret – *(verb) lament; repine (noun) anguish; sorrow*
ri-**gret**

Reading Plan: I Samuel 4-8

Your reading today has a central theme that is at the heart of every person or group in the story. The narrative is driven by an experience of **regret** that brought God's judgment on each situation. Israel had been badly defeated by the Philistines. Many of the Israelites were killed, and the Ark was captured. They were filled with **regret** for not seeking the Lord. The Philistines were **regretful** for taking the Ark away from the Israelites. They would return the Ark with an offering trying to remove God's judgment on them. Eli and his sons would die as a result of their unfaithfulness to God. Samuel would warn the Israelites they would **regret** asking for a king to lead them.

Reflect on these thoughts:
- You can't live victorious without obedience to God.
- You can't control or contain God.
- You can't force God on anyone.
- You must be a voice for God's truth to others.

Take this to the next level: Live your life with no regrets!

regret: say it, believe it, avoid it!

This is my perspective for today, Pastor Scott

Dr. Scott Payne

Day One Hundred
The Pastor's Perspective: Your word for the day!

luminary – *(noun)* ***VIP; superstar***
loo-muh-ner-ee

Reading Plan: I Samuel 9-12

Samuel knew, as soon as he set eyes on Saul, that Saul was to be the first king of Israel. Samuel would tell Saul that he would be Israel's king. Saul believed the confirmation of his king-appointment by the fulfillment of Samuel's directions given to him for returning home. Everything Samuel told Saul happened! The appointing of Saul as king came with some reservation by the people, but they quickly discovered he was to be their called-out leader. Saul's first act of leadership would be to defeat the Ammonites that besieged Jabesh Gilead. Samuel was a **luminary** as a judge among his people. During Samuel's farewell speech to the Israelites he challenged them to remain faithful to God and resist evil.

Reflect on these thoughts:
- It pays to talk to a man of God.
- If you're a godly person you will show leadership.
- God will approve and bless what He is doing.
- Take the integrity challenge, and live a life of godly character.

Take this to the next level: Encourage the doubters to trust in God and faithfully live for him!

luminary: say it, believe it, live it!

This is my perspective for today, Pastor Scott

Day One Hundred-One
The Pastor's Perspective: Your word for the day!

castigate – *(verb) **rebuke; chastise***
kas-ti-geyt

Reading Plan: I Samuel 13-14

Samuel did not hesitate to **castigate** Israel's first king. In a moment of impatience King Saul assumed the role of Samuel in making an offering to the Lord. The consequence for this sin meant Saul's kingdom would not endure, and the Lord would seek out a man after God's own heart.

King Saul's son, Jonathan, along with his armor-bearer, slipped out of the Israelite camp and attacked the Philistines, killing twenty men. As panic struck the Philistines, Saul and all his men joined the battle and the enemy had to retreat beyond Beth Aven. Saul then placed the Israelites under a vow not to eat, but Jonathan ate some honey while the army was in the woods. Saul had made a decree that any one who ate would surely be put to death. Once the king discovered his son ate the honey the people came to Jonathan's defense, and Saul backed off from his decree. So the men rescued Jonathan.

Reflect on these thoughts:
- It's dangerous to step outside your God-called assignment.
- You should call out sin when you see it.
- The Lord is in the battle with you.
- Make sure the pledges you make are God-directed.
- Don't hesitate to draft faithful help for the tasks you are given.

Take this to the next level: What characterizes your walk before God and others?

castigate: say it, believe it, avoid it!

This is my perspective for today, Pastor Scott

Dr. Scott Payne

Day One Hundred-Two
The Pastor's Perspective: Your word for the day!

waylay – *(verb)* ***ambush; bushwhack***
wey-ley
Reading Plan: I Samuel 15-17

Saul and the Israelite army would **waylay** the Amalekites. Samuel informed Saul that this was God's order because of what the Amalekites did to the Israelites when they left Egypt. Once again Saul failed to follow the complete orders of God, and, in so doing, became a rejected king by God.

God sent Samuel on a mission to anoint a new king, the youngest son of Jesse, David. A defining series of actions performed by David would birth great jealousy in the heart of Saul.

Reflect on these thoughts:
- You reap what you sow.
- Partial obedience will always fall short of pleasing God.
- You had rather live by God's provisions than man's provisions.
- God looks at your heart not your physical appearance.
- Let no one offend God in your presence!

Take this to the next level: Rid yourself of anyone or anything that causes you to sin!

waylay: say it, believe it, practice it against sin!

This is my perspective for today, Pastor Scott

Day One Hundred-Three
The Pastor's Perspective: Your word for the day!

blood brother – *(noun) best friend*
bluhd **bruhth**-er

Reading Plan: I Samuel 18-20; Psalm 11, 59

King Saul's son, Jonathan, became a **blood brother** to David. Their close friendship would serve God's purposes in keeping David protected from the destructive jealousies of a king. David's popularity was growing by the day, and King Saul was outraged by the threat he felt David had become to his kingship. On several occasions Saul tried to kill David. Once Jonathan was convinced that his father was trying to kill David, he assisted in David's escape. David would thank God for His faithful watch care over him during those days of threat from Saul.

Reflect on these thoughts:
- God places friends in your life to make a difference. Who are your friends and to whom are you a friend?
- Jealously is a destructive companion. Are you having problems with another's success?
- You can't handle all the threats in life. Are you asking for God's strength?
- You are making it because of God's favor on your life. Do you find the time to praise God?

Take this to the next level: Pause and thank God for the friendships He has given you!

blood brother: say it, believe it, indentify one!

This is my perspective for today, Pastor Scott

Dr. Scott Payne

Day One Hundred-Four
The Pastor's Perspective: Your word for the day!

supererogatory – *(adjective)* ***beyond requirement; excessive***
soo-per-uh-**rog**-uh-tawr-ee, -tohr-ee

Reading Plan: I Samuel 21-24

In your reading today, David was living out a season in his life where he was **supererogatory** in his servant leadership. David was dodging the intention of King Saul to kill him. Saul's growing sense of the threat David posed was very misplaced. Saul's insecurity related to his insufficient relationship with God. Saul had deceived himself so much about David's threat that he had eighty-five priests killed for supporting David. When given the opportunity to kill King Saul, David chose to prove his loyalty to the king by not seizing the moment. David had gotten close enough to cut a piece of cloth off the king's garment to prove how much he respected the king and his office.

Reflect on these thoughts:
- Flee every opportunity to sin.
- Bad things can happen to good people.
- Be ready to help those in need.
- Love those who would mistreat and take advantage of you.

Take this to the next level: Serve God by going beyond the call of duty in all your responsibilities!

supererogatory: say it, believe it, live it!

This is my perspective for today, Pastor Scott

Day One Hundred-Five
The Pastor's Perspective: Your word for the day!

emancipate – *(verb) **free; release***
ih-**man**-s*uh*-peyt

Reading Plan: Psalm 7, 27, 31, 34, 52

David cried out to God asking to be **emancipated** from the enemy's hold on him and the evil the enemy would inflict on him. Even in the midst of the enemy's assaults on his life, David found refuge in God's protection. David confessed that God provided him light in the darkest moments and salvation was from the Lord. Placing his trust in God, he remained confident that God would not fail him. The days may be bad, but David knew that God was good and His love would endure forever. Period!

Reflect on these thoughts:
- The enemy wants to destroy you. Satan is your enemy!
- God will provide a safe place for those who seek Him. God is your shelter!
- The Lord will drive away the darkest of times. The Lord is your light and salvation!
- You can stand strong even during hard times. God never fails!

Take this to the next level: What is your source of help in time of trouble?

emancipate: say it, believe it, live it!

This is my perspective for today, Pastor Scott

Dr. Scott Payne

Day One Hundred-Six
The Pastor's Perspective: Your word for the day!

convey – *(verb)* ***bring; transfer***
k*uh*-n-vey

Reading Plan: Psalm 56, 120, 140-142

The Psalms you've read today related to a period of time when David was on the run to save his life. He found himself in the camp of the enemy, the Philistines, as he fled the wrath of King Saul. He cried out to God to **convey** his enemy to a place of wrath, and himself to a place of peace and provision. David pledged to be a man on guard from the assaults of evil, and gave thanks to God for hearing his confessions of trust and calls of praise to the Lord.

Reflect on these thoughts:
- During hard times remember that God is for you.
- Distance yourself from those that war with God.
- Deliverance is discovered in the presence of God.
- Discipline yourself to avoid evil.

Take this to the next level: When your enemy is chasing you, you chase God!

convey: say it, believe it, live it!

This is my perspective for today, Pastor Scott

Day One Hundred-Seven
The Pastor's Perspective: Your word for the day!

juncture – *(noun)* ***moment; crisis point***
juhngk-cher

1. a point of time, especially one made critical or important by a concurrence of circumstances: *At this juncture, we must decide whether to stay or to walk out.*

Reading Plan: I Samuel 25-27

Samuel had died and David had moved into the Desert of Paran. There he encountered Nabal and Nabal's wife Abigail. Nabal's arrogance cost him his life, while Abigail's humility gained her a position in the heart of a future king.

Hearing about David's position on the hill of Hakilah, Saul moved his three thousand select troops into the area to find and kill this popular hero. David and Abishai at this **juncture** secretly entered the camp of Saul by night and took his sword and water jug. When Abishai asked David if he might thrust Saul through with his sword, David refused to do so. Instead they left the camp and assumed a spot on top of the hill some distance away and called out to the army of Saul. Because David could have killed Saul but chose not to, the threat of David was removed from Saul's mind and the two went their separate ways.

Reflect on these thoughts:
- You must return good for good. What goes around comes around.
- Evil will be judged. In God's time and in God's way.
- It's good to show others your willingness to do life God's way.
- Live with your guard up and your eyes open.

Take this to the next level: … be wise as serpents and harmless as doves! (Matthew 10:16b)

juncture: say it, believe it, live it!

This is my perspective for today, Pastor Scott

Dr. Scott Payne

Day One Hundred-Eight
The Pastor's Perspective: Your word for the day!

citadel – *(noun) fortress; refuge*
sit-*uh*-dl, *uh*-del

Reading Plan: Psalm 17, 35, 54, 63

David believed that God would be his **citadel** during difficult and threatening days. His enemy arrogantly opposed God and the work of His servant. David who wanted their plans to backfire on them and the evil they would do against him, would instead, visit them. Then rather than fearing the enemy, David would turn his attention to praising God. God's presence and love would provide all the protection David would need.

Reflect on these thoughts:
- God will answer your prayers.
- Only God can truly satisfy.
- God provides for His people.
- Seek God with all your heart and He will uphold you.

Take this to the next level: Build your life on the strong rock of God!

citadel: say it, believe it, live there!

This is my perspective for today, Pastor Scott

SéanceDay One Hundred-Nine
The Pastor's Perspective: Your word for the day!

séance – *(noun)* ***session to attempt contact with spirits of dead people***
sey-ahns

Reading Plan: I Samuel 28-31; Psalm 18

Saul learned of his fate through a **séance** performed by a medium at En Dor. The medium called on the spirit of Samuel who came and spoke to Saul. Samuel told Saul that he and his sons would die the next day, and the army of Israel would fall to the Philistines. David was with the Philistine army at the time, but was sent back to Ziklag by the princes of the Philistines. When he returned to Ziklag, David discovered it had burned to the ground and the Amalekites had taken the people captive. He pursued them and defeated the Amalekites, rescuing the people of Ziklag. Saul and his sons came to the tragic end that Samuel had forecasted.

David celebrated the faithfulness of God. It was God who had protected him and delivered the enemy into his hand. He gave thanks and praise to the God of his salvation!

Reflect on these thoughts:
- Be careful what you ask for.
- God works in mysterious ways.
- Seek God's will before pursuing your enemy.
- The victory is the Lord's, so share it with others.
- Always be ready to give God praise and glory!

Take this to the next level: God will use all things to accomplish His plans.

séance: say it, believe it, trust God!

This is my perspective for today, Pastor Scott

Dr. Scott Payne

Day One Hundred-Ten
The Pastor's Perspective: Your word for the day!

surety – *(noun)* ***certain assurance; certain security***
shoo r-i-tee, **shoo** r-tee, **shur**-i-tee, **shur**-tee

Reading Plan: Psalm 121, 123-125, 128-130

David repeated with confidence the **surety** God was to those who loved Him. God was there for those who would seek Him. God's children were to humbly call out to Him for relief. The One who made heaven and earth would come to the defense of those who called out to Him and blessed His name. God would give strength to His people. God gave victory over the enemy of Israel and ultimate victory would come soon.

Reflect on these thoughts:
- The guarantee of God is enough.
- God is the Father who wants to hear from His children.
- God will act on behalf of those who put their faith in Him.
- God's faithful children always win!

Take this to the next level: Recall the times God has seen you through.

surety: say it, believe it, live it!

This is my perspective for today, Pastor Scott

Day One Hundred-Eleven
The Pastor's Perspective: Your word for the day!

bemoan – *(verb) **mourn; lament***
bih-**mohn**

Reading Plan: 2 Samuel 1-4

The twenty-four chapters of 2 Samuel recorded the highlights of David's reign. David and the nation would **bemoan** the death of Saul and Jonathan. The nation experienced years of division because some sought a spiritual direction for king while others would seek a natural progression for king. God confirmed David's position as the new king, and the people of Judah anointed him. However, Saul's son, Ishbosheth, was made king over Israel. This would create several years of conflict until Ishbostheth died.

Reflect on these thoughts:
- Mourning those you love is natural.
- It's a dangerous thing to take the life of God's anointed.
- Infighting has negative consequences.
- Murdering another person is just wrong!

Take this to the next level: God's timing is perfect. You never want to take things into your own hands.

bemoan: say it, believe it, you will live it!

This is my perspective for today, Pastor Scott

Dr. Scott Payne

Day One Hundred-Twelve
The Pastor's Perspective: Your word for the day!

sovereign – *(noun) supreme authority; supreme ruler*
sov-rin, **sov**-er-in, **suhv**-

Reading Plan: Psalm 6, 8-10, 14, 16, 19, 21

God was the **sovereign** of all things! David struggled with the grief his enemy caused, but there was no doubt in his mind that God ruled and at some point would execute judgment on all that was evil. David reflected on the majesty of God. He declared that God was a fair judge and knew that even though the wicked prospered, he should not be deceived! God would reward the righteous and rebuke the unrighteous.

Reflect on these thoughts:
- All people must navigate difficult times.
- Look around you and celebrate an awesome Creator.
- God will make things right.
- Don't worry about why the wicked prosper; rather make sure you're doing life the right way.
- It's good to place your hope in God. He will never fail!

Take this to the next level: Are you living an acceptable life before God?

sovereign: say it, believe it, honor Him!

This is my perspective for today, Pastor Scott

Day One Hundred-Thirteen
The Pastor's Perspective: Your word for the day!

genealogy – *(noun)* ***lineage; family tree***
jee-nee-**ol**-uh-jee

Reading Plan: 1 Chronicles 1-2

1 and 2 Chronicles covers a period of about 3,500 years of human history. The primary purpose of both books was to give a priestly and spiritual perspective of God's people.

The first few chapters of 1 Chronicles began the **genealogy** of God's people from Adam. The driving reason behind the detailed record was to bring the reader to the royal line of David, who became the righteous king of Israel. You can also see the birth lines of the unrighteous, and the names and families associated with forsaking God.

Reflect on these thoughts:
- You are part of God's BIG family.
- Your choices have consequences.
- You leave a legacy.
- Your family is important.

Take this to the next level: Know where you came from and decide where you are going.

genealogy: say it, believe it, live it!

This is my perspective for today, Pastor Scott

Dr. Scott Payne

Day One Hundred-Fourteen
The Pastor's Perspective: Your word for the day!

hubris *(noun)* ***arrogance; cockiness***
hyoo-bris, **hoo**-

Reading Plan: Psalm 43-45, 49, 84-85, 87

The Psalmist realized that only God could save His people from the threat of their enemy. It was unthinkable the **hubris** of a person that could turn against God. Only God was worthy of blessing and honor. The Psalmist confessed his dependency on the Lord to provide for his needs. The greatest citizenship was that of Heaven, and there was nothing better than dwelling in the presence of God!

Reflect on these thoughts:
- God's offer to His creation is salvation.
- Never turn your back on God.
- The presence of God is something you should celebrate.
- God will provide for the needs of His people.
- Discover the dwelling places of God, and spend some time there on a regular basis.

Take this to the next level: Life with God is better than life without Him.

hubris: say it, believe it, avoid it!

This is my perspective for today, Pastor Scott

Day One Hundred-Fifteen
The Pastor's Perspective: Your word for the day!

exponential – *(adjective)* ***rapidly changing numbers***
ek-spoh-**nen**-sh*uh* l, -sp*uh*-

Reading Plan: 1 Chronicles 3-5

The three chapters in your reading today focused on the tribal growth of almost half of the nation of Israel. Men of valor, faith, and commitment to God stand in sharp contrast to those who played the harlot after other gods. God would bless the faithful and judge the unfaithful. It's amazing how God blessed His people in the area of procreation. The tribes of Israel for the most part experienced **exponential** growth, and their tribal assets were rapidly increasing. Jabez's prayer demonstrated that prayer and a God who answers prayer could overcome the threat of evil.

Reflect on these thoughts:
- History serves to show you God will complete His promises.
- Stay faithful to the one and only God.
- Ask God to direct and bless your life.
- God will complete what He starts.

Take this to the next level: Believe God for His very best!

exponential: say it, believe it, live it!

This is my perspective for today, Pastor Scott

Dr. Scott Payne

Day One Hundred-Sixteen
The Pastor's Perspective: Your word for the day!

magnanimous – *(adjective)* ***generously forgiving; noble***
mag-**nan**-*uh*-muh s

Reading Plan: Psalm 73, 77-78

There was an age-old question that seemed to confound most people, "why did the wicked seem to prosper and the righteous struggle?" The conviction of the Psalmist was that the wicked would face the judgment of God and receive their day of reckoning, and the righteous would, in due season, receive their favorable reward. The righteous understood they must turn from their wicked ways and seek God; then they would discover Him as a **magnanimous** Lord. The Psalmist would trust God and bless His wondrous ways.

It was the responsibility of the people to teach the faithfulness of God to their children and expect their children would pass those teachings on to the next generation. This process would insure that each generation would be reminded of God's ways, and they would also be faithful during their own journey of trusting in God.

Reflect on these thoughts:
- You may not understand God's ways, but you can trust His ways will lead to your good.
- Be willing to confess your sins and affirm your trust in God.
- Establish times of teaching the Word of God to your children.
- Do not provoke God with sinful behavior or thoughts.
- Celebrate the goodness and greatness of your God!

Take this to the next level: Tell others your stories of God's faithfulness and continue living out the ways of the Lord.

magnanimous: say it, believe it, live it!

This is my perspective for today, Pastor Scott

Day One Hundred-Seventeen
The Pastor's Perspective: Your word for the day!

latent – *(adjective)* ***hidden or concealed presence***
leyt-nt

Reading Plan: 1 Chronicles 6

Your reading started with a partial genealogy of the chief priests. Then a listing of the extended family of Levi followed.

King David brought the ark of God from the house of Obed-Edom to Jerusalem. He put it in a special tent. God was **latent** in this special tent until Solomon built the temple. King David assigned worship leaders for God's house. It was the people's place of worship. They brought their sacrifices there, and the priests burned them on the altar. Only the priests would go inside the holy tent.

A record of Aaron's descendants was given. The Levite families of Kohath, Gershon and Merari received 48 towns.

Reflect on these thoughts:
- God provides spiritual leaders for His people.
- God demonstrates His desire to be with His people.
- God's people should provide for God-called servants.
- You experience God's presence in the place He calls His people to gather.

Take this to the next level: Where will you meet with God, and who will be there with you?

latent: say it, believe it, live in it!

This is my perspective for today, Pastor Scott

Dr. Scott Payne

Day One Hundred-Eighteen
The Pastor's Perspective: Your word for the day!

preeminent – *(adjective)* ***unequalled; superior; unmatchable***
pree-**em**-*uh*-n*uh* nt

Reading Plan: Psalm 81, 88, 92-93

The **preeminent** God was clearly experienced in the way He delivered His people from captivity in Egypt. The Israelites cried out to God, and He brought them out of bondage, and required they serve only Him. They were to have no false gods in their midst.

There were times or seasons when the Psalmist felt that God no longer remembered him. Even in the moment of questioning God's presence, the Psalmist was calling out to Him every morning. When all failed there was still hope that God would deliver.

Mourning was turned into praise and thanksgiving. The Lord truly reigned, and He was faithful to those who declared Him to be the rock of their salvation.

Reflect on these thoughts:
- God is the only true source of life.
- Don't buy into the lies that God is dead or that He doesn't care for you.
- God is your only hope.
- Praise and thanksgiving expressed to God has a great return for your life.

Take this to the next level: God is BIGGER than your fears or frustrations.

preeminent: say it, believe it, live it!

This is my perspective for today, Pastor Scott

Day One Hundred-Nineteen
The Pastor's Perspective: Your word for the day!

debacle – *(noun) fiasco; total failure*
dey-**bah**-k*uh* l

Reading Plan: 1 Chronicles 7-10

Your reading completed the genealogies of the remaining families of Israel. Special attention was given to the tribes of Judah and Benjamin, mainly because of their loyalty to the Davidic line.

Emphasis was placed on Gibeon where the central sanctuary stood during most of Saul's reign and from then on until Solomon built the temple. It represented the **debacle** caused by the people making choices without consulting God. Gibeon was not God's chosen place of worship! The Gibeon site was the people's choice, and Saul was their choice for King. God's choices were neither. (2 Chron. 6:6).

The organizational structure of the temple came into focus: the priests, the Levites, and the temple servants Chapter 10 was almost a verbatim repetition of Saul's defeat as recorded by the writer of Samuel (1 Samuel 31). The reason the writer of Chronicles recorded the death of Saul at such length seemed to have been to show that David had no hand in it.

Reflect on these thoughts:
- God pays attention to your actions.
- It is far better to do life God's way than yours.
- God expects order and preparation to be present in His House.
- Don't touch what God's tells you to leave alone!

Take this to the next level: Life is better when you have a heart for God.

debacle: say it, believe it, avoid it!

This is my perspective for today, Pastor Scott

Dr. Scott Payne

Day One Hundred-Twenty
The Pastor's Perspective: Your word for the day!

provocation – *(noun) incitement; instigation; troublemaking*
prov-*uh*-**key**-shun n

Reading Plan: Psalm 102-104

The righteous may be overwhelmed with afflictions. It was in the exhorting words of the Psalmist that people had a duty and interest to pray. Their only source of hope was the Lord. Humanity was a dying part of creation, but God was an everlasting God. Today's reading contained a happy end to all the believer's trials.

Think of the **provocation**; it was sin, and yet God was ready to pardon. God was good to all while His creation was rebellious and prideful. God's mercy was better than life, for it would outlive it.

Every object we might observe would call on us to bless and praise the Lord, who was great. His eternal power and Godhead were clearly shown by the things that He had made. Man's glory was fading; God's glory was everlasting. Man changes, but with the Creator there was no variableness.

Reflect on these thoughts:
- Life is hard but God is good!
- Only God can change the outcome from bad to good.
- Sin will destroy, but God is ready to forgive and restore those who seek Him.
- God's creation points to His power and eternal glory.

Take this to the next level: An unchanging God is ready to change your sin for His success.

provocation: say it, believe it, avoid it!

This is my perspective for today, Pastor Scott

Day One Hundred-Twenty One
The Pastor's Perspective: Your word for the day!

agnize – *(verb) **acknowledge; accept; approve***
ag-**nahyz**, ag-nahyz

Reading Plan: 2 Samuel 5; 1 Chronicles 11-12

After Saul's death, Israel would now **agnize** David as king. The leaders of Israel came to him at Hebron and made him the God-appointed king. David and the army of Israel quickly moved to take Jerusalem from the Jebusites, and made it the City of David.

Today's biblical narrative listed the great warriors of King David and traced his mighty men all the way back to Ziklag. Hundreds of thousands of men joined him at Hebron to strengthen his reign as king over God's people.

Reflect on these thoughts:
- God's plans are irreversible.
- God will always supply what you need to complete the task He calls you to do.
- Keep godly warriors around you not wayward wimps.
- Let God strengthen your influence over others!

Take this to the next level: Acknowledge God in all your ways!

agnize: say it, believe it, live it!

This is my perspective for today, Pastor Scott

Dr. Scott Payne

Day One Hundred-Twenty Two
The Pastor's Perspective: Your word for the day!

sacerdotal – *(adjective)* ***holy; spiritual; ministerial***
sas-er-**doht**-l

Reading Plan: Psalm 133

This psalm was a song of blessing or wisdom. It declared a blessing on those who lived in unity. It was sung as the people gathered for one purpose: to worship the Lord in Jerusalem, most likely in unity during one of the annual feasts.

The oil was **sacerdotal** and would have been associated exclusively with priestly service. The abundance of oil and dew represented the wonderful joy of abundant life God gives His people.

Remember I Peter 2:9, "But you are a chosen race, a royal priesthood, a holy nation, a people for his own possession, that you may proclaim the excellencies of him who called you out of darkness into his marvelous light."

Reflect on these thoughts:
- Worship of God must be done in unity when you are among other believers.
- There is always an abundant blessing to those who worship in unity.
- God has anointed all his children to be worshippers.
- Celebrate the life given you that is eternal!

Take this to the next level: Live, lead, and serve as an anointed priest of the most holy God.

sacerdotal: say it, believe it, live it!

This is my perspective for today, Pastor Scott

Day One Hundred-Twenty Three
The Pastor's Perspective: Your word for the day!

cyclic – *(adjective)* ***regularly recurring; periodic; repeated***
sahy-klik, **sik**-lik

Reading Plan: Psalm 106-107

Israel's history of disobedience was once again recounted. By the nature of its creation, physical Israel was a portrayal of how anyone could become God's "chosen people" if and when they truly lived according to His way.

You saw the beginning of the consequence of Israel's sin; God handed them over to the nations. That became the blueprint through 300+ years. The plea was for restoration.

Notice the **cyclic** nature of the disobedience among God's people. The history of Israel's pattern of disobedience was a vivid picture of God's people disobeying down through the ages. Remember the continuous repetition found in this reading: Israel disobeyed, God chastised them, they repented, and God delivered them.

Reflect on these thoughts:
- God's people will live God's way.
- The consequences of sin are great.
- Break the cycle of sin by staying faithful to God.

Take this to the next level: Avoid repeating the sins of your past!

cyclic: say it, believe it, avoid it!

This is my perspective for today, Pastor Scott

Dr. Scott Payne

Day One Hundred-Twenty Four
The Pastor's Perspective: Your word for the day!

plurality – *(noun) **majority; preponderance***
ploo-**ral**-i tee

Reading Plan: 1 Chronicles 13-16

David sought a **plurality** of support from the leaders and people of Israel for moving the ark from Kirjath Jearim to Jerusalem. With God's approval the ark began the journey. David failed to move the ark as prescribed by God to Moses, and the attempted move cost Uzza his life. The ark was left with the family of Obed-Edom because of David's fear of God after mishandling it. After defeating the Philistines several times, and establishing his military dominance, David built his houses in the City of David and prepared the Levites to move the ark. The ark was successfully placed in the Tabernacle and David's song of thanksgiving was delivered. Regular worship would be maintained by the Levites.

Reflect on these thoughts:
- God will confirm His work through His people.
- Don't just do what God says, but do it God's way.
- Spiritual people learn from their mistakes.
- God must always get the glory for success!

Take this to the next level: Unity and obedience to God equals success!

plurality: say it, believe it, live it!

This is my perspective for today, Pastor Scott

Day One Hundred-Twenty Five
The Pastor's Perspective: Your word for the day!

depose – *(verb)* ***dethrone; overthrow***
dih-**pohz**

Reading Plan: Psalm 1-2, 15, 22-24, 47, 68

The psalmist opened his writing by affirming the blessedness of the righteous and the desperation of the wicked. Nations were waging war against God, but He was not moved by their vain attempts to **depose** Him.

God was interested in the spiritual building going on in His people rather than a physical building.

David was a key ancestor of Jesus Christ, and at times became a prophet of the coming Messiah.
The psalmist provided a key for interpreting the message of Jesus' passion and death. David saw the Lord as his shepherd.

Psalms raised the standard of readiness for corporate worship. The sign of a spiritually healthy heart was gratitude and affection. After time was spent with God, a deep sense of gratitude would be central in your heart.

The final chapter of your reading brought the climactic celebration of God's greatness.

Reflect on these thoughts:
- Those that live for God will discover God's favor.
- It's hopeless to fight against the Lord.
- David saw the future Messiah providing all God's people would need for victory.
- God is worthy of praise and glory!

Take this to the next level: Great is the Lord and worthy to be worshipped!

depose: say it, believe it, not gonna do it!

This is my perspective for today, Pastor Scott

Dr. Scott Payne

Day One Hundred-Twenty Six
The Pastor's Perspective: Your word for the day!

segregated – *(verb) separated; singled out*
seg-ri-geyt

Reading Plan: Psalm 89, 96, 100-101, 105, 132

God would be **segregated** from all others. No one compared to God and His greatness or glory. His people were to give faithfully to their Lord, because a giving life was an expected response from those who truly loved and followed the Lord. God's grace, guidance, and goodness should always be recognized in the life of His followers.

The Israelites had an expression, I will … (let my life reflect the purposes of God); I will not … (allow my life to respond to evil's temptations). There was to be 100% faithfulness and loyalty to God, and in turn, He would continue to bless those who wholly called on His name and committed to live in a relationship with Him. God would dwell with His people!

Reflect on these thoughts:
- Consider the overwhelming nature of God.
- Celebrate the faithfulness of God in your life.
- Count your blessings.
- Conduct your life in a way that reflects your love for the Lord.
- Commune with God on a daily and regular basis.

Take this to the next level: What song comes to mind that helps you connect with God and expresses your praise to Him?

segregated: say it, believe it, live it!

This is my perspective for today, Pastor Scott

Day One Hundred-Twenty Seven
The Pastor's Perspective: Your word for the day!

dynasty – *(noun)* *line of familial rulers*
dahy-n*uh*-stee

Reading Plan: 2 Samuel 6-7; 1 Chronicles 17

The ark of the Lord was moved incorrectly from the house of Abinadab. It was moved on a cart rather than with the poles held by the Levites. Uzzah's motive was good in trying to balance the ark when it was slipping off the cart, but he forgot the command of God that stated it should not be touched. This cost him his life. David left the ark at the house of Obed-edom because he feared the Lord, and he soon learned that Obed-edom's house was blessed because the ark was there. David acted quickly to take the ark to Jerusalem in the proper way, and celebrated its arrival with music and dancing. His wife Michal rebuked him for his unkingly way of appearing before the people.

David's desire to construct a house for God brought God's disapproval. Rather than David building God's house, God would build David a house, a **dynasty** for eternity. David's son, Solomon, would build the house of God. David closed out your reading with his prayer of gratitude.

Reflect on these thoughts:
- Deal with the things of God the exact way you're instructed.
- God wants obedience birthed out of a sincere heart.
- God loves a heart of worship not a well-dressed worshipper.
- Be thankful you are part of God's forever family!

Take this to the next level: A simple person can worship the Holy God, and become a part of God's eternal plan!

dynasty: say it, believe it, live it!

This is my perspective for today, Pastor Scott

Dr. Scott Payne

Day One Hundred-Twenty Eight
The Pastor's Perspective: Your word for the day!

lament – *(verb)* ***grieve; express regret***
l*uh*-**ment**

Reading Plan: Psalm 25, 29, 33, 36, 39

The psalmist and other worshippers would **lament** their shortcomings and troubles. There was recognition that only God could rescue His people from the circumstances they were facing. Their request for forgiveness and protection was grounded in God's goodness and mercy.

The call to praise God was shaped by a sense of God as Creator and Ruler of all things. His chosen people would be filled with gladness, peace and hope.

It was hard not to become discouraged when the wicked opposed the faithful. His people knew the antidote was to pray for God's protection and strength.

Reflect on these thoughts:
- Confession of sin and dependency on God are essential to worship.
- If God is for you, then you have nothing to worry about.
- Fill your heart with gratitude for an awesome and loving God.
- The wicked will not have their way much longer!

Take this to the next level: Trade your regrets for God's glorious future!

lament: say it, believe it, experience it, then leave it!

This is my perspective for today, Pastor Scott

Day One Hundred-Twenty Nine
The Pastor's Perspective: Your word for the day!

subjugation – *(noun) **enslavement; conquest; bondage***
suhb-j*uh*-**gey**-sh*uh* n

Reading Plan: 2 Samuel 8-9; 1 Chronicles 18

Your reading today focused on the **subjugation** of the enemies of Israel, the Philistines to the Transjordan nations, which went all the way to the Euphrates River. David was a great and feared warrior, but his victories were the results of God's gift not his strength.

David would honor his commitment to Saul and Jonathan by not destroying their descendants. David discovered that one of Jonathan's sons, Mephibosheth, was alive. Mephibosheth was brought to Jerusalem, and David provided for his wellbeing.

Reflect on these thoughts:
- Don't fear man, rather fear God.
- Always give God the glory for the victories in your life.
- Don't leave things in your life that the enemy can use later to defeat you.
- God has made a covenant with all His children to give them a future and a hope!

Take this to the next level: Never become a slave to man; let God lead your life to victory!

subjugation: say it, believe it, avoid it!

This is my perspective for today, Pastor Scott

Dr. Scott Payne

Day One Hundred-Thirty
The Pastor's Perspective: Your word for the day!

oracle – *(noun)* ***revelations; truths; prophecies***
awr-uh-kuh l, or-

Reading Plan: Psalm 50, 53, 60, 75

The psalmist spoke of the **oracles** of God. The people of God were to live His pronouncements because they were His covenant family. Israel was being reminded that they would be judged as His people and could not live apart from Him. The majority of the world did not seek after God and had no respect for those who did. Mankind had to realize God would judge the just and the unjust.

The nation of Israel learned the value of pre-war prayer. It was prayer that prepared them to receive the victory God had prepared for them. A response of praise always followed the recognition of God's word and the assurance of His final judgment, a judgment that would vindicate His people.

Reflect on these thoughts:
- God's precepts are to be faithfully followed.
- God's people must worship Him from a sincere heart.
- The wicked will not avoid God's judgment.
- Prayer is a spiritual remedy to not trusting God.
- Praise is a spiritual response to worshipping God!

Take this to the next level: Prayer is power for God's people!

oracle: say it, believe it, live it!

This is my perspective for today, Pastor Scott

Day One Hundred-Thirty One
The Pastor's Perspective: Your word for the day!

denigrate – *(verb) degrade; mock*
den-i-greyt

Reading Plan: 2 Samuel 10; 1 Chronicles 19; Psalm 20

Hanun, the Ammonite king, would **denigrate** the representatives of Israel that David had sent to console him after the death of his father. The Ammonites then hired the Syrians to join them in doing war against the Israelites. After two conflicts the Syrians cut their ties with the Ammonites and became subject to Israel.

God's people united in petitioning God to protect and bless their leader, King David. The people were aware that God, not chariots and horses, would give the victory to their king.

Reflect on these thoughts:
- Ask God to reveal the motives of those who approach you.
- You can disagree with someone and still show respect.
- Be careful with whom you partner.
- God gives His anointing on His people and His leaders!

Take this to the next level: Are you praying for those who provide spiritual leadership in your life?

denigrate: say it, believe it, avoid it!

This is my perspective for today, Pastor Scott

Dr. Scott Payne

Day One Hundred-Thirty Two
The Pastor's Perspective: Your word for the day!

invocation – *(noun) **prayer, petition, or plea to God for help***
in-vuh-**key**-shuh n

Reading Plan: Psalm 65-67, 69-70

It was natural for God's people to respond to Him with hearts filled with thanksgiving. When there was an increase or return experienced in life, God would get the praise from His people for it. God was responsive to His people when they would call out to Him for help.

The **invocation** of God was the hope of every Israelite. There was a sense that failure drew the judgmental attention of others. Calling on God for help during these unfair judgments by others encouraged and sustained the child of God.

Reflect on these thoughts:
- Reflect on the goodness of God and His delivering hand.
- Only God is worthy of your worship.
- Journal through your prayers, and you'll discover His answers.
- Call out to God in your time of trouble.

Take this to the next level: Call out to the One who can help!

invocation: say it, believe it, do it!

This is my perspective for today, Pastor Scott

Day One Hundred-Thirty Three
The Pastor's Perspective: Your word for the day!

admonition – *(noun)* ***warning; reprimand***
ad-m*uh*-**nish**-uh n

Reading Plan: 2 Samuel 11-12; I Chronicles 20

During a time when kings should have been at war, David stayed home and found himself in deep trouble because of an adulterous relationship with Bathsheba (the wife of Uriah). She became pregnant with David's child. Since Uriah had been at war, and could not have been the child's father, David had him placed at the front line of the battle against Rabbah, and Uriah was killed. David then took Bathsheba to be his wife. The **admonition** of David for these sinful acts came from the prophet Nathan. David would pay a high price for his sin and would witness the death of this child conceived in sin. David and Bathsheba would give birth to another child and his name would be Solomon. Ultimately David and the Israelites defeated Rabbah, and the Israelite people returned to Jerusalem.

Reflect on these thoughts:
- Avoid being in the wrong place by doing what is right.
- You can always have the strength to say no to temptation.
- You can't cover sin or live a deceitful life.
- Forgiveness of sin doesn't mean you will necessarily avoid the consequences of sin.
- Repentance is good regardless of how or when you experience it.

Take this to the next level: Welcome correction from others and avoid the failures of your past!

admonition: say it, believe it, receive it!

This is my perspective for today, Pastor Scott

Dr. Scott Payne

Day One Hundred-Thirty Four
The Pastor's Perspective: Your word for the day!

contrition – *(noun) sorrow; repentance; remorse*
k*uh*-n-**trish**-*uh* n

Reading Plan: Psalm 32, 51, 86, 122

Contrition was a central theme among early worshippers. There was great joy in the experience of having their sins forgiven. Confession of sin was an appeal to God's gracious character by seeking His forgiveness and future blessing. The worshipper understood that sacrifices only benefited those who used them in humble and sincere faith.

There was another central aspect of worship that was clearly expressed in Psalm 86: there was only one God, to whom all peoples must come. He was good and forgiving to all who seek Him.

Jerusalem was a very important place of worship. It was there where "the house of the Lord" and the security and strength of the Lord could be celebrated.

Reflect on these thoughts:
- God will not accept a proud spirit when you approach Him.
- God will restore the broken relationship sin causes anyone.
- God will not share the throne of your life with another.
- God still dwells in His house (the body of Christ, the church).

Take this to the next level: Confession is good for the soul. Try it!

contrition: say it, believe it, live it!

This is my perspective for today, Pastor Scott

Day One Hundred-Thirty Five
The Pastor's Perspective: Your word for the day!

retaliation – *(noun)* ***revenge; retribution***
ri-tal-ee-**ey**-sh*uh* n

Reading Plan: 2 Samuel 13-15

Absalom and Amnon were both King David's sons. In **retaliation** for the rape of his sister by his half-brother Amnon, Absalom had him killed at Ball-hazor. Fearful of his father's response to this act, Absalom spent several years in a self-imposed exile from David.

Absalom returned to Jerusalem but still avoided a meeting with his father David. After two years, David summoned Absalom and a poor attempt of reconciliation occurred. Absalom left David's presence and began a conspiracy to overthrow David and become Israel's new king. David would flee Jerusalem because of Absalom's popularity.

Reflect on these thoughts:
- Guard your heart from doing evil to satisfy your wants.
- Dealing honestly with your failures improves your opportunity for healing.
- It's always dangerous to take matters into your own hands.
- Popularity with people is no substitute for God's approval.

Take this to the next level: Let God be the judge and executioner of righteousness!

retaliation: say it, believe it, let God handle it!

This is my perspective for today, Pastor Scott

Dr. Scott Payne

Day One Hundred-Thirty Six
The Pastor's Perspective: Your word for the day!

treacherous – *(adjective)* ***deceitful; dangerous; traitorous***
trech-er-*uh* s

Reading Plan: Psalm 3-4, 12-13, 28, 55

David modeled genuine faith in the worst of circumstances. Trust in God was the focus of his attention during difficult times.

Many times David found that liars in positions of authority dominated the people's perception of right or wrong. Good people could be turned against good people by the motives of evil leaders.

David suggested that when threatened by evildoers the best course of action for the faithful was to call out to God for help. The **treacherous** actions of those close to them were painful to face. The psalmist assured the reader that God would deliver His faithful children through these times of disappointment.

Reflect on these thoughts:
- The faithful are the most trusting of God during dire times.
- Joy is so much more than material prosperity.
- Test the words of others and ask God to reveal any lies.
- Close friends are not God; they will let you down and may even betray you.

Take this to the next level: God will lead you in all truth and deliver you from the world's lies!

treacherous: say it, believe it, avoid it!

This is my perspective for today, Pastor Scott

Day One Hundred-Thirty Seven
The Pastor's Perspective: Your word for the day!

coup – *(verb)* ***takeover; revolution***
koo

Reading Plan: Psalm 26, 40, 58, 61-62, 64

David was on the run from his son Absalom. Absalom had entered Jerusalem, and the people of Israel were ready to accept him as their new king. Hushai became a trusted counselor to Absalom but secretly remained true to David. He warned David of the impending attack Absalom was planning in hopes of killing David.

Absalom's attempt at a **coup** ended in disaster for him and thousands of his followers. David was a great warrior; Absalom together with his army was no match for David and his mighty men. Twenty thousand Israelites were killed during the battle, and Absalom was killed as well. David would mourn the death of his son.

Reflect on these thoughts:
- Humbly follow the Lord, and He will deal with you and your enemies.
- God will place people in your life to guard you and give you His counsel.
- You are the strongest when you are the most dependent on God.
- It's ok to mourn for those that would do you harm.

Take this to the next level: You can't possess what God doesn't want you to have!

coup: say it, believe it, avoid it!

This is my perspective for today, Pastor Scott

Dr. Scott Payne

Day One Hundred-Thirty Eight
The Pastor's Perspective: Your word for the day!

exonerate – *(verb)* ***absolve; vindicate; pardon***
ig-**zon**-*uh*-rety

Reading Plan: Psalm 26, 40, 58, 61-62, 64

The psalmist declared the faithfulness of God to **exonerate** those who righteously sought His ways.
When pressured by the influence of false leaders to comply with their desires, God's people would prayerfully conform to His will and experience His blessings. God would vindicate His people even though they were not perfect. Their worship would declare God's faithfulness through music and personal confession.

The Israelites related their well being with that of their king (David). It was the responsibility of God's people to pray for their leader. As the king was blessed, so would the people be blessed.

Reflect on these thoughts:
- The righteous wins!
- Don't fall prey to false leaders.
- Wait on the Lord and His helping hand will deliver you.
- Pray for and protect godly leaders.

Take this to the next level: Bad times and bad people will pass, but God's love and faithfulness is eternal!

exonerate: say it, believe it, experience it!

This is my perspective for today, Pastor Scott

Day One Hundred-Thirty Nine
The Pastor's Perspective: Your word for the day!

ambidexterity – *(noun) **deceitfulness; hypocrisy***
am-bi-dek-**ster**-i-tee

Reading Plan: 2 Samuel 19-21

Joab rebuked David for publicly expressing his grief over the death of Absalom, when the people expected him to be celebrating the victories they had won for him. David accepted the correction of Joab and made peace with his men. The people of Judah accompanied David back to Jerusalem, while there was a lack of support from the other tribes of Israel.

The **ambidexterity** of many Israelites would come back to haunt David and the nation. The rebellion of Sheba served as a precursor to the eventual split of God's people into two kingdoms.

David sought God for an answer to the purpose of the drought the kingdom was experiencing. God told him it was because of Saul's earlier mistreatment of some Gibeonites. David would reconcile this action with the Gibeonites by handing over seven sons of Saul.

Reflect on these thoughts:
- Never overlook the respect you should have for those who have your back.
- Keep your friends close and your enemies as far away as possible.
- You must call out deceit.
- Seek God's direction during difficult times.

Take this to the next level: Honesty shows the true character of a child of God!

ambidexterity: say it, believe it, avoid it!

This is my perspective for today, Pastor Scott

Dr. Scott Payne

Day One Hundred-Forty
The Pastor's Perspective: Your word for the day!

supplication – *(noun)* ***plea; prayer; petition***
suhp-li-**key**-sh*uh* n

Reading Plan: Psalm 5, 38, 41-42

The psalmist called out for God's justice and judgment to fall on the evildoers. Those who righteously followed God would rejoice in the Lord. People of faith should give thanks to God for having heard their **supplications.**

Sin would reap trouble! The enemy was ready to attack at the point of a person's failure. However, one's source of help was found in God.

Even those who helped the poor could find themselves facing serious suffering. This amplified the great need for a dependency upon God.

Reflect on these thoughts:
- Evil people are not out for your best interests. Guard yourself!
- Righteous people never stop doing the right thing. Encourage yourself!
- Prayerful people discover God's will. Humble yourself!
- Dependent people choose to trust God. Entrust yourself!

Take this to the next level: Life is hard but God is good!

supplication: say it, believe it, live it!

This is my perspective for today, Pastor Scott

Day One Hundred-Forty One
The Pastor's Perspective: Your word for the day!

nettle – *(verb) provoke; aggravate; rile*
net-l

Reading Plan: 2 Samuel 22-23, Psalm 57

This Psalm related to how the enemy would **nettle** the lives of the righteous. Evildoers set traps and made accusations against the righteous in an attempt to undermine the faith of God's people. The songs of David were sung to encourage those who trusted in God. God would deliver them from the evil designs of the enemy. The faithful would get the last word, and the evildoers would fall into their own traps.

David spoke as a prophet. His words and lyrics were from God, and were meant to build up God's people. David loved his mighty men! He recalled thirty-seven mighty men and their great heroism.

Reflect on these thoughts:
- Where good men serve, bad men seek to destroy.
- Praising God will keep your focus on the right path (you will not stumble)!
- Evildoers reap what they sow!
- Loyalty to God and His people is an honorable thing!

Take this to the next level: Guard yourself against the evil plans of others.

nettle: say it, believe it, avoid it!

This is my perspective for today, Pastor Scott

Dr. Scott Payne

Day One Hundred-Forty Two
The Pastor's Perspective: Your word for the day!

loathed – *(verb)* ***detested; despised***
loh*th* d

Reading Plan: Psalm 95, 97-99

God **loathed** the generation that refused to trust Him and take the Promise Land. They spent forty years in the wilderness for their acts of disobedience, and the psalmist was encouraging the people not to repeat their rebellious actions. The new generation was to be one of faith ready to heed God's voice.

It was the high calling of those who followed God to hate evil and worship only Him! This was an opportunity offered to all nations and all people. The Israelites were to set the example and call on other nations to follow their lead. They would sing of God's salvation for all people. God was Creator and King over everyone and everything. People were to celebrate His glory and majesty.

Reflect on these thoughts:
- A perfect God expects obedience to His perfect commands. You can't direct your life better than your creator!
- The results of your disobedience will be painful. You can't remove the consequences of poor decisions!
- You can't save yourself and there are no gods that can. You can call out to the true God for salvation!
- You can't create something from nothing. You can honor God as Creator!

Take this to the next level: Be true to God, and worship Him in spirit and truth.

loathed: say it, believe it, avoid it!

This is my perspective for today, Pastor Scott

Day One Hundred-Forty Three
The Pastor's Perspective: Your word for the day!

sedition – *(noun)* ***rebellion; insubordination***
si-**dish**-*uh*-n

Reading Plan: 2 Samuel 24; 1 Chronicles 21-22; Psalm 30

David's act of **sedition** against God was brought on by the temptation of the Devil. Satan challenged David to place his confidence in the size of his nation (by taking a census) rather than the greatness of his God. This offense would cause God to react with judgment on the leadership of David and the people.

With a repentant heart David would purchase a place where he would build an altar to the Lord and make offerings. God responded to David's humble actions and the strength and length of the plague was averted.

David began the preparation of the construction of the Temple. He gathered resources, materials, and challenged the people to follow the directions of his son, Solomon, in building the Temple. David would also prepare a worship song to be used in the dedication of the Temple.

Reflect on these thoughts:
- Only listen to God's voice and you'll avoid the wrong actions.
- Act quickly when you fall into sin; confess the sin, correct the course, and commit to God.
- A sacrifice to God must cost you something!
- May the song in your heart always be one of praise to the Lord!

Take this to the next level: Think like Christ and the outcome will be God-honoring.

sedition: say it, believe it, avoid it!

This is my perspective for today, Pastor Scott

Dr. Scott Payne

Day One Hundred-Forty Four
The Pastor's Perspective: Your word for the day!

accuse – *(verb)* ***blame; implicate; charge***
*uh-***kyooz**

Reading Plan: Psalm 108-110

God's children were to live courageously before their enemies. If they looked at life from a strictly human perspective, they would lose heart. But as they focused on the promises of God, they could give thanks in a victorious outcome.

The enemies of God would **accuse** the faithful even when they were living a righteous life. There was an expressed confidence that the accusations of the enemies towards the righteous would backfire. The enemies would receive the judgment they had projected on the righteous.

The Israelites were looking forward to a greater day, a time when the house of David would provide the Messiah! Their songs and worship would celebrate God's promises to David, a time when the Gentiles would receive the light and the faithfulness required of them until that day came.

Reflect on these thoughts:
- Don't let your circumstance determine your outlook.
- Look at life with your spiritual eyes and not your physical eyes.
- Stay pure to God and let the accuser experience the final guilty judgment!
- Worship looks at the past, present, and the great prospects of the future!

Take this to the next level: Celebrate God's gift available to anyone who will receive Him!

accuse: say it, believe it, live free from it!

This is my perspective for today, Pastor Scott

Day One Hundred-Forty Five
The Pastor's Perspective: Your word for the day!

correlate – *(verb)* ***link; connect***
kawr-*uh*-leyt

Reading Plan: 1 Chronicles 23-25

David continued preparation for Solomon's reign as his predecessor. David would **correlate** the leadership of Israel, the priests, and the Levites to the successful preconstruction of the Temple. David placed great emphasis on the organizational structure of the Levites, and the priestly administrative and worship responsibilities for temple worship. These were important structural issues that were precursors to the coming temple.

Reflect on these thoughts:
- Leadership is a critical foundation to building a successful spiritual future.
- Coordinating the efforts of leaders will advance God's purposes for His people.
- Leaders should assume a variety of responsibilities in order to advance spiritual plans!
- God takes seriously the preparations made in building His house!

Take this to the next level: You are the New Testament temple of the Holy Spirit!

correlate: say it, believe it, live it!

This is my perspective for today, Pastor Scott

Dr. Scott Payne

Day One Hundred-Forty Six
The Pastor's Perspective: Your word for the day!

Selah – *(noun) possibly a pause to praise, lift up, reflect*
see-l*uh*, s**e**l-*uh*

Reading Plan: Psalm 131,138-139, 143-145

In spite of the difficulties faced by God's people, they discovered God could calm and quiet the soul. The Lord gave hope!

Selah was an appropriate expression for the worshipper who repeated the psalms. At times there was no other response to an awesome God other than raising loud praises to Him. Other times the worshipper was struck by a sense of reflection and would therefore take a moment to consider the greatness of God. The Lord knew the hearts of those who worshipped Him, and a natural response to that fact was to submit to Him!

The Lord was responsive to the needs and requests of His children. He would deal with the enemies of His people and secured the direction of those who trusted Him. God was the security and provision for His followers. They loved to declare, "Great is the Lord!"

Reflect on these thoughts:
- The soul can be steady even when during tempestuous times.
- Make a joyful shout to the Lord then pause and listen for His voice.
- The Lord knows you better than you know yourself.
- Make your requests known to the Lord and begin to thank Him for His provisions!

Take this to the next level: Be a part of God's creation that praises His wonderful works!

Selah: say it, believe it, live it!

This is my perspective for today, Pastor Scott

Day One Hundred-Forty Seven
The Pastor's Perspective: Your word for the day!

idolatrous – *(adjective)* ***pagan or unholy worship***
ahy-**dol**-*uh*-tr*uh* s

Reading Plan: 1 Chronicles 26-29; Psalm 127

The gatekeepers were a vital part of the Levitical service among God's people. Their responsibilities included safeguarding the sanctuary, avoiding **idolatrous** worship, managing the treasury, and maintaining the facilities and equipment.

The Chronicler addressed the military and political structures for the kingdom. King David would instruct the leaders once they were assigned their respective places of service. The first book would conclude with an accounting of the Temple offerings and David's prayer in the assembly of the people. Solomon was anointed as the new king, and David's reign of forty years would come to an end.

The Psalmist challenged the people to remember that human effort was worthless unless God gave them wisdom, which in turn, motivated them to faithful living and sincere worship.

Reflect on these thoughts:
- As a part of the priestly family you are to stand as a gatekeeper on spiritual matters.
- God's people should never hesitate being generous at offering times.
- God is actively at work during transitions in leadership.
- Living life based on Godly wisdom will reap a good harvest!

Take this to the next level: Are you putting God first in ALL things at ALL times?

idolatrous: say it, believe it, avoid it!

This is my perspective for today, Pastor Scott

Dr. Scott Payne

Day One Hundred-Forty Eight
The Pastor's Perspective: Your word for the day!

redemptive – *(adjective)* ***delivering; saving; rescuing***
ri-**demp**-tiv

Reading Plan: Psalm 111-118

Today you have read a group of **redemptive** praise hymns. There was a celebration of God's great works describing the calling and protecting of the people of God. You also noticed a pattern of prayer, praise, and instruction for worship.

The Israelites would frequently remember God's delivering hand that set them free. He brought them out of Egypt and gave them a great land to possess. No other god could have done that! Other gods were made of man's hands and had no power. On the other hand, God was life and was the giver of life to all. It was no hard thing for a person relating to the true God to realize He was worthy of praise. Only God, His faithfulness, and love would endure forever.

Reflect on these thoughts:
- Only the lost need to be found. Only the sinner needs to be saved.
- Godly patterns of worship will deliver Godly power in the life of the worshipper.
- God is ready to set the captives free. If sin is holding you a prisoner, then ask God to set you free.
- The physical will pass away, but the Lord God will continue for eternity!

Take this to the next level: Have you asked God to set you free from your past?

redemptive: say it, believe it, experience it!

This is my perspective for today, Pastor Scott

Day One Hundred-Forty Nine
The Pastor's Perspective: Your word for the day!

obstinate – *(adjective)* ***stubborn; headstrong; unyielding***
ob-st*uh*-nit

Reading Plan: 1 Kings 1-2; Psalm 37, 71, 94

Adonijah was an **obstinate** son of King David. He sought to set himself up to become king after his father's pending death. The problem was he knew his younger brother, Solomon, was to succeed his father. God did not bless his ambitions, and his actions would eventually cost him his life. Before King David's death God made sure Solomon was installed as Israel's king with his kingdom firmly established.

The psalmist once again would remind God's people to remain faithful. Even though it seemed the wicked prospered, their judgment day was coming. The righteous should patiently wait on the Lord. Regardless of the difficulties in life, the righteous would always have the strength to praise God. God would never forsake His people.

Reflect on these thoughts:
- Doing life your way will get you in trouble.
- You can be sure your sins will find you out.
- God will keep His promises.
- Never grow weary in doing well.
- Live life God's way and you'll be regret free.

Take this to the next level: Make sure you know the difference in conviction and stubbornness.

obstinate: say it, believe it, avoid it!

This is my perspective for today, Pastor Scott

Dr. Scott Payne

Day One Hundred-Fifty
The Pastor's Perspective: Your word for the day!

precepts – *(noun) **principles; guidelines; teachings***
pree-sept s

Reading Plan: Psalm 119

The **precepts** of this psalm were written and celebrated as an awesome gift and perfect guide to life. This was the longest psalm penned with the intent to shape the character and conduct of the worshipper. This would be accomplished as the participant realized the value of God's instructions.

It was so encouraging for God's children to know that He would be with them as they faced trials or suffered bad treatment for their faithfulness. This psalm became a prayer or song for the children of God to use in private and public situations to draw attention to and affection for God's Word. His Word in turn would become the lifeblood of the relationship between man and God.

Reflect on these thoughts:
- Store up God's Word in your heart for a great foundation for life.
- You can't negotiate with God's instructions.
- God is faithful and His Word can be trusted.
- Your life must be a witness to the reliability of God and His Law.

Take this to the next level: Is your life a consistent declaration to God's righteous truth?

precepts: say it, believe it, live it!

This is my perspective for today, Pastor Scott

Day One Hundred-Fifty One
The Pastor's Perspective: Your word for the day!

wisdom – *(noun)* ***righteous knowledge; godly understanding***
wiz-d*uh* m

Reading Plan: 1 Kings 3-4

Solomon made several missteps during his early days as king: he formed an alliance with Egypt by marrying Pharaoh's daughter, and he continued worship in the high places. In contrast, one of the strongest faith steps was taken early in his kingship as well. When given the opportunity to ask anything from God he wanted, he asked for **wisdom**. God granted his request and added to the gift of wisdom, riches and honor.

Solomon established an administrative structure to effectively execute his reign. His reign became so great that rulers from all nations came to hear the wisdom and counsel from Solomon.

Reflect on these thoughts:
- Even godly leaders can make foolish decisions.
- God loves distributing wisdom to those who ask for it.
- Wisdom will detect true love.
- Effective leadership includes others.
- Wisdom seeks God's way not man's way.

Take this to the next level: What is the greatest desire of your heart?

wisdom: say it, believe it, live it!

This is my perspective for today, Pastor Scott

Dr. Scott Payne

Day One Hundred-Fifty Two
The Pastor's Perspective: Your word for the day!

interceded – *(verb) intervened; mediated*
in-ter-**seed**-ed

Reading Plan: 2 Chronicles 1; Psalm 72

Solomon requested of God that He grant him wisdom to rule well. God gave him wisdom and much more. God provided Solomon with such wealth, materials, and workers that he could build the Temple with no obstacles.

King David did a beautiful thing as he **interceded** for his son's (Solomon) future as king. David knew that the blessing of a nation was determined in large part by its leadership. He earnestly prayed that God would bless Solomon and make him a success as he cared for Israel.

Reflect on these thoughts:
- Seek God's blessing on your life.
- Ask God to give you the assets needed to build a strong Christian life.
- Pray that God will give wisdom to those that lead and influence you.
- God will bless you in order that you might be a blessing to others.

Take this to the next level: Can you name three people for whom you are praying?

interceded: say it, believe it, live it!

This is my perspective for today, Pastor Scott

Day One Hundred-Fifty Three
The Pastor's Perspective: Your word for the day!

fidelity – *(noun)* ***loyalty; faithfulness***
fi-**del**-i-tee, fahy

Reading Plan: Song of Solomon

Today you have read one of the most questionable and controversial books in the Bible. Let's try and keep this simple. The book focused on a relationship driven by love and a physical desire for another person. The **fidelity** of two lovers would have been a given to the reader. The major movements in the book were: the desire they have for one another, the female's dreams for the man of her choice, the growing passion they expressed for one another, and the eventual union. Key themes of the book were God's expectation for sexual purity and God's gift of marriage as the means to experience loyalty and commitment to another. The book could also be a reflection of God's love for His people and their love for Him.

Reflect on these thoughts:
- God has a plan for individuals to express their love for one another.
- God created humans to be attracted to one another.
- The courtship is an important part of building a strong future.
- A physical relationship should be the result of a God-blessed marriage.

Take this to the next level: Are you practicing fidelity in your love relationship with God and other personal relationships?

fidelity: say it, believe it, live it!

This is my perspective for today, Pastor Scott

Dr. Scott Payne

Day One Hundred-Fifty Four
The Pastor's Perspective: Your word for the day!

duped – *(verb)* ***deceived; tricked; fooled***
doop, dyoop

Reading Plan: Proverbs 1-3

Solomon was the wisest man who ever lived. His care for the people was foundational in God's preservation of his wise words of counsel. An early caution was given to the reader to avoid being **duped** by the ways of those that would seek to draw people away from God. Solomon advised the people to avoid places, people, and purposes that were not God-centered. He taught that if you truly desired wisdom, you should ask for it and seek it. This would be the best way to secure God's blessing on your life.

Reflect on these thoughts:
- A wise person wants more wisdom.
- Wisdom makes good choices.
- Greed does not match the character of a giving God.
- A healthy respect for God is the beginning of wisdom.

Take this to the next level: From whom do you seek counsel and direction for living?

duped: say it, believe it, avoid it!

This is my perspective for today, Pastor Scott

Day One Hundred-Fifty Five
The Pastor's Perspective: Your word for the day!

exhort – *(verb)* ***urge; encourage; spur***
ig-**zawrt**

Reading Plan: Proverbs 4-6

A father would **exhort** his son to listen to his instruction. The son was not to forsake the teachings of his father. The loving father knew the son must seek wisdom and hold fast to wise counsel. The lure of evil must be avoided, and the son must guard his heart against the destructive forces at work around him. By listening to the wisdom a father has offered, the son could stay clear of the enticing activity of evil.

The son was to flee the temptations of adultery. The consequences of such an offense were deadly.

Idleness must be avoided and time needed to be filled with godly activities to guard the heart and one's actions.

Reflect on these thoughts:
- Fathers that love their children will instruct them in godly things.
- Children can learn a great deal from their parents.
- God is the best Father a person can have.
- Avoid evil and anything that draws your attraction away from God.
- Poor choices reveal a lack of sense and leads to destruction.

Take this to the next level: Are you taking godly counsel from your spiritual mentors?

exhort: say it, believe it, learn from it!

This is my perspective for today, Pastor Scott

Dr. Scott Payne

Day One Hundred-Fifty Six
The Pastor's Perspective: Your word for the day!

sentinel – *(noun)* ***guard; lookout***
sen-tn-l

Reading Plan: Proverbs 7-9

It was profoundly important that **sentinels** be posted in the lives of God's people. A **sentinel** would be someone or something that reminded the child of God to honor and keep God's words, seek wisdom and understanding, and avoid any lie that would lead to destruction.

The proverbs warned people to be careful when considering any temptation to participate in ungodly activities. They needed to realize there was a high price to pay for chasing evil. The best prescription to deny evil was to stay close to God, value wisdom, and wait on the Lord; then it would be well with their soul.

Reflect on these thoughts:
- Use what you can to remind yourself to stay faithful to God and avoid evil.
- Maintain a healthy relationship with God.
- Stay away from the paths that lead to ungodly actions.
- The tempter will never tell you what's waiting on the other side of the offer.

Take this to the next level: God will not tempt you.

sentinel: say it, believe it, live it!

This is my perspective for today, Pastor Scott

Day One Hundred-Fifty Seven
The Pastor's Perspective: Your word for the day!

maxim – *(noun)* ***adage; truthful saying***
mak-sim

Reading Plan: Proverbs 10-12

Your reading today was filled with **maxims** related to personal righteousness versus wicked rebellion. The Lord provided for those who practiced righteousness, and judgment awaited those who pursued their own prideful desires. The righteous would provide fairly for those around them, and the wicked would manipulate others for their own gain. The wicked had a distorted and false view of their possessions and power. They would realize at some point in the future their assets would not save them. The righteous would live in peace with God and others, and at some point in the future, find God's abundant provisions overwhelming.

Reflect on these thoughts:
- God speaks to life issues with precise truth.
- Living life God's way provides a hope that will be completely satisfying.
- A humble life is the exemplary pattern and practice of God's people.
- God-followers will embrace correction and discipline.

Take this to the next level: What does your conduct say about your commitment to God?

maxim: say it, believe it, live it!

This is my perspective for today, Pastor Scott

Dr. Scott Payne

Day One Hundred-Fifty Eight
The Pastor's Perspective: Your word for the day!

elocution *(noun)* **articulation; vocalization; oral delivery**
el-*uh*-**kyoo**-sh*uh* n

Reading Plan: Proverbs 13-15

Elocution revealed a lot about the character of a person. The proverbs acknowledged a profound truth that the speech of a person revealed the true content of their heart. The language of the wicked declared their guilt; likewise, the words of the righteous declared their innocence.

The wise would keep counselors close and would listen to the thoughts of others before making decisions. The wicked were driven to experience life without consideration of others in their choices and directions for life. Proverbs repeatedly characterized people in two categories: the wicked who were proud and the wise who were humble.

Reflect on these thoughts:
- Do you seek counsel from others?
- Do your words encourage others or minimize them?
- Do you love righteousness or enjoy making your own way?
- Do you fear the Lord or favor your freedom?

Take this to the next level: Is your tongue a friend to God or does it declare your independence?

elocution: say it, believe it, understand it!

This is my perspective for today, Pastor Scott

Day One Hundred-Fifty Nine
The Pastor's Perspective: Your word for the day!

persuasive – *(adjective)* ***convincing***
per-**swey**-siv, -zip

Reading Plan: Proverbs 16-18

The person that exercised wisdom would produce a very **persuasive** life testimony. This was more valuable than any other treasure one could possess.

Wisdom would follow the direction of God over the plans of the heart. The proverb warned the heart was deceptive, and a person should faithfully seek God's plans for life. The Lord tested the heart and provided wisdom to those who asked.

A fool isolated himself, but the wise would seek the Lord and become hopeful.

Reflect on these thoughts:
- Turn from evil and seek God.
- The greatest treasure is wisdom.
- The wise heart is characterized by good speech.
- Let God define right from wrong.
- Guard your public speech or risk humiliation.

Take this to the next level: Does your life add value or extract value from others?

persuasive: say it, believe it, live it!

This is my perspective for today, Pastor Scott

Dr. Scott Payne

Day One Hundred-Sixty
The Pastor's Perspective: Your word for the day!

equivocate – *(verb) **mislead intentionally; lie; falsify***
ih-**kwiv**-*uh*-keyt

Reading Plan: Proverbs 19-21

The person who would **equivocate** deceived himself, destroyed the lives of others, and deconstructed his own future. A fool used deceitful speech to manipulate others for personal gain.

The lazy found no profit and only made contributions for their ruin. Wisdom was better than wealth, because it had an objective value rather than a subjective worth that was misleading.

Good things came to those who waited. God looked at the motive and heart of a person. Outward appearances failed to impress God, but a humble heart that honestly lived to please God had a reward.

Reflect on these thoughts:
- Truthful living has a great return.
- Avoid deceiving yourself by listening to God.
- Invest your life by actively working out your faith through serving God and others.
- Giving is far better than receiving.

Take this to the next level: Are your words buildings up others or seeking to control others?

equivocate: say it, believe it, avoid it!

This is my perspective for today, Pastor Scott

Day One Hundred-Sixty One
The Pastor's Perspective: Your word for the day!

disingenuous – *(adjective)* ***misleading; insincere***
dis-in-**jen**-yoo-*uh* s

Reading Plan: Proverbs 22-24

Parenting was not an art but an act of humility. Parent wisely and your children would be drawn to God. Training up a child in a Godly environment was essential to the development of the child.

The **disingenuous** person was no friend of God and should not be the friend of God's people. Seeking to benefit on the backs of others would only bring God's judgment on that person. The sincere faithful servant of the Lord would prosper in all his ways.

Your home was to be established with wisdom and an abundance of counsel. In contrast, the foolish person valued his opinion above all and never stopped talking.

Your plans for life were to be for good and not evil. Much of the calamity of life could be avoided if the wisdom of God is sought and one lived a righteous life.

Reflect on these thoughts:
- Parenting God's way brings God's favor.
- Trust God to handle the judging of others, and know that He will deal rightly with you.
- Honesty will reap a great harvest.
- Wisdom is good for the soul and satisfying to the heart.

Take this to the next level: "People may doubt what you say, but they will always believe what you do."

disingenuous: say it, believe it, avoid it!

This is my perspective for today, Pastor Scott

Dr. Scott Payne

Day One Hundred-Sixty Two
The Pastor's Perspective: Your word for the day!

precursor – *(noun) forerunner; indication; predecessor*
pri-**kur**-ser, **pree**-kur-

Reading Plan: 1 Kings 5-6; 2 Chronicles 2-3

King Hiram's loyal relationship with King David served as a **precursor** for Solomon's ability to construct the Temple. Solomon requested King Hiram to make preparations and provide materials for the construction of God's Temple. King Hiram of Tyre cheerfully agreed and had his people harvest the timber (cedar and cypress). Hiram also had masons cut and prepare stone that would be used. The materials were then sent to Mount Moriah in Jerusalem where the Temple was erected.

It took the people seven years to construct the Temple under Solomon's direction. He was faithful to construct "the house of the Lord" in a manner fitting to the true God. The Temple was a perfect reflection of a Holy God with all the materials, construction, structural integrity, and designated areas completed according to specifications.

Reflect on these thoughts:
- God's timing is everything.
- Working for the Lord is a joy not a burden.
- Honor God in everything you do.
- God indwells the living temples of His people (their bodies).

Take this to the next level: God's presence is still looking for a place to dwell.

precursor: say it, believe it, honor it!

This is my perspective for today, Pastor Scott

Day One Hundred-Sixty Three
The Pastor's Perspective: Your word for the day!

consociation – *(noun) **association of like-minded members; partnership***
k*uh* n-soh-see-**ey**-sh*uh* n

Reading Plan: 1 Kings 7; 2 Chronicles 4

The **consociation** of Solomon and Hiram completed the physical construction of Solomon's Palace and the house of the Lord. The entire Temple complex included the House of the Forest of Lebanon, the Hall of the Throne, the Hall of Pillars, the House of Pharaoh's Daughter, Solomon's House, the Court, and the main Temple area.

Reflect on these thoughts:
- More can be accomplished when people work together.
- Complete what you start.
- The greatest investments in life are those that honor God.
- Give God your best.

Take this to the next level: Take a moment and thank God for those people who help you accomplish God's plan for your life.

consociation: say it, believe it, celebrate it!

This is my perspective for today, Pastor Scott

Dr. Scott Payne

Day One Hundred-Sixty Four
The Pastor's Perspective: Your word for the day!

ubiquity – *(noun)* ***omnipresent; pervasiveness***
yoo-**bik**-wi-tee

Reading Plan: 1 Kings 8; 2 Chronicles 5

His dwelling in the Temple did not compromise the **ubiquity** of God. Solomon pronounced that God could not be held in a single place or in a particular house. What Solomon requested from God was that His presence would be in the Temple, and His favor and willingness to forgive would permeate the Temple.

Solomon called for the Ark to be brought to its permanent location in the Temple along with the holy vessels. After the people assembled Solomon dedicated the Temple, challenged the people to faithfulness, and made great sacrifices to God. After a week of Temple dedication the people returned to their homes.

Reflect on these thoughts:
- A place means little without the presence of God there.
- You can't be possessive with God because He is everywhere.
- Holy things should be used for holy purposes.
- Dedicating something to God must be taken seriously.

Take this to the next level: May God inhabit the praises of His people. Praise Him now!

ubiquity: say it, believe it, celebrate it!

This is my perspective for today, Pastor Scott

Day One Hundred-Sixty Five
The Pastor's Perspective: Your word for the day!

exculpate – *(verb) acquit; exonerate*
ek-skuhl-peyt, ik-**skuhl**-peyt

Reading Plan: 2 Chronicles 6-7; Psalm 136

Solomon asked the Lord that He **exculpate** the people. Solomon exhorted the people to seek God's forgiveness by approaching the Temple to seek forgiveness of their sin. The people's humble request would find God's favor and forgiveness.

God's response to His repentant people would be restoration. The Temple was God's visible symbol of His mercy and grace. The Temple would become a foreshadowing of God's forgiveness of sin through faith in His Son, Jesus Christ. God's presence in the Old Testament was understood to be the actual temple building. In the New Testament, God arrived in the flesh providing forgiveness from sin by faith in Jesus Christ. PTL!

Reflect on these thoughts:
- All sin, but few repent.
- God's love for His creation is demonstrated by His presence with us.
- God responds to the confessions from a humble heart.
- God's love never waivers.

Take this to the next level: When is the last time you cried out to God and asked for His favor?

Exculpate: say it, believe it, live it!

This is my perspective for today, Pastor Scott

Dr. Scott Payne

Day One Hundred-Sixty Six
The Pastor's Perspective: Your word for the day!

laudable – *(adjective)* ***admirable; praiseworthy***
law-d*uh*-b*uh* l

Reading Plan: Psalm 134, 146-150

God only was the true **laudable** Lord! Your reading today declared the greatness of God. He was worthy to be praised because He was creator, could be trusted, and would heal the brokenhearted.

The goodness of the Lord was so overwhelming that those who worshipped Him should do so with a new song.

The people of God discovered the joy of joining all creation and praising the Lord!

Reflect on these thoughts:
- No one or nothing compares to the glory of the Lord.
- Better to trust in the Lord than people or things.
- Keep a new song in your heart.
- Join His creation in giving Him praise!

Take this to the next level: You worship your highest priority. Evaluate what consumes your time and treasure, and you'll discover what you are declaring is worthy of your praise.

laudable: say it, believe it, let God receive it!

This is my perspective for today, Pastor Scott

Day One Hundred-Sixty Seven
The Pastor's Perspective: Your word for the day!

dubious – *(adjective)* ***unconvinced; questionable***
doo-bee-*uh* s

Reading Plan: 1 Kings 9; 2 Chronicles 8

The Lord appeared to Solomon and blessed him for completing the house of the Lord and the king's house. God would challenge Solomon to continue his faithful walk and pledged to establish his royal rule over Israel.

One thing that struck the reader was Solomon's **dubious** gift to Hiram. The emphasis on this fact might have served to remind the people that Hiram was not the principal in all these matters. God was working through Solomon on behalf of His people and His covenant promise. Solomon would build the house of the Lord not Hiram! But Hiram was given something for his service.

Solomon would continue to build his empire by using the forced labor of conquered nations. The people of Israel would serve as administrators and managers as the growth of their nation continued. Solomon would faithfully continue the expectation of worship as his father, David, had done.

Reflect on these thoughts:
- Good stewardship produces godly results.
- God will bless His people with the assets of others.
- God appoints people in their places of service.
- God loves a heart of worship.

Take this to the next level: No gift is a bad gift. Doing God's work is an honorable thing!

dubious: say it, believe it, accept what God gives!

This is my perspective for today, Pastor Scott

Dr. Scott Payne

Day One Hundred-Sixty Eight
The Pastor's Perspective: Your word for the day!

sluggard – *(noun)* ***slouch; slacker***
sluhg-erd

Reading Plan: Proverbs 25-26

The **sluggard** considered himself wise, but his careless ways would be his demise. A warning was given to the one who thinks of himself too highly versus encouragement that was given to the person who humbly seeks truth from God. Humble people rejected the temptation to indulge in high opinions of themselves. The wise chose righteous living over foolish behavior. God's people would be people of integrity who treat all redemptively.

Reflect on these thoughts:
- Treat your enemy with respect.
- Laziness invites evil.
- Don't listen to any voice other than God's.
- Integrity is based on what God thinks about you, rather than what people say about you.

Take this to the next level: Ask God to direct the activity of your life.

sluggard: say it, believe it, avoid it!

This is my perspective for today, Pastor Scott

Day One Hundred-Sixty Nine
The Pastor's Perspective: Your word for the day!

inveigle – *(verb) **con; trick; lure***
in-**vey**-g*uh* l, -vee-

Reading Plan: Proverbs 27-29

The wicked attempted to **inveigle** God's people into idolatry. Pride was a primary tool used to draw them away from God and truth. A great number of the proverbs cautioned about placing too much confidence in one's own self. The proverbs warned God's people to guard themselves against feeding their ego through deceptive thoughts and behavior.

Relationships were to be grounded in truth and honesty seeking to build up others. A person should be ready to accept correction and be quick to seek understanding, knowledge, and justice. When sin was detected the best remedy was to quickly confess it.

Reflect on these thoughts:
- Seek wisdom from God in order to avoid evil temptations.
- Avoid a lot of personal pronouns in your conversations.
- Be a friend and have a friend.
- Fear the lie and faith the truth.
- Confession is good for the soul.

Take this to the next level: Wisdom will say no to the lure of the wicked.

inveigle: say it, believe it, avoid it!

This is my perspective for today, Pastor Scott

Dr. Scott Payne

Day One Hundred-Seventy
The Pastor's Perspective: Your word for the day!

vanity – *(noun)* ***anything with the property of worthlessness, meaninglessness, unproductiveness***
van-i-tee

Reading Plan: Ecclesiastes 1-6

Solomon was convinced all attempts to make a meaningful contribution to life was nothing but **vanity**.
He had all the assets to expand his sense of accomplishment in many areas of living, but came to the conclusion it didn't matter. There was nothing new under the sun. God was the only One that mattered so He should be feared and respected.

Reflect on these thoughts:
- The value of your existence must be understood from God's perspective not yours.
- Just because you can't understand something doesn't mean it has no value.
- Life will bring many changes and challenges.
- The physical things of this world are fleeting, but the spiritual things are eternal.

Take this to the next level: Human understanding is limited; therefore, you must trust God.

vanity: say it, believe it, avoid it!

This is my perspective for today, Pastor Scott

Day One Hundred-Seventy One
The Pastor's Perspective: Your word for the day!

capricious – *(adjective)* ***unpredictable; fickle***
k*uh*-**prish**-*uh* s, -**pree**-sh*uh* s

Reading Plan: Ecclesiastes 7-12

Solomon observed that life was so **capricious** there was no way you could know how to prepare for, or even react to, its experiences. He expressed all you could do is make the best of each situation.

The only true way to find any joy in life would be to fear God and respect His laws. The priority of a wise person was to fear the Lord; only the fool would seek to live without respect for God.

The most significant challenge a person faced was sin. It was man's sin that robbed him of the value and joy of life.

Reflect on these thoughts:
- There is no way you can anticipate what tomorrow holds.
- God sees ahead, and it is wise to trust Him.
- Avoid sin by loving God's Word.
- A person prepares for eternity by living God's way now.

Take this to the next level: Life is difficult but God is your hope.

capricious: say it, believe it, you can deal with it!

This is my perspective for today, Pastor Scott

Dr. Scott Payne

Day One Hundred-Seventy Two
The Pastor's Perspective: Your word for the day!

impiety – *(noun) sinfulness; irreverence; ungodliness*
im-**pahy**-i-tee

Reading Plan: 1 Kings 10-11; 2 Chronicles 9

Solomon welcomed the queen of Sheba to his royal house. She came with many questions and found that Solomon's wisdom surpassed her wildest imagination. He also impressed her with his great wealth. The queen responded with lavish gifts to the wise king.

The **impiety** of Solomon would bring the judgment of God upon him. His disobedient relationships with women from foreign nations angered the Lord. God raised up adversaries that challenged Solomon's rule and would ultimately divide the nation of Israel. What a sad state of affairs that the wise king Solomon allowed his personal weakness for women to trump his loyalty to God.

Reflect on these thoughts:
- Wisdom does not have to impress anyone.
- Identify your weaknesses, and confess them to God.
- Obey God regardless of your feelings.
- Disobedience to God always comes at a high personal price.

Take this to the next level: Your actions declare your faithfulness to God. Are you faithful?

impiety: say it, believe it, avoid it!

This is my perspective for today, Pastor Scott

Day One Hundred-Seventy Three
The Pastor's Perspective: Your word for the day!

guerdon – *(noun) **repayment; reward***
gur-dn

Reading Plan: Proverbs 30-31

A righteous life could expect the **guerdon** to be wisdom. God's words and ways were the truth that provided meaning and purpose to those who sought him. Doing life without God was foolish and caused weariness. Judgment followed those who lied, and, in contrast, peace followed those who spoke truth and avoided lies.

The character of the woman who feared the Lord proved to be one of excellence in all areas of life and was the expectation for all children of God. She became the model for all those who sought wisdom.

Reflect on these thoughts:
- Tell God you are tired of doing life your way.
- Confess you are ready to obey His Words.
- Deny the lie, and trust the Truth.
- Only the humble can attain a respectable place among others.
- Commit your life to the highest standards which reflect the character of God.

Take this to the next level: Are you doing life God's way? If so you are at peace.

guerdon: say it, believe it, seek it from God!

This is my perspective for today, Pastor Scott

Dr. Scott Payne

Day One Hundred-Seventy Four
The Pastor's Perspective: Your word for the day!

infidelity – *(noun)* **unfaithfulness; betrayal; rebellion**
in-fi-**del**-i-tee

Reading Plan: 1 Kings 12-14

After the death of Solomon God's people would be divided into two kingdoms; Rehoboam would lead Judah, and Jeroboam would lead Israel. The **infidelity of** Rehoboam and Jeroboam led to the spiritual downfall of both kingdoms.

Jeroboam failed to trust God during the early days of his kingship. He leaned on his own plans to save his position of authority. His fears drove him to create new places of worship that focused on false gods. Even after being called out by the prophet of God he refused to forsake the worship of false gods. Jeroboam failed to obey God, and it cost him his life.

Rehoboam had no heart for God and saw God's people as his servants, rather than a nation to love and lead. He forsook God and built places of false worship to idols.

Reflect on these thoughts:
- God calls out servant leaders not prideful masters.
- Listen to God's appeal to turn from sin.
- Obey God's word rather than man's.
- Serve the true God and share His love with others.

Take this to the next level: Does God drive your life and influence your decisions?

infidelity: say it, believe it, avoid it!

This is my perspective for today, Pastor Scott

Day One Hundred-Seventy Five
The Pastor's Perspective: Your word for the day!

consultation – *(noun) **discussion; discourse***
kon-s*uh* l-**tey**-sh*uh* n

Reading Plan: 2 Chronicles 10-12

There was some **consultation** between King Rehoboam and the old men of Israel. He sought their insight to the question of relieving the burdens that had been placed on the people by King Solomon. The king failed to listen to the advice given him, and he announced the burdens would be increased. The people rebelled, and they killed the king's taskmaster over the forced labor. There was constant infighting between those who supported Rehoboam and those who would not. Rehoboam abandoned the law of God. Therefore, God allowed Egypt to plunder Jerusalem and made them servants to the Egyptians.

Reflect on these thoughts:
- Listen to wise counsel.
- Don't increase the burdens of others.
- Remember God will not share His throne with another.
- There are consequences to sin.

Take this to the next level: Are you seeking the counsel of wise people? Do you listen?

consultation: say it, believe it, seek it!

This is my perspective for today, Pastor Scott

Dr. Scott Payne

Day One Hundred-Seventy Six
The Pastor's Perspective: Your word for the day!

piety – *(noun) **devoutness; reverence***
pahy-i-tee

Reading Plan: 1 Kings 15; 2 Chronicles 13-16

A lack of **piety** characterized the kings of both Israel and Judah. The hope of the Chronicler was that the kings would follow the faithfulness of David. However, most succumbed to the faithlessness and idolatry of Solomon.

Nada and Baasha followed King Jeroboam of Israel. Abijam and Asa followed King Rehoboam of Judah. The conflict between Israel and Judah polarized the people of God.

King Asa of Judah was reportedly a good king, calling the people back to the true God. He removed the false idols and repaired the Lord's altar. However, he had two great failures: he failed to destroy the high places, and when threatened by Israel, he sought help from Syria rather than God.

Reflect on these thoughts:
- God wants fully devoted followers.
- The enemy is Satan not your brother.
- Influencers and leaders must follow after God.
- Be faithful, start strong, and finish strong.

Take this to the next level: Daily confess your need for God. Keep His ways your highest priority!

piety: say it, believe it, live it!

This is my perspective for today, Pastor Scott

Day One Hundred-Seventy Seven
The Pastor's Perspective: Your word for the day!

preponderance – *(noun) majority; prevalence; dominance*
pri-**pon**-der-*uh*- ns

Reading Plan: 1 Kings 16; 2 Chronicles 17

The 1 Kings reading focused on the demise of Baasha and his house. Because Baasha had led the people of Israel away from God and caused them to sin, the Lord would destroy him. Elah, his son, would reign in his place. Zimri conspired against Elah and killed him. Omri overthrew Zimri's rule. Omri continued to do evil in the sight of the Lord. After his death, his son Ahab ruled, and he was the most evil king of all kings.

The 2 Chronicles reading reflected on the transition of King Asa of Judah to his son Jehoshaphat after his forty-year reign. Even though Jehoshaphat's influence was mixed with good and bad decisions, there was a **preponderance** of good. He walked in the earlier ways of David, and God blessed the kingdom of Judah.

Reflect on these thoughts:
- God will ultimately judge sin.
- Don't leave a bad heritage to your family.
- The traitor will be betrayed.
- Turn from evil before things get worse.
- Good leaders will bless the people they serve, and have great influence.

Take this to the next level: What does your life declare about God?

preponderance: say it, believe it, live it for God!

This is my perspective for today, Pastor Scott

Dr. Scott Payne

Day One Hundred-Seventy Eight
The Pastor's Perspective: Your word for the day!

oblation – *(noun) sacrifice; offering*
o-**bley**-sh*uh* n

Reading Plan: 1 Kings 17-19

The prophet Elijah predicted a drought would come to Israel. God told Elijah to go hide east of the Jordan at the brook Cherith. The prophet would find provisions there from the ravens, and eventually, from a widow. He would raise the widow's son from a death experience before returning to confront Ahab and the false prophets of Baal.

Elijah challenged the false prophets to a contest to see whose god was the true God. They accepted the challenge but found their acts of sacrifice made no difference. They received no response from their gods. The **oblation** made by Elijah to God on Mount Carmel was totally acceptable. God completely consumed the offering, the altar and all the water. The people fell on their faces and worshipped the Lord. They seized the false prophets of Baal and killed them.

Elijah announced to the king and the people that God would soon release the rains from the heavens. King Ahab returned to Jezreel and reported to Jezebel all that had happened. She sent a messenger to Elijah letting him know she would have him killed within a day. Elijah fled and ended up in a cave, where the Lord spoke to him and told him to anoint Elisha to become the prophet to Israel.

Reflect on these thoughts:
- God provides for His obedient children.
- False gods are no matches for the true God.
- Acceptable sacrifices please God.
- A lie will die.
- God is making ready His servants.

Take this to the next level: What and to whom are you making sacrifices?

oblation: say it, believe it, live it!

This is my perspective for today, Pastor Scott

Day One Hundred-Seventy Nine
The Pastor's Perspective: Your word for the day!

nefarious – *(adjective)* ***evil; reprehensible***
ni-**fair**-ee-*uh* s

Reading Plan: 1 Kings 20-21

Even with the evil actions of King Ahab, God would protect the nation of Israel from a Syrian invasion. God would lead a prophet to prepare Ahab for the battle and give him directions to win the war. Ahab ends up letting the king of Syria go free. A prophet of God condemned that decision, and Ahab returned to his house upset.

Ahab wanted Naboth's vineyard, because it was close to his house. After Naboth refused to sell his vineyard Jezebel had Naboth killed. When Jezebel informed Ahab of Naboth's death he seized the vineyard. The Lord condemned the **nefarious** behavior of Jezebel and Ahab, but responded to Ahab's repentant heart.

Reflect on these thoughts:
- God's love pursues sinners.
- God sends others into your life to share His love and plans.
- Don't make friends with the enemy.
- Confessing sin gets God's attention.

Take this to the next level: Let God fulfill the desires of your heart; never take matters into your own hands.

nefarious: say it, believe it, avoid it!

This is my perspective for today, Pastor Scott

Dr. Scott Payne

Day One Hundred-Eighty
The Pastor's Perspective: Your word for the day!

alliance – *(noun)* ***pact; partnership; association***
uh-**lahy**-*uh* ns

Reading Plan: 1 Kings 22; 2 Chronicles 18

Ahab asked Jehoshaphat to enter into an **alliance** that could challenge Syria. Ahab wanted Jehoshaphat to join forces to take back Ramoth-gilead from the Syrians. After seeking the approval of the prophets of God Jehoshaphat agreed. There was only one problem. Four hundred prophets agreed that God would give the combined forces Ramoth-gilead, but one revealed the truth, the prophet Micaiah. Micaiah declared the word of the Lord to the two kings; Syria would defeat them, and Ahab would be killed.

Reflect on these thoughts:
- Guard the alliances you make with others.
- The majority may not have it right.
- God's ways need no deception.
- Listen to what God has to say rather than what you want to hear.

Take this to the next level: Ask God to reveal His ways directly to you.

alliance: say it, believe it, live it with God!

This is my perspective for today, Pastor Scott

Day One Hundred-Eighty One
The Pastor's Perspective: Your word for the day!

recant – *(verb)* ***renounce; retract; disown***
ri-**kant**

Reading Plan: 2 Chronicles 19-23

Jehoshaphat would **recant** his disobedient ways towards God and reclaim the fear of the Lord for the people of Judah. He re-established the service of the Levites and the duties of the priests. But he left the high places and allowed the hearts of the people to turn toward the Lord, but not be transformed by the Lord.

God stepped in and delivered Judah from the warring people of Edom. God alone totally destroyed the invading armies and the spoils went to Judah. Jehoshaphat's reign ended short of seeing God's blessings because he continued to align himself with Ahaziah, king of Israel.

Judah would struggle under the leadership of wicked kings. Then Jehoiada, the priest, rallied the people and spiritual leaders to refocus their attention on executing godly ways. Joash was anointed king. Athaliah was killed and the people enjoyed peace and a renewed desire for living as God's children.

Reflect on these thoughts:
- Never do a job half way.
- Genuine transformation is internal.
- God may be ready for battle on your behalf.
- Get rid of the evil thing, and you'll discover God's peace.

Take this to the next level: Are you willing to leave anything that harms your relationship with God?

recant: say it, believe it, live it!

This is my perspective for today, Pastor Scott

Dr. Scott Payne

Day One Hundred-Eighty Two
The Pastor's Perspective: Your word for the day!

thwart – *(verb) impede; obstruct; prevent*
thwawrt

Reading Plan: Obadiah; Psalm 82-83

God's judgment was inevitable. Those who lived for God would be restored, and those who denied Him would be judged guilty. Because God forgave and restored His people, they were to use their position to service the needs of others.

God assured His people He would restore Israel and had doomed Edom. The Edomites were descendants of Jacob's brother Esau. Their partnership with Babylon had assisted in the defeat of Israel. Their activities in helping the Babylonians had sealed their fate. God would deal with them directly.

The people of God cried out that He would **thwart** the plans of the enemy, and those who did not know Him would recognize His glory.

Reflect on these thoughts:
- Everyone must face God's judgment.
- Service is a calling for all God's people.
- Only God can restore the broken.
- Your partnerships should do no harm to others.

Take this to the next level: Ask God to stop evil wherever it raises its head.

thwart: say it, believe it, use it against evil!

This is my perspective for today, Pastor Scott

Day One Hundred-Eighty Three
The Pastor's Perspective: Your word for the day!

mentor – *(noun) **adviser; coach; teacher***
men-tawr, -ter

Reading Plan: 2 Kings 1-4

Israel continued her spiritual slide away from God under the leadership of King Ahaziah. Ahaziah sought the blessing of the prophet Elijah, but received the verdict of God's judgment instead of approval.

Elisha discovered his **mentor** was Elijah. The two men walked out their prophetic work together until God took Elijah by a whirlwind to heaven. Before Elijah's departure Elisha had asked for a double portion of his spirit. After Elijah went to be with the Lord, it became obvious that Elisha's request was granted. He performed amazing works that could only be attributed to God. He assured Israel of victory over the Moabites, he provided for the needs of a widow, he raised the Shunammite's son from the dead, and he purified the stew. God was at work in the prophet's life!

Reflect on these thoughts:
- Evil leadership begets negative results.
- Turn from sin and humbly approach the Lord seeking forgiveness.
- Invest in others, and allow others to invest in you.
- Boldly ask God for His abundant blessings.

Take this to the next level: Are you making a contribution in the lives of others?

mentor: say it, believe it, live it!

This is my perspective for today, Pastor Scott

Dr. Scott Payne

Day One Hundred-Eighty Four
The Pastor's Perspective: Your word for the day!

portent – *(noun) premonition; forewarning; prediction*
pawr-tent, **pohr**-

Reading Plan: 2 Kings 5-8

Elisha continued to perform miracles of **portent**. He had requested a blessing of double portion of Elijah's prophetic work, and he had definitely received it. The scriptures record a series of mighty works by the prophet: the healing of Naaman, floating the axe head, the chariots of fire, the blessings of the four lepers and the people of Israel, the provisions of the Shunammite woman, and the prediction of transitions in leadership. God had anointed Elisha for a great work, and anyone who came in contact with the prophet knew he was a man of God.

Reflect on these thoughts:
- Obey God, and discover the miraculous.
- Greed always had a negative return.
- Only spiritual eyes can see the provisions of God.
- Take a step of faith, and do something.
- Share the benefits of God's blessings in your life.

Take this to the next level: Are you living up to God's potential for your life?

portent: say it, believe it, live it!

This is my perspective for today, Pastor Scott

Day One Hundred-Eighty Five
The Pastor's Perspective: Your word for the day!

eradicate – *(noun) **eliminate; destroy; annihilate***
ih-**rad**-i-keyt

Reading Plan: 2 Kings 9-11

After the prophet Elisha anointed Jehu the king of Israel, Jehu assassinated King Joram and King Ahaziah. He also had Jezebel executed. During Jehu's campaign to **eradicate** King Ahab's family, he killed the seventy descendant sons who lived in Samaria. He didn't stop there. Next he struck down all the people and prophets that followed Baal. He reigned over Israel twenty-eight years and then died.

Joash would become the heir to the throne of Judah. He was miraculously spared from the attempts of Athaliah to destroy all the royal family. Jehoiada, the priest, was the spiritual leader that gave direction to King Joash and the people. After Athaliah's death the people rejoiced, and all was well.

Reflect on these thoughts:
- An evil house cannot stand.
- God's people need spiritual leaders willing to serve as God directs.
- You can be sure your sins will find you out.
- God's people can make no room for sin.

Take this to the next level: Are you serving God regardless of the cost?

eradicate: say it, believe it, live it against sin!

This is my perspective for today, Pastor Scott

Dr. Scott Payne

Day One Hundred-Eighty Six
The Pastor's Perspective: Your word for the day!

neglect – *(noun)* ***inattention***   **neglected***(verb)* ***ignored***
ni-**glekt**

Reading Plan: 2 Kings 12-13; 2 Chronicles 24

During his reign, King Jehoash of Judah discovered the Temple was in great **neglect** and in need of many repairs. He ordered the priests use funds from the Temple offerings to handle the upkeep of the Temple. By the twenty-third year of the king's reign, he learned the Temple was still being **neglected**, so the king's secretary took charge of the project, managed the money, and paid the workers. The Temple was successfully refurbished. After a forty-year reign Jehoash was struck down by two conspirators and died.

The readings today recorded the death of a great prophet of God, Elisha. After he was buried, a dead man was thrown into his tomb because of the threat of an approaching group of marauders to the burial party. When the dead man's body touched Elisha's bones he was revived and stood up.

Reflect on these thoughts:
- You must take care of God's House.
- You are also the Temple of God's Spirit.
- Manage your resources well, and God will provide for your needs.
- Elisha was a type of Christ. Let Jesus' life touch yours, and you will live!

Take this to the next level: Are you neglecting the House of God?

Neglect(ed): say it, believe it, avoid it!

This is my perspective for today, Pastor Scott

Day One Hundred-Eighty Seven
The Pastor's Perspective: Your word for the day!

irresolute – *(adjective)* ***indecisive; unsure; vacillating***
ih-**rez**-*uh*-loot

Reading Plan: 2 Kings 14; 2 Chronicles 25

Even though Amaziah sought to do right in the eyes of the Lord, his commitment to God was **irresolute**. He failed to bring down the high places of pagan worship and went from bad to worse in wholeheartedly seeking and serving the Lord. However, for a brief period of time during Amaziah's reign, there was resurgence in the significance of Judah.

The two kingdoms of God's people (Judah and Israel) continued their furious conflict and rivalry. The conflict between Judah and Israel was the product of the aggression of Amaziah even though his counterpart, King Johash of Israel, wanted to remain neutral. Johash would eventually defeat Amaziah. His son Azariah would replace Amaziah after his death. Jeroboam would replace his father Johash as king of Israel.

Reflect on these thoughts:
- A halfhearted commitment to anything or anyone is worthless.
- Sins ultimately reap failures.
- You reap what you sow.
- Righteous leaders are made, not born.

Take this to the next level: A divided heart only creates conflict and eventually defeat. Are you serving God wholeheartedly?

irresolute: say it, believe it, avoid it!

This is my perspective for today, Pastor Scott

Dr. Scott Payne

Day One Hundred-Eighty Eight
The Pastor's Perspective: Your word for the day!

relented – *(verb) yielded; softened; eased off*
ri-**lent**

Reading Plan: Jonah

Jonah was called by God to go to Nineveh and declare a pending judgment for their evil ways. He neglected the word of the Lord and ran the opposite direction from Nineveh. After being consumed by a great fish he was vomited up on the shores of Nineveh. He then proclaimed the coming judgment of the Lord. The Ninevites repented from their sins and asked God to forgive them. God **relented** and then dealt with Jonah's disobedience and resentment. It seemed Jonah cared more for a plant than he did for 120,000 persons who did not know right from wrong.

Reflect on these thoughts:
- Running from God's call never works out well.
- God knows your heart and will work to change it for good.
- People are more important than things.
- God wants to use you to reach others with His plans to save!

Take this to the next level: What will you do when God comes calling?

relent: say it, believe it, believe God will do it!

This is my perspective for today, Pastor Scott

Day One Hundred-Eighty Nine
The Pastor's Perspective: Your word for the day!

respite – *(noun)* ***lull; reprieve***
res-pit

Reading Plan: 2 Kings 15; 2 Chronicles 26

Judah would experience one of the longest tenures of her kings. King Azariah reigned for fifty-two years. Because of God's judgment on him, he would live in isolation as a leper. His son Jotham would govern on behalf of his father. He sought the Lord but kept the high places of false worship.

Israel may have experienced a **respite** from external conflict but the internal war was on! The nation went through reign after reign of bad leaders that progressively led the nation away from God. The kings of Israel were not seen as even trying to do what was right in the eyes of the Lord. They just were flat out corrupt.

Reflect on these thoughts:
- God will judge sin when He is ready.
- Don't let the lull in a battle deceive you, evil is always on the attack.
- Evil begets evil.
- Right versus wrong is a choice!

Take this to the next level: Is your desire to seek God and do what is right?

respite: say it, believe it, watch out for it!

This is my perspective for today, Pastor Scott

Dr. Scott Payne

Day One Hundred-Ninety
The Pastor's Perspective: Your word for the day!

sacrilege – *(noun)* ***irreverence; desecration; profanity***
sak-ruh-lij

Reading Plan: Isaiah 1-4

Isaiah came before the people of Judah calling out their lives and worship as a **sacrilege** before the Lord. They had gone so far away from God they did not realize their sin and just how corrupt their worship and society had become. God was rejecting their worship and rebuked their hypocritical expressions of sacrifice. The prophet made it clear, if the people would repent, they still had the opportunity to please God and reach the nations. Judgment was coming on Judah, and the Lord would starve the people of spiritual leaders. Irresponsible children would replace former leaders, and God would not step in to help. But God would preserve a remnant to declare His faithfulness.

Reflect on these thoughts:
- God is not interested in your form of worship, but He does look for your heart of worship.
- Worship must be pure and unadulterated.
- Hypocrisy can't be tolerated among God's people.
- Stay faithful, and God will declare His glorious name through you!

Take this to the next level: Are you part of the core group of people remaining faithful to God?

sacrilege: say it, believe it, avoid it!

This is my perspective for today, Pastor Scott

Day One Hundred-Ninety One
The Pastor's Perspective: Your word for the day!

craving – *(noun)* ***longing; hunger***
krey-ving

Reading Plan: Isaiah 5-8

The **craving** for something other than God revealed the corrupt heart of Judah. Their deep spiritual decline would bring the judgment of God upon them. They were compared to an evil vineyard that must be destroyed.

Through a vision given to Isaiah during an awesome time of worship, God promised a new future for His people: a messianic kingdom that would fulfill the purpose for which He had called them and a miracle child who would rule forever from the throne of David. From human failure God alone would accomplish this!

The coming Assyrian invasion would be the defining moment of judgment against the wickedness of God's people. The prophet was to fear the Lord and faithfully wait upon Him. Isaiah was to bind up the teaching among the true disciples and hope in the Lord. Others would realize their hopelessness and helplessness in the face of the coming judgment.

Reflect on these thoughts:
- You will feed your desires. What do you want?
- You are either advancing or declining. Which direction are you moving?
- You worship something or someone. Will you worship the true God?
- You have a choice when facing oppression. Will you trust the Lord?

Take this to the next level: What are the top priorities of your life?

craving: say it, believe it, avoid it if not God-centered!

This is my perspective for today, Pastor Scott

Dr. Scott Payne

Day One Hundred-Ninety Two
The Pastor's Perspective: Your word for the day!

atrocious – *(adjective)* ***appalling; dreadful; heinous***
uh-**troh**-sh*uh* s

Reading Plan: Amos 1-5

Amos was God's prophet called to speak out against the Northern Kingdom (Israel). God's judgment was first spoken out towards other nations that had negative influences on God's people, nations that had **atrocious** practices. Unfortunately Israel had joined these nations' patterns of behavior.

Judgment was declared against Aram, Philistia, Phoenicia, Edom, Ammon, Moab, Judah and Israel. All had practiced the callous oppression of the poor, profane religious worship, systems of rules that favored the rich and neglect of the poor. Israel would not avoid God's wrath, but a repentant remnant could find forgiveness and God's favor. The unrepentant would not be able to avoid God's just reaction to their evil ways.

Reflect on these thoughts:
- Listen to God's instruction from the voice of His agent.
- God will judge the evil influences that non-believers place on God's people.
- God's people have a choice to follow God's ways or the ways of the wicked.
- Promote the well being of others!
- If you're reading this you still have the opportunity to turn to God and forsake evil.

Take this to the next level: Make sure your ways are not offensive to God.

atrocious: say it, believe it, avoid it!

This is my perspective for today, Pastor Scott

Day One Hundred-Ninety Three
The Pastor's Perspective: Your word for the day!

imitate – *(verb) mimic; replicate;*
im-i-teyt

Reading Plan: Amos 6-9

Assyria was on the march conquering other nations. Judah and Israel were next. The only defense that could turn the Assyrians would be a repentant heart, and that was unlikely. The Israelites would **imitate** King David's love for music but had no passion for the ways of God. The pride and arrogance of God's people pronounced defeat and doom.

Amos brings his prophecy to an end by sharing visions of a final judgment. In the finale of the book, Amos pictured God's judgment with a note of hope.

Reflect on these thoughts:
- God may use the enemy to humble His people.
- God's desire is to bring His people to repentance and restoration.
- Pride comes before the fall!
- God always makes a way out for those who seek Him.

Take this to the next level: Are you relying on your assets or God's?

imitate: say it, believe it, live it godly!

This is my perspective for today, Pastor Scott

Dr. Scott Payne

Day One Hundred-Ninety Four
The Pastor's Perspective: Your word for the day!

adversary – *(noun)* ***enemy; foe*** **adversarial** – *(adjective)* ***combative; antagonistic***
ad-ver-ser-ee   ad-ver-**sair**-ee-uh l

Reading Plan: 2 Chronicles 27; Isaiah 9-12

Jotham ruled in Judah for sixteen years. He was a good king who sought the Lord, but the people still followed corrupt practices. He conquered the Ammonites, and they served Judah during his reign.

Isaiah 9 ushers in a mighty encouragement to God's people. Isaiah announced the coming of Messiah, Jesus Christ. Messiah would be a divine gift of God's grace to an undeserving people. God's grace to Israel would come first through judgment and then through a remnant of His people who would overcome their **adversarial** nations. The prophet revealed to God's people the transformation coming to the world through Messiah. Isaiah concluded this section of reading with the foretelling of a time when God's people would experience the joy of salvation.

Reflect on these thoughts:
- God's people should follow godly leaders.
- God will deliver His people, in His time and in His way.
- The Messiah is the only One who can transform a person.
- Salvation comes from the Lord and brings complete joy.

Take this to the next level: Trust God and what rules you now will be overcome by His power!

adversarial: say it, believe it, avoid it!

This is my perspective for today, Pastor Scott

Day One Hundred-Ninety Five
The Pastor's Perspective: Your word for the day!

dispersion – *(noun) scattering; distribution; dispersal*
dih-spur-zh*uh* n

Reading Plan: Micah

The prophet Micah came on the scene to announce that God's judgment was coming on Judah and Israel. He was quick to tell of the forgiving nature of God, and that His people would experience both judgment and divine forgiveness and protection. God would keep His covenant with His people. The Assyrian's would be prone to God's judgment. In defeat the Israelites would experience the **dispersion** tactic used by many conquering nations. But God would protect a remnant of His people who would reestablish the reign and rule of their true God.

Micah called out the sins of the people by name: idolatry, seizure of property, unfaithful civil and religious leadership, corrupt sacrifice, and evil business practices. The ultimate goal of the prophet was to show Israel that God was at work with the purpose to restore them to a renewed and sincere faithful relationship with Him.

Reflect on these thoughts:
- Will you rightly declare truth to your generation?
- Do you understand a loving God will punish sin?
- Are you ready to follow God with a pure heart rather than phony sacrifice?
- Can you let others call out sin in your life?
- Are you ready to receive God's forgiveness and walk faithfully with Him?

Take this to the next level: Confess your sin and receive God's forgiveness, grace, and mercy.

dispersion: say it, believe it, avoid it!

This is my perspective for today, Pastor Scott

Dr. Scott Payne

Day One Hundred-Ninety Six
The Pastor's Perspective: Your word for the day!

mitigated – *(verb)* ***alleviated; lessened***
mit-i-geyt-ed

Reading Plan: 2 Chronicles 28; 2 Kings 16-17

Ahaz was a very wicked king to the people of Judah. He totally turned his back on God and chased after the false gods of other nations. As a judgment from God, the king of Syria first defeated Judah. Then Judah's fellow countrymen (Israel) defeated them. One hundred twenty thousand men of valor from Judah died in one day at the hand of the Israelite Pekah. The army of Israel also planned to take two hundred thousand people from Judah captive. Judah's sin was ushering in God's fierce judgment.

The decline of Judah was **mitigated** by the action of Israel. The prophet Oded warned Israel not to take their two hundred thousand relatives captive. He counseled them that they too had sinned against God and did not need their mistreatment of their relatives hanging over their heads. So Israel released the captives to return home.

Ahaz started poorly and ended his sixteen years of kingship even worse. He turned the whole city of Jerusalem into a pagan altar.

Reflect on these thoughts:
- Leaders will answer to God for their influence on His people.
- You always have a choice in the way you respond to God's correction.
- Be careful how you relate to other believers.
- It pays to listen to godly counsel.

Take this to the next level: Judgment is a God thing not a man thing. Avoid a judgmental spirit!

mitigated: say it, believe it, live it!

This is my perspective for today, Pastor Scott

Day One Hundred-Ninety Seven
The Pastor's Perspective: Your word for the day!

indignation – *(noun)* ***outrage; fury***
in-dig-**ney**-sh*uh* n

Reading Plan: Isaiah 13-17

The nations had stirred up God**'s indignation**. He was the sovereign ruler of the world, and all nations answered to Him! He pronounced His judgment over Babylon, Assyria, Philistia, Moab, and Damascus. God would hold all peoples accountable for their deeds. Through the judging of the nations, God would restore Israel to His purpose of grace. There was coming a reversal of influence, purpose and prominence. The nations would see Israel resuming her place as God's chosen people.

Reflect on these thoughts:
- None can stand against the Lord God.
- God has a plan for the world that cannot be dismissed.
- God will use His people to influence His outcome for creation.
- Stay faithful and strong in the Lord even when things may seem bleak.
- The Lord's grace and mercy will rescue the repentant child of God.

Take this to the next level: God will punish the offense of evil committed by people and nations.

indignation: say it, believe it, avoid it!

This is my perspective for today, Pastor Scott

Dr. Scott Payne

Day One Hundred-Ninety Eight
The Pastor's Perspective: Your word for the day!

imploding – *(verb) collapsing inward; caving in*
im-**plohd**

Reading Plan: Isaiah 18-22

Continuing the theme of judgment pronounced on the nations, Isaiah called out Cush and Egypt. Egypt was **imploding** from corrupt leadership and wicked defiance. Isaiah spoke of a time when Cush, Egypt and Israel would experience a season of coming together and God using them to impact the world for His greater purpose. Isaiah lived naked and without sandals as he prophesied against Egypt and Cush. The Assyrians would take them into captivity, and they would go naked into slavery.

Babylon would experience God's judgment as well. Its false gods would be no match for the power of the true God. Isaiah saw a destroyed Babylon and the failure of her illegitimate gods.

Isaiah would see the ultimate destruction of Jerusalem. The people had become too self-reliant.

Reflect on these thoughts:
- You can't hide sin. It will destroy you.
- Life is seasonal. Stay close to God during all seasons.
- Sin will make a fool out of you. Repent from it before it's too late.
- False gods are just that. They are incapable of truth.

Take this to the next level: Are you allowing God to have consistent control of your life?

imploding: say it, believe it, avoid it!

This is my perspective for today, Pastor Scott

Day One Hundred-Ninety Nine
The Pastor's Perspective: Your word for the day!

apocalyptic – *(adjective)* ***fateful; ominous; prophetic***
uh-pok-*uh*-**lip**-tik

Reading Plan: Isaiah 23-27

In the beginning of this reading, Isaiah addressed the judgment and eventual redemptive work of God in Tyre. After a seventy-year period God would use Tyre and her assets to supply the needs of those who follow Him.

The reading transitions and would appear to be clearly connected to an **apocalyptic** writing depicting a final conflict with evil and God's victory. The prophet declared the day when God would judge the whole world and yet protect and provide for His people. Eventually, there would be no more death and perfect peace would prevail. In that day the redemption of Israel would become a reality.

Reflect on these thoughts:
- God works in all things for His glory.
- God can benefit His people from the harvest of others.
- God lets us know the final results of this world.
- God will redeem His work and purpose with Israel being a major focus.

Take this to the next level: Are you living in light of God's future declarations?

apocalyptic: say it, believe it, understand it!

This is my perspective for today, Pastor Scott

Dr. Scott Payne

Day Two Hundred
The Pastor's Perspective: Your word for the day!

reformer – *(noun) **improver; crusader***
ri-**fawr**-mer

Reading Plan: 2 Kings 18; 2 Chronicles 29-31; Psalm 48

The great **reformer** of Judah was King Hezekiah. He was a king who followed in the ways of King David. Hezekiah sought and followed the ways of the Lord and removed the high places of false worship. He defied the king of Assyria and declared the independence of Judah.

King Hezekiah restored the pure act of worship to the One and only true God. As king he recalled the Levites and priests to their places of service in the temple. He had them cleanse the temple and follow the prescribed patterns of consecrating the place, priests, and people for holy worship. He also reinstituted the Passover celebration.

Reflect on these thoughts:
- Make a God-difference where you live.
- Ground your life in God's ways not man's ways.
- Prepare yourself for a life worthy of God's use.
- Repentance and spiritual cleansing are mandatory.
- Never stop celebrating God's deliverance.

Take this to the next level: Are you a conformer or a reformer?

reformer: say it, believe it, live it!

This is my perspective for today, Pastor Scott

Day Two Hundred One
The Pastor's Perspective: Your word for the day!

promiscuous – *(adjective) **sexually immoral; engaged in casual sex with a number of partners***
pruh-**mis**-kyoo-uh s

Reading Plan: Hosea 1-7

The prophet Hosea was told by God to take a **promiscuous** woman to be his wife. Her unfaithfulness to her husband became a sign to the Israelites of their forsaking the Lord. The children of Hosea and Gomer were given names that exampled ways God's people betrayed Him. God would use the judicial system of dealing with an adulterous wife to reveal His plans to deal with Israel. Hosea accused Israel's rulers of leading the people away from God. Hosea used several things to continue to illustrate the unfaithfulness of Israel: an oven, a cake, a dove, and a bow.

Reflect on these thoughts:
- Listen to God and obey Him even if it doesn't make sense.
- Consider the ways a person can be unfaithful to God.
- Corrupt rulers will influence people to break away from God.
- Ultimately the individual must answer to God for his life.

Take this to the next level: Are you staying faithful to God in all areas of your life?

promiscuous: say it, believe it, avoid it!

This is my perspective for today, Pastor Scott

Dr. Scott Payne

Day Two Hundred Two
The Pastor's Perspective: Your word for the day!

reliance – *(noun) **dependence; confidence***
ri-**lahy**-uh ns

Reading Plan: Hosea 8-14

Israel was being judged for her lack of **reliance** in the Lord. The people were far from God, but their pride had convinced them they could gain His approval by their sacrifices. The prophet Hosea declared that God would judge their unfaithfulness. Their places of worship were empty, and their gods were false. God would cause the people and leaders to remember the past days of His glory and provisions for them, and they would mourn for those days.

In spite of Israel's sins, God loved them with an everlasting love. He would not give up on them. He would get their attention, and they would tremble in fear for their waywardness. Even though they must be judged, God's purpose to call His people back to an obedient faith walk with Him was the goal. Hosea pleaded for a repentant nation to once again walk in the ways of God.

Reflect on these thoughts:
- Do you trust in the things of man or the truth of God?
- Are you being deceived into thinking God does not know your heart?
- Do you long for the days when God was everything to you?
- Are you aware that God's love is still pursuing you?
- Do you know that God is ready and willing to welcome you home?

Take this to the next level: Submitting to God requires commitment and discipline. Are you trusting in God or something/someone else?

reliance: say it, believe it, place it in God!

This is my perspective for today, Pastor Scott

Day Two Hundred Three
The Pastor's Perspective: Your word for the day!

omnipresent – *(adjective)* ***ever-present; pervasive; inescapable***
om-n*uh*-**prez**-*uh* nt

Reading Plan: Isaiah 28-30

The prophet appealed to Judah not to follow the same mistakes Israel made. He spoke to them like a teacher would to small children, and that offended them. They would refuse to listen to his words. Judah was fearful of the Assyrians and chose to place their trust and security in someone other than God. God would have delivered them just like He did Joshua and David, but they had to trust Him.

Ariel was a pseudo name for Jerusalem. The people in Jerusalem had convinced themselves that God was not **omnipresent**. They believed they could hide their thoughts and actions from Him. They were wrong! God became very displeased with His people, because they sought power and protection from other kings. He even warned them not to seek protection from Egypt or other nations. Their faith had turned into a religion of routine rather than a real relationship with their Lord.

Reflect on these thoughts:
- Strong drink will impede the judgment of God's wise counsel.
- It's a sad day when no one understands doctrine or is in a position to teach truth.
- A biblical foundation for life is imperative.
- You can't escape God's judgment! When you leave His path He will correct you.

Take this to the next level: God knows your heart, so why not be honest with yourself. Seek Him!

omnipresent: say it, believe it, live it!

This is my perspective for today, Pastor Scott

Dr. Scott Payne

Day Two Hundred Four
The Pastor's Perspective: Your word for the day!

hypocrite – *(noun) phony; pretender; imposter*
hip-uh-krit

Reading Plan: Isaiah 31-34

The **hypocrite** will face God's judgment regardless of who they are or where they live. Judah had fallen to the same demise as other nations and was trusting in man instead of God. They sought protection from powerless sources. Both Egypt and Judah would fall to God's consuming power and judgment.

The prophet announced a time coming when the people would throw away their idols. Judah would seek a strong king who would rule effectively, and that desire would be fulfilled in Jesus Christ. The people would realize that peace and prosperity would only come when God's Spirit was with them. If Judah would change directions, attitudes, and actions, God would be their salvation.

Idumea was home to the Demotes. The Israelites were descended from Jacob and the Edomites from Esau. They were enemies! The destruction of Idumea was a picture of the ultimate end to all who oppose God and His people.

Reflect on these thoughts:
- You might fool some of the people some of the time, but never God.
- When God is with you, things will be ok.
- If you have been a doubter it's time to become a believer.
- You can experience the Spirit of God with you at all times.
- There are no matches to God's power.

Take this to the next level: Are you sincerely connected to God through faith in His Son?

hypocrite: say it, believe it, avoid it!

This is my perspective for today, Pastor Scott

Day Two Hundred Five
The Pastor's Perspective: Your word for the day!

ransomed – *(adjective)* *exchanged; redeemed*
ran-suh m

Reading Plan: Isaiah 35-36

Chapter 35 began a strong transition that focused on God's mercy and His forgiveness to those who sincerely loved and obeyed Him. It spoke of a time when the judgment of God had passed and the people experienced a time of lasting peace. There would be a highway of safety for the righteous pilgrims to travel as they returned to Jerusalem. The **ransomed** children of God would return home to Jerusalem.

The prospect of an Assyrian assault on Judah was imminent. Even with Egypt's help, Judah was no match for the judgment of God being imposed on them by Assyria. Judah's only hope was God! With the offer made by the Assyrian army to spare Judah if they would pay allegiance to the Assyrian king, the people of God refused to do so and remained silent.

Reflect on these thoughts:
- Hold on! God will make a way out.
- It is important to know and trust God's eternal promises.
- Obey God and follow Him and He will fight your battles.
- Resist the deals others offer you, and seek the Lord!
- There's only One King!

Take this to the next level: Let God do for you what you cannot do for yourself.

ransom: say it, believe it, accept it!

This is my perspective for today, Pastor Scott

Dr. Scott Payne

Day Two Hundred Six
The Pastor's Perspective: Your word for the day!

blasphemed – *(verb) spoke about God disrespectfully or irreverently; profaned*
blas-feem

Reading Plan: Isaiah 37-39; Psalm 76

King Hezekiah turned to God and waited for Him to come to Judah's aid. He realized the only hope Judah had was God. Because the servants of Assyria had **blasphemed** the Lord, their fate was sealed. Assyria had insulted God, and, therefore, they would not be His instrument of correction against Jerusalem.

At some point King Hezekiah became deathly ill, but his prayerful approach to God gained him fifteen more years of life. Even with that blessing, he battled with pride which was a constant struggle. The prophet would pronounce God's eventual judgment on Judah at the hands of the Babylonians. But that will not happen until almost 100 years later.

King Hezekiah was one of Judah's most faithful kings and did what He could to lead Judah to faithful worship of God and a destruction of idol worship.

Reflect on these thoughts:
- Wait on the Lord. He will come to your aid.
- Blaspheming the Lord guarantees His judgment.
- Pray for God's deliverance through difficult times.
- Share your faith with family and others.

Take this to the next level: Don't turn your back on God, and He will never turn His back on you!

blasphemed: say it, believe it, avoid it!

This is my perspective for today, Pastor Scott

Day Two Hundred Seven
The Pastor's Perspective: Your word for the day!

manumit *(verb)* ***liberate; emancipate***
man-yuh-mit

Reading Plan: Isaiah 40-43

The prophet spoke of a time when God would restore the glory of His chosen people. He would **manumit** them from the wicked influence of the world, and reunite Israel and Judah. Even though the encouraging word of Isaiah will not come true for 100 years, his words would serve as comfort and the promise needed to endure. The people were told to wait on the Lord and He would renew their strength!

God was in total control of the events and affairs on earth. God expected His people to declare His glory to the world. He, in turn, would provide the strength, help, and the ultimate success for those who served Him. The promise of the coming Messiah, Jesus, would complete the prophetic words from Isaiah to the people. In spite of the spiritual decay among God's people, He would show mercy to them and bring them back from captivity. The victory offered to the people could only come from God. Sin had separated the people from God, but He would send a Savior to reunite them.

Reflect on these thoughts:
- God will comfort you through times of adversity.
- God is indescribable, and His power and provisions are readily available.
- God is a friend like no other!
- Jesus is the fulfillment of God's promise to be with us and provide for our every need.
- God's forgiveness of your sin comes through Jesus Christ.

Take this to the next level: God has set you free. Are you totally devoted to Him?

manumit: say it, believe it, live it!

This is my perspective for today, Pastor Scott

Dr. Scott Payne

Day Two Hundred Eight
The Pastor's Perspective: Your word for the day!

transgress *(verb) **disobey; sin; violate***
trans-**gres**

Reading Plan: Isaiah 44-48

Isaiah gave many examples of how people made their own gods. A man-made god could have no power. The prophet was calling people to serve the true God, because He was the only One that could free a person from their sin and failure.

God would take no pleasure in evil. As ruler over all, only He could turn good out of bad situations. It was important for the people to look for God's purpose in every life experience.

All who **transgress** God's Word would suffer loss, but He offered forgiveness and salvation to all that would seek Him. Isaiah spoke of deliverance as present and future tense.

Isaiah foretold of the fall of Babylon more than one hundred and fifty years before the event. The captors of Judah would become captives themselves. God had used Babylon to punish the sins of Judah, and He would eventually punish the Babylonians by way of the Medo-Persians. The advantage Babylon had accumulated by wickedness would not save them from God's judgment. God would offer peace to the righteous and defeat to the wicked.

Reflect on these thoughts:
- How can you honor God with your life?
- Are your assets really capable of helping you escape God's judgment?
- Have you broken away from your dependence on God?
- Will you confess your need for God's forgiveness and commit to faithfully obey Him?
- Seek God and live!

Take this to the next level: Living contrary to God's Law brings nothing but pain and loss.

transgress: say it, believe it, avoid it!

This is my perspective for today, Pastor Scott

Day Two Hundred Nine
The Pastor's Perspective: Your word for the day!

taunted – *(verb) insulted; jeered; mocked*
tawnt, tahnt

Reading Plan: 2 Kings 19; Psalms 46, 80, 135

Isaiah announced the victory of Judah over Assyria. With the odds against him, Judah's King Hezekiah went into the Temple to seek God's help. The king of Assyria had **taunted** God with his behavior and words. God would prove to the Assyrians that He was in control of the destiny of all His creation. The Assyrians would be defeated, and King Sennacherib would die by the sword of his own children.

The psalmist celebrated the power and help God provided His children. God would always reach out to deliver those who loved Him and obeyed Him. When times were tough and failure was ready to destroy God's people, they could turn to Him and find hope for salvation. Praise filled the hearts of those who worshipped the true and living God. Idols would fail, but God would be victorious.

Reflect on these thoughts:
- Don't put off asking God for help.
- Approach God with a humble spirit grounded in respect and honesty.
- No one is self-made.
- Ask God to enlarge your faith.
- Live a life filled with daily praise to God.
- Confession of sin is good for the soul.
- God inhabits the praises of His people.

Take this to the next level: Are you acknowledging God by confessing sin and consecrating living?

taunt: say it, believe it, avoid it!

This is my perspective for today, Pastor Scott

Dr. Scott Payne

Day Two Hundred Ten
The Pastor's Perspective: Your word for the day!

omnipotent – *(adjective)* ***all-powerful; almighty; invincible***
om-**nip**-*uh*-t*uh* nt

Reading Plan: Isaiah 49-53

The prophet revealed the coming of the servant. The servant he spoke of was the Lord Jesus Christ. God's people could take assurance that the servant would lead them to salvation. Unlike the people, the servant would be submissive to God and would complete the mission of God victoriously. God's restored people would become shockingly numerous.

The Jews needed to hear this message of assurance because they had felt abandoned by God. This was a consequence of their unfaithfulness, not God's failure. Isaiah saw the servant as a rejected prophet. The servant would accept the suffering he must endure because he believed in God's **omnipotent** rule over all the earth!

Isaiah gave several incentives for following the direction of the servant: it would make them a great nation; the truth would be shared with all nations, and those that followed God would be eternally vindicated. God, through the servant, would set His people free.

Isaiah finished this section with a clear picture of the suffering servant, Jesus Christ, Messiah. Only this servant could deliver the people from their sins.

Reflect on these thoughts:
- Salvation can only be achieved from God through His servant Jesus Christ.
- Once forgiven and restored before the Lord, you will prosper.
- God wants a close relationship with His people, but sin will separate them.
- The Lord not only forgives sin, He takes our punishment for sin.

Take this to the next level: Are you allowing the power of God to direct your life?

omnipotent: say it, believe it, God is it!

This is my perspective for today, Pastor Scott

Day Two Hundred Eleven
The Pastor's Perspective: Your word for the day!

revive – *(verb) resuscitate; restore; rejuvenate*
ri-**vahyv**

Reading Plan: Isaiah 54-58

Isaiah spoke of the rebuilding of Israel. This forecast would include a lifting of God's judgment on the nation. With this, His blessing would be released for national prosperity to return in all areas of life. As the people repented of their sin, God would **revive** their nation. Other nations would once again fear Israel.

The prophet declared he would accept anyone who turned to God, and they would find a place in His forever family. God would gather the outcasts and bless even the gentiles who turned to Him. Those that refused His provisions would be judged, and those who sought His forgiveness would live in peace. God's offer for salvation was a true gift that no one could earn or achieve on their own. This gift required simple faith and trust in Him.

Reflect on these thoughts:
- Are you experiencing the joy that comes when God has forgiven you of your sins?
- Does God spiritually feed you?
- Are you inclusive with all people in sharing the gospel story?
- Are you free from trying to earn God's love and favor?
- Do you make worship ritual, or is it relational with God?

Take this to the next level: A loving God is ready to renew, rebuild, and restore broken lives. He alone can offer abundant life to anyone who seeks Him!

revive: say it, believe it, live it!

This is my perspective for today, Pastor Scott

Dr. Scott Payne

Day Two Hundred Twelve
The Pastor's Perspective: Your word for the day!

Redeemer – *(noun) Savior; rescuer*
ri-**dee**-mer

Reading Plan: Isaiah 59-63

It was amazing how evil the people had become. They were taking advantage of one another, even in the courts of law. The prophet was pointing out the personal responsibility the people had to assume for their failure and sin. They had rejected justice. Therefore, God was rejecting them. The sins of the people required a **Redeemer**. This **Redeemer** was the coming Messiah who would turn the wrath of God and usher in a rebirth of God's glory. God's people would become the great influencers in the world and nations would come to honor Him and them.

The coming Messiah would lead the people into salvation, and they would experience a renewed position of blessings and prosperity. God's ultimate victory over evil and His final day of vengeance were coming. Those who sought mercy from the Lord would find it, and those who didn't would reap His judgment. Judgment and salvation were on the way!

Reflect on these thoughts:
- Don't allow sin to create a barrier between you and God.
- Only God can take away the guilt of your sin.
- God will include His people in His ultimate victory.
- God keeps His promises.
- God is at work in seasons of judgment and blessing for your good.

Take this to the next level: Acknowledge only Jesus Christ can remove sin and restore joy.

redeemer: say it, believe it, accept it!

This is my perspective for today, Pastor Scott

Day Two Hundred Thirteen
The Pastor's Perspective: Your word for the day!

recompense – *(verb)* ***payback; reparation; repayment***
rek-*uh* m-pens

Reading Plan: Isaiah 64-66

Isaiah seemed so ready for God to put an end to the unrighteous behavior of the people. The actions of the people had brought the collapse of a nation and the house of God. The response of God to an unholy people was **recompense**; they had truly become His enemy.

God seemed ready to grant eternal joy to those who faithfully loved Him and judgment to those who had rejected Him. The prophet saw a time coming when life would offer an abundance of peace, prosperity, and prolonged years of fulfillment. False and phony worship would be replaced with true and sincere worship. Those who heard this message and purified themselves would discover a satisfying relationship with God and those who refused God's offer to walk with Him would surely die.

Reflect on these thoughts:
- The time is coming when God will rectify injustice and unrighteousness.
- There will be joy when the presence of the Lord is welcomed.
- There is a difference in the form of worship and the heart of worship.
- God will give life abundant and eternal to those who love Him.
- Live with God and not the ungodly.

Take this to the next level: Plant seeds of faith in God and reap a harvest of joy!

recompense: say it, believe it, avoid it!

This is my perspective for today, Pastor Scott

Dr. Scott Payne

Day Two Hundred Fourteen
The Pastor's Perspective: Your word for the day!

despicable – *(adjective) **disgraceful; vile; reprehensible***
des-**pi**-k*uh*-b*uh* | dih-**spik**-uh

Reading Plan: 2 Kings 20-21

The prophet Isaiah warned Hezekiah of his pending death. Hezekiah immediately prayed with a humble heart asking God to spare him. God heard his sincere request and added another fifteen years to his life.

King Hezekiah struggled with the sin of pride, and it would cost his children and the nation a dear price. When he died, his son Manasseh ruled as king for fifty-five years. He was the worst king of Judah. He was a **despicable** king and did abominable things in the eyes of the Lord. After his death, his son Amon would rule for two years. He followed in the footsteps of his father and was struck down by conspirators.

Reflect on these thoughts:
- How do you react when God calls you out for sin in your life?
- Do you find yourself repeating the same sins?
- What legacy will you leave your family and others?
- Is your life a blessing or a curse to others and God?

Take this to the next level: Is your life a testimony that honors or grieves God?

despicable: say it, believe it, avoid it!

This is my perspective for today, Pastor Scott

Day Two Hundred Fifteen
The Pastor's Perspective: Your word for the day!

ambivalent – *(adjective)* ***unsure; indecisive; contradictory***
am-**biv**-*uh*-l*uh* nt

Reading Plan: 2 Chronicles 32-33

The writer of Chronicles portrayed Hezekiah as an **ambivalent** king. On the one hand he sought the Lord during difficult days, but he also allowed room for plenty of evil influences in his life and within the nation. After God's display of awesomeness in rebuffing the Assyrians, King Hezekiah became sick to the point of death. He cried out to God and asked for his health to be restored. God granted this request but Hezekiah returned to his prideful ways.

After Hezekiah's death two of his sons, Manasseh and Amon, would rule. They were both evil kings and did much harm to the people of God.

Reflect on these thoughts:
- A divided heart will bring troublesome days.
- Never take for granted the purposes of God for your life.
- You are no match for God.
- Evil has its reward, and it's not good.

Take this to the next level: Are you serving God with your whole heart?

ambivalent: say it, believe it, avoid it!

This is my perspective for today, Pastor Scott

Dr. Scott Payne

Day Two Hundred Sixteen
The Pastor's Perspective: Your word for the day!

arrogant – *(adjective)* ***cocky; overconfident***
ar-*uh*-*guh* nt

Reading Plan: Nahum

Nahum understood that God had completed His judgment on the people of Judah and pronounced the liberation of His people, and the pending judgment on the Assyrians and their capitol city, Nineveh. God would no longer tolerate an **arrogant** response from the Assyrians. The Assyrians had resisted God's rule and authority, and were about to face the overwhelming judgment of God. The evil done by the Assyrians had sealed their ultimate defeat. There would be no avoiding the destruction of a corrupt and evil people.

Reflect on these thoughts:
- Disobey God and you will face His wrath.
- God will always honor His relationship with His people.
- No one is a match for God.
- Sin leads to death and obedience leads to life.

Take this to the next level: God never fails!

arrogant: say it, believe it, avoid it!

This is my perspective for today, Pastor Scott

Day Two Hundred Seventeen
The Pastor's Perspective: Your word for the day!

Pentateuch – *(noun)* **Torah; first 5 books of the Old Testament**
pen-t*uh*-took

Reading Plan: 2 Kings 22-23; 2 Chronicles 34-35

Josiah ruled for thirty-one years in Jerusalem. He was a king that did right in the sight of the Lord and ruled well. He commanded the House of the Lord be rebuilt and the places of false worship be destroyed. It was believed that Hilkiah, the priest, discovered the **Pentateuch** in the House of the Lord at Jerusalem when reconstruction of the Temple began. Josiah not only removed the false places of worship, but he had the priests of Baal destroyed as well. King Josiah's death came during the battle with Egypt, even though he was warned not to fight. Josiah did good in the eyes of the Lord and his people.

Reflect on these thoughts:
- Righteous people will do right things.
- Good must be restored and evil must be destroyed.
- God's Word needs a central place in the hearts of His people.
- God's message may be delivered in unusual ways and from unexpected people.

Take this to the next level: Do you have a strong appetite for God's Word?

Pentateuch: say it, believe it, read it!

This is my perspective for today, Pastor Scott

Dr. Scott Payne

Day Two Hundred Eighteen
The Pastor's Perspective: Your word for the day!

absolve – *(verb) forgive; pardon; acquit*
ab-**zolv**

Reading Plan: Zephaniah

The prophet declared there was only one way to escape God's judgment - the people would have to confess their sins and declare their dependency on God. God was ready to judge Judah and **absolve** those who would trust in Him, thereby making way for His blessings. Sin had a destructive and deadly influence on the people, and God was ready to purge sin from the nation. His greater purpose was to re-establish a nation of people that would love and honor Him.

Reflect on these thoughts:
- Is confession of sin a routine practice in you life?
- Are you ready for God to forgive your sins and provide a hope for your future?
- Do you see God at work in your present circumstances to accomplish His purposes?
- Will you seek God while there is still time?

Take this to the next level: Only sinners need the salvation God offers. Are you a sinner?

absolve: say it, believe it, accept it!

This is my perspective for today, Pastor Scott

Day Two Hundred Nineteen
The Pastor's Perspective: Your word for the day!

ominous – *(adjective)* ***menacing; threatening***
om-uh-nuh s

Reading Plan: Jeremiah 1-3

Jeremiah was God's prophet to the people of Judah. He spoke out against their sins and false leaders. He prophesied about their pending 70-year captivity in Babylon. The prophet was speaking out to Judah and the entire world about God's coming judgment on their sin. Jeremiah's words were rather **ominous** for the nation, yet the people had an opportunity to turn from their sin and seek God. The prophet declared there was no lasting hope or security apart from a genuine relationship with the eternal God.

Reflect on these thoughts:
- God calls some to speak the truth to the multitude.
- Judgment leads to repentance and a promised future of blessings to the disciple.
- Dark days require the light only God provides.
- Hope is in the Lord!

Take this to the next level: Leave the darkness of sin, and seek the light of God's truth.

ominous: say it, believe it, avoid it!

This is my perspective for today, Pastor Scott

Dr. Scott Payne

Day Two Hundred Twenty
The Pastor's Perspective: Your word for the day!

belied – *(verb)* ***contradicted; disproved***
bih-**lahy**

Reading Plan: Jeremiah 4-6

Jeremiah stated the pending judgment of God against the evil ways of Judah. Even Jerusalem could not avoid God's correction. But God continued to leave the door open for anyone to repent, turn from their false worship of pagan gods and trust Him.

The people's actions **belied** their respect for the Lord by declaring His announcements false and their desires superior over God's. They had arrived at the place where they believed their own lies. They were to find they were no match for God. There was no respect for God, and He was done with their irreverence.

Reflect on these thoughts:
- How do you approach God?
- Dare you continue to deny the Word of God?
- Believing it so doesn't make it so.
- Many people simply can't handle the Truth.

Take this to the next level: Does your life express a reverence for God?

belied: say it, believe it, avoid it!

This is my perspective for today, Pastor Scott

Day Two Hundred Twenty-One
The Pastor's Perspective: Your word for the day!

ritual – *(noun)* ***ceremonial; procedural; rite***
rich-oo-*uh* |

Reading Plan: Jeremiah 7-9

The prophet was sent to the gates of the Temple to pronounce God's judgment against those who came to worship the Lord with an insincere or phony heart. The people and their leaders were practicing empty **ritual** instead of genuine worship. Jeremiah warned that the practice of attending worship at the Temple was worthless if there was no heart for God. The people were given false assurance that God would overlook sin if they would keep their religious practices. God would offer forgiveness for this sin, but He would not force it upon the people.

Reflect on these thoughts:
- Is your heart right with God?
- Why do you attempt to follow God's Word?
- Do you believe God can be manipulated?
- What do you want people to think about you?

Take this to the next level: Does sin and hypocrisy break your heart?

ritual: say it, believe it, avoid it!

This is my perspective for today, Pastor Scott

Dr. Scott Payne

Day Two Hundred Twenty-Two
The Pastor's Perspective: Your word for the day!

covenant – *(noun) agreement; pledge; pact*
kuhv-*uh*-n*uh* nt

Reading Plan: Jeremiah 10-13

There were many false gods, and none of them breathed or had created anything; the hands of man created them. The Lord was the God of creation. The shepherds had brought this evil rebellion towards God on the people (the sheep) by their false teaching. Jeremiah was challenging the people to remember the **covenant** they had made with God. The people had promised to listen to God's voice and obey His commands. Their only salvation was to return to their **covenant** relationship with God. Jeremiah was ready for God to act, but God taught him the importance of patience. If the people would not heed the call of the prophet to return to God, then they would find themselves conquered and placed into captivity.

Reflect on these thoughts:
- Don't trust in the created things - trust in the Creator.
- Follow leaders that direct you to God.
- If you can call on God for help it's not too late.
- A prideful person cannot see God.

Take this to the next level: Our actions speak louder than our words. Are you living for God?

covenant: say it, believe it, live it!

This is my perspective for today, Pastor Scott

Day Two Hundred Twenty-Three
The Pastor's Perspective: Your word for the day!

divination *(noun) foretelling; prediction*
div-uh-**ney**-shuh n

Reading Plan: Jeremiah 14-17

The prophets of God were far from being the men they were called to be. Their false **divination** had served to mislead the people and had brought about a drought on Judah. God's judgment continued to be His means to call the people to repentance. Because of the people's wicked ways, God would not listen to their calls for help; His lack of response angered Jeremiah. Jeremiah warned the people of the wickedness in the human heart and the real need for obedience to God.

Reflect on these thoughts:
- Do you see God as your only hope?
- Can you really trust a god of your own-making to answer your prayers?
- Is God number one in your life?
- What are you allowing to reside in your heart?

Take this to the next level: God hates the hypocrite. Lead and serve with a sincere heart that is loyal to Him!

divination: say it, believe it, avoid it!

This is my perspective for today, Pastor Scott

Dr. Scott Payne

Day Two Hundred Twenty-Four
The Pastor's Perspective: Your word for the day!

hostile – *(adjective)* ***antagonistic; contentious***
hos-tl

Reading Plan: Jeremiah 18-22

Jeremiah faced the hard reality that people living in sin many times despise those that call out their sin. His own people became **hostile** to him and the Lord. They loved their sin more than they loved God. The message God had given the prophet would challenge their actions both socially and spiritually. Because of the corruption among the leadership and the people, God was ready to destroy them. Jeremiah's message to them was one of repentance towards God and He would relent. The leaders and people became angry with Jeremiah and sought to silence him. But his captors were the ones in real trouble with God not Jeremiah. Judgment would come, and God would rise up a righteous king and a people that would love and listen to Him.

Reflect on these thoughts:
- Are you soft clay in the hands of the potter (God)?
- Do you have a humble and teachable spirit before God?
- Are you quick to turn from evil and confess your sin?
- Will you only listen to what you want to hear, or are you listening for God's voice?
- Will you remain faithful to God regardless of the cost?

Take this to the next level: Will you be the voice of God to those who need to hear His Word?

hostile: say it, believe it, avoid it!

This is my perspective for today, Pastor Scott

Day Two Hundred Twenty-Five
The Pastor's Perspective: Your word for the day!

indictment – *(noun) charge; accusation*
in-**dahyt**-m*uh* nt

Reading Plan: Jeremiah 23-25

God brought an **indictment** against His people, the false prophets and priests who led the people astray. God declared He would hold those, who claimed to be His servants, responsible for the evil within the nation of Judah and Israel. Jeremiah prophesied God would judge His people by placing them in captivity for 70 years, but would restore a remnant served by genuine godly leaders. God's judgment would extend to those outside His people. Evil would be punished, and all people must give an account for denying God and rejecting His truth.

Reflect on these thoughts:
- Is there anything in your life God is not pleased with?
- Are you following godly leaders that are faithful to His Word?
- If you find yourself being rejected by God turn from your way and follow His.
- Sin has an inevitable consequence, God's judgment!

Take this to the next level: Let God's Word speak into your life.

indictment: say it, believe it, avoid it!

This is my perspective for today, Pastor Scott

Dr. Scott Payne

Day Two Hundred Twenty-Six
The Pastor's Perspective: Your word for the day!

inimical – *(adjective)* ***hostile; unfavorable; adverse***
ih-**nim**-i-k*uh* l

Reading Plan: Jeremiah 26-29

Jeremiah found himself in an **inimical** place in his life. His pronouncement of God's coming judgment became an offense to most. A few of the civil leaders and people came to his defense, but the priests and prophets were ready to have him killed. In fact, he was captured and held for some time for declaring the truth. After his release, the prophet continued to declare the message God was placing on his heart. Jeremiah spoke of a yoke-like submission that must be given to Babylon during a 70-year exile. His message condemned the lies of the false prophets and gave a great caution to all who listened to those lies.

Reflect on these thoughts:
- Serving God may place you in dangerous places.
- God may use the most unlikely people or things to accomplish His purpose.
- God loves the truth and hates the lies!

Take this to the next level: Are you trusting in God's provisions as you live for Him?

inimical: say it, believe it, trust God through it!

This is my perspective for today, Pastor Scott

Day Two Hundred Twenty-Seven
The Pastor's Perspective: Your word for the day!

flagrant *(adjective)* ***blatant; obvious***
fley-gr*uh* nt

Reading Plan: Jeremiah 30-31

God sent Israel into captivity because their sins had been **flagrant**. The season of punishment was coming to an end, and God was ready to restore the people back to their homeland and the covenant relationship they had once enjoyed. The covenant relationship would actually be a new one with a deeper level of commitment by the people. God would now turn His wrath on the enemies of His people.

Reflect on these thoughts:
- God's punishment for sin is directed to bring the sinner home.
- Only God can make things all right.
- God's forgiveness and presence always makes you a better person.
- Sin never goes unpunished.

Take this to the next level: God may be calling you home. Are you ready to return?

flagrant: say it, believe it, avoid it!

This is my perspective for today, Pastor Scott

Dr. Scott Payne

Day Two Hundred Twenty-Eight
The Pastor's Perspective: Your word for the day!

forlorn – *(adjective)* ***despondent; pitiful; lonely***
fawr-**lawrn**

Reading Plan: Jeremiah 32-34

The prophet had difficulty with God's command to buy property in Judah. With his knowledge of the pending exile it just didn't make sense to own real estate. God explained this was a foreshadowing of the return of Judah from exile to reclaim the land. Jeremiah made an all too true statement when he declared nothing was too hard for God, and that if God wanted to restore His people, it would happen.

Jeremiah would pronounce the judgment of God on the people, and they would become a **forlorn** people. Their cities became empty, and their houses were burned to the ground. The Babylonians would take King Zedekiah with them, and he would die in Babylon. But he would die in peace, and the people would declare favor on him after his death.

Reflect on these thoughts:
- God may ask you to do an unreasonable thing. Will you?
- God may declare the impossible is about to happen. Does He?
- God may restore the lost and declare there's hope. Believe Him?
- God may bring good from the bad. Let Him?

Take this to the next level: Do you feel abandoned and alone? Call out to God!

forlorn: say it, believe it, avoid it!

This is my perspective for today, Pastor Scott

Day Two Hundred Twenty-Nine
The Pastor's Perspective: Your word for the day!

insouciance – *(noun)* ***apathy; unconcern***
in-**soo**-see-*uh* ns

Reading Plan: Jeremiah 35-37

God used the faithfulness of the Rechabites to illustrate to Judah how unfaithful they had been. Then God gave words of judgment for Jeremiah to deliver to King Jehoiakim of Judah with the hope of a national tone of repentance as a response.

The scribe Baruch wrote on the scroll God's judgment as Jeremiah spoke the words God said to him. At first reading of the scroll to the people and leaders, there was a favorable response, but once it reached the king, the message of God was totally rejected.

The **insouciance** expressed by Johoaikim kindled the anger of God. Zedekiah followed Jehoiakim as king of Judah. He would send for Jeremiah only to find God's judgment was still impending.

Reflect on these thoughts:
- Do you honor the spiritual counsel of others in your life?
- Do you listen to God's Word and obey it?
- Do you avoid a prideful spirit that would show no concern for God's ways?

Take this to the next level: Honor godly influences in your life.

insouciance: say it, believe it, avoid it!

This is my perspective for today, Pastor Scott

Dr. Scott Payne

Day Two Hundred Thirty
The Pastor's Perspective: Your word for the day!

preemptive – *(adjective)* ***precautionary; preventive***
pree-**emp**-tiv

Reading Plan: Jeremiah 38-40; Psalm 74, 79

Many of the officials of Judah decided it was best to silence Jeremiah by killing him. They threw him into a cistern hoping he would starve to death. An Ethiopian appealed to King Zedekiah for Jeremiah's deliverance, and he was granted permission to free him.

Jeremiah told King Zedekiah there were **preemptive** measures that could be taken to minimize the effects of God's judgment against Judah. Zedekiah continued to reject the prophet's counsel and paid a heavy price for it. Even though Jerusalem would fall to the Babylonians, Jeremiah was spared and remained in Judah.

The psalmist pled with God to defend His honor and His purposes. God was asked to judge the nations that had mocked Him and denied His power. The psalmist also recalled the disasters that had fallen on the disobedient nation of Judah, yet asked for forgiveness and promised faithfulness from the people.

Reflect on these thoughts:
- God will protect those He calls to share His truth.
- You are either being delivered, or you are one delivering others.
- When you're given the option to avoid painful consequences, take it!
- God will fulfill His plans and has no equal to His power.

Take this to the next level: Celebrate those God places in your life to give you His counsel.

preemptive: say it, believe it, live it!

This is my perspective for today, Pastor Scott

Day Two Hundred Thirty-One
The Pastor's Perspective: Your word for the day!

vassal *(noun)* **bondman; servant**
vas-*uh* |

Reading Plan: 2 Kings 24-25; 2 Chronicles 36

A **vassal** king was established by King Nebuchadnezzar to provide stability and accountability to Babylon. Judah's kings never fared well because they refused to listen to the true prophets, and they constantly disobeyed God.

Zedekiah was one of the vassal kings appointed by Nebuchadnezzar. He rebelled against Babylon, but his rebellion was met by a devastating response. His children were killed before him, and then his eyes were put out. He spent the rest of his life exiled in Babylon.

Reflect on these thoughts:
- Being a child of God is far better than being a vassal of another.
- Listening and obeying the Lord God is better than being a slave to an evil lord.
- Notice God's patience versus the quick reaction of controlling people.
- Life separated from God offers no pleasure or joy.

Take this to the next level: Whom do you serve? Where you invest your time, talent and treasure will tell you.

vassal: say it, believe it, avoid it!

This is my perspective for today, Pastor Scott

Dr. Scott Payne

Day Two Hundred Thirty-Two
The Pastor's Perspective: Your word for the day!

forgotten – *(verb) **abandoned; disremembered***
fer-**got**-n

Reading Plan: Habakkuk

The prophet Habakkuk struggled with God's silence during the rebellious and turbulent times of the nation of Judah. His ministry was directed at God rather than the people. Habakkuk thought God had **forgotten** His people and had abandoned His character. The prophet questioned the seemingly good times the people and nations of evil were experiencing while the righteous were left to suffer. He then asked God how He could use corrupt nations to judge His people. God answered the prophet by letting him know He was at work even though the prophet could not see it. God also declared that all evil would be punished in due time. The prophet learned the valuable lesson of trusting and faithing God.

Reflect on these thoughts:
- Do you talk to God when you have questions about His work?
- Are you willing to patiently wait on God's answers to your concerns about life?
- How can God let evil be overlooked in any people?
- Is there a better option than placing your faith in God?

Take this to the next level: When you feel God is not there remember to let your faith and the facts about God drive your feelings.

forgotten: say it, believe it, you must avoid it!

This is my perspective for today, Pastor Scott

Day Two Hundred Thirty-Three
The Pastor's Perspective: Your word for the day!

rebellion – *(noun)* ***disobedience; dissent; defiance***
ri-**bel**-y*uh* n

Reading Plan: Jeremiah 41-45

Governor Gedaliah was appointed by King Nebuchadnezzar, and was assassinated by Ishmael. Ishmael continued his crusade by killing all those associated with the governor. Johanan and others pursued Ishmael. They were able to rescue some of the hostages Ishmael had taken, but Ishmael avoided Johanan.

Even after the warnings by Jeremiah, to the leaders and people of Judah, not to enter Egypt, their **rebellion** against God continued, and they rejected the words of His prophet. This was a complete denial of faith and trust in God and a decision to rely on someone other than Him. It would cost them dearly. God would judge Judah for their idolatry and refusal to repent from their sinful ways. God had the power to correct and even judge what He had created.

Reflect on these thoughts:
- Crime never pays.
- Righteous people should stand up for the innocent.
- All God's ways have spiritual value. Only the spiritually minded can understand His ways.
- God will have the final word.

Take this to the next level: Are there any areas in your life where you might be showings signs of rebellion towards God? Confess them now!

rebellion: say it, believe it, avoid it!

This is my perspective for today, Pastor Scott

Dr. Scott Payne

Day Two Hundred Thirty-Four
The Pastor's Perspective: Your word for the day!

haughty – *(adjective)* ***arrogant; cavalier; pompous***
haw-tee

Reading Plan: Jeremiah 46-48

A series of judgments came against the nations. Their **haughty** attitudes played a big role in their demise. They had totally rejected the true God and had embraced their own evil and wicked egos, fueling a disastrous future.

Egypt's mighty army would be no match for the judgment God declared against her. Egypt's false gods and kings would be put to shame. Egypt would survive, and a small remnant would be given a chance to turn to God.

God then turned His attention on Philistia. The Philistines were one of Israel's great nemeses. God pronounced their total destruction by hands from the north (Babylon).

Moab answered to God and His judgment. God judged their prideful attitudes and their worship of false gods, but eventually restored Moab.

Reflect on these thoughts:
- God has no equals.
- Physical strength and assets are no match for God's power.
- Don't be deceived by what would appear to be a lack of God's judgment. Sin will not go unpunished.
- As long as you have life there is an opportunity to discover God's forgiveness.

Take this to the next level: Are you able to do life without acknowledging God? It won't last!

haughty: say it, believe it, avoid it!

This is my perspective for today, Pastor Scott

Day Two Hundred Thirty-Five
The Pastor's Perspective: Your word for the day!

fate – *(noun)* ***destiny; inevitability***
feyt

Reading Plan: Jeremiah 49-50

God was continuing to use the prophet Jeremiah to declare the **fate** of many nations. Judgment was spoken out against Ammon because of their worship of the false god Molech, Edom because of their self-relent nature, Damascus because of their weak dependence on others, Kedar and Hazor because of their independence through trade, Elam because of their military strength, and Babylon because of the evil done against Israel. All these nations became an offense to God because of their rejection and refusal to see Him as the only true Creator and acknowledge His ways.

Reflect on these thoughts:
- God rules and decides what the day holds.
- God does hold the nations accountable for their ways.
- Offend God's people and you will reap His wrath.
- God looks for faithful people.

Take this to the next level: Anything that comes before God is wrong!

fate: say it, believe it, trust it to God!

This is my perspective for today, Pastor Scott

Dr. Scott Payne

Day Two Hundred Thirty-Six
The Pastor's Perspective: Your word for the day!

condemnation – *(noun) censure; strong disapproval*
kon-dem-**ney**-sh*uh* n

Reading Plan: Jeremiah 51-52

God's **condemnation** on Babylon was coming to fruition, and the nation's days were numbered. God was preparing an invader from the north that would totally destroy the Babylonian nation forever!

Even though God had sent many judgments on Judah and Israel, He had not forgotten them, and He would bring them back together and bless His people once again.

The prophet closed out his book with the story of Judah's defeat and the harsh consequence King Zedekiah paid for his unfaithfulness to God.

Reflect on these thoughts:
- The wicked must perish.
- God holds His own people accountable for their sins.
- God is always acting to bring His people to repentance.
- To whom much is given, much is required.

Take this to the next level: Are there areas in your life that God is condemning? Confess them now!

condemnation: say it, believe it, avoid it!

This is my perspective for today, Pastor Scott

Day Two Hundred Thirty-Seven
The Pastor's Perspective: Your word for the day!

enemy – *(noun)* ***adversary; foe***
en-uh-mee

Reading Plan: Lamentations 1-2

The writer of Lamentations began with a clear picture of the destruction of Jerusalem and the horrible aftermath of her defeat. Because of Judah's sins, the **enemy** (Babylon) had conquered God's people, and the persecution of an enslaved nation became evident. The people had not listened to the cry for repentance and a return to faith in God, and they paid for it. Because the people had forsaken God, He turned His back on them and intensified His judgment. There was no escaping the wrath of God.

Reflect on these thoughts:
- A defeat is NEVER pretty.
- There's always an enemy ready to attack.
- God's judgment will break you only to remake you into what He desires.
- The fires of correction are always the hottest ones to face.

Take this to the next level: Do you take the enemy for real?

enemy: say it, believe it, avoid it!

This is my perspective for today, Pastor Scott

Dr. Scott Payne

Day Two Hundred Thirty-Eight
The Pastor's Perspective: Your word for the day!

complicit – *(adjective)* ***conniving; conspiring with another party to perform unethical acts***
kuh m-**plis**-it

Reading Plan: Lamentations 3-5

The prophet of Lamentations realized God would punish sin, but would also restore and bless His people in the future. That gave him great confidence to trust in God with his future. He was willing to come under God's discipline that he might benefit and grow into the person God would bless.

God's anger towards Judah had been satisfied by Babylon's conquest, but Edom became a **complicit** partner with Babylon. Edom would now pay a price for her evil done against Judah.

As God's people returned to Him in confession and repentance their lives and future were reestablished.

Reflect on these thoughts:
- Learn from your mistakes and humbly accept correction.
- With a repentant heart you can trust better days are ahead.
- A partnership with evil never works out well.
- Run from evil and run towards God.

Take this to the next level: Evaluate your relationships. Are they God-honoring?

complicit: say it, believe it, avoid it!

This is my perspective for today, Pastor Scott

Day Two Hundred Thirty-Nine
The Pastor's Perspective: Your word for the day!

siege – *(noun) surrounding, isolating and restrictive blockade*
seej

Reading Plan: Ezekiel 1-4

Ezekiel was a prophet, called of God, while in exile in Babylon. He experienced a very unique call through a divine vision. God prepared His message for Ezekiel on a scroll, and then had him eat it. The words became a part of the life of the prophet. His responsibility would be to share the message with the people regardless of whether they received it or not. Ezekiel would only be judged if he failed to tell the message. God set him as a watchman over Israel, so they would hear the truth.

God then had Ezekiel act through a series of role-playing that demonstrated the **siege** that would befall Jerusalem and Judah.

Reflect on these thoughts:
- God calls His children to be Ezekiel today.
- God has prepared a message for His children to share with the world.
- You are only responsible to deliver the message, not make the people accept it.
- Stand guard and sound the warning, Satan is on the loose.

Take this to the next level: Are you willing to be a God voice into the lives of others?

siege: say it, believe it, avoid it!

This is my perspective for today, Pastor Scott

Dr. Scott Payne

Day Two Hundred Forty
The Pastor's Perspective: Your word for the day!

detestable – *(adjective) **despicable; vile; loathsome***
dih-**tes**-t*uh*-b*uh* l

Reading Plan: Ezekiel 5-8

Even in exile God's people continued their **detestable** ways and further withdrawal from God. They had aroused the anger of God, and He would not relent from increased judgment for their abominations. Idol worship had become a great offense to God, and now He would bring a hard judgment on the people for cheating on Him. The more God revealed to Ezekiel, the greater the offense of the people and her leaders. It broke Ezekiel's heart to see the evil committed by those who claimed to know God and be His people. To make it worse, they seemed to be snubbing their nose at God.

Reflect on these thoughts:
- When God's correction comes you have a choice as to how you will respond.
- Putting anything before God is just wrong.
- You can always make things worse.
- Ignoring God is not a smart thing.

Take this to the next level: Is there anything in your life that is not pleasing to God? Confess it and leave it.

detestable: say it, believe it, avoid it!

This is my perspective for today, Pastor Scott

Day Two Hundred Forty-One
The Pastor's Perspective: Your word for the day!

dissuade – *(verb) discourage; advise against*
dih-**sweyd**

Reading Plan: Ezekiel 9-12

Ezekiel continued his attempts to **dissuade** God from harshly judging the people and possibly exterminating the nation. The prophet was brought to a vivid understanding that God would judge the guilty but spare the repentant.

Jerusalem would be destroyed by fire, and the Spirit and glory of the Lord would leave the temple. The spiritual bankruptcy of the people would be totally disclosed. God would judge the evil counselors. He promised to give the people a new heart and spirit. Their captivity (exile) would become the womb of new birth and deliverance for a restored future in Israel.

Reflect on these thoughts:
- God's ways are beyond our comprehension.
- Staying close to God will give you peace of mind.
- Turn your back on God, and you will face His judgment.
- God is ready to transform the heart and soul of any repentant person.

Take this to the next level: Changing God's plans won't work. Faithfully seeking to understand His ways is profitable.

dissuade: say it, believe it, can't do it with God!

This is my perspective for today, Pastor Scott

Dr. Scott Payne

Day Two Hundred Forty-Two
The Pastor's Perspective: Your word for the day!

syncretism – *(noun)* ***attempted merging of opposing principles***
sing-kri-tiz-*uh* m

Reading Plan: Ezekiel 13-15

The Prophets had become manipulators of the people rather than men of God. They claimed to hear a word from God, yet God had not been speaking to them. God would judge these impostors and their controlling influences over the people.

The Elders would discover that **syncretism** was impossible with God's holiness. Their actions were totally empty as representatives of God's ways. They had chased after idols and neglected any relationship with God. These leaders were leading the people away from God's plans for them. The people would answer for their dependency on these unfaithful leaders.

Because Jerusalem had acted faithlessly, they would reap the judgment of God. Because they had turned their backs on God, He would turn from them and judge their sins.

Reflect on these thoughts:
- You must test the words of a prophet.
- Prophets point you to God's truth and not seek to control your life.
- Don't allow your leaders to compromise the truth of God.
- You are responsible for the choices you make and the leaders you follow.

Take this to the next level: Inventory your affections and discard anything that points you away from God.

syncretism: say it, believe it, avoid it!

This is my perspective for today, Pastor Scott

Day Two Hundred Forty-Three
The Pastor's Perspective: Your word for the day!

prostitution – *(noun)* ***harlotry; whoredom***
pros-ti-**too**-sh*uh* n

Reading Plan: Ezekiel 16-17

God had Ezekiel use a disgusting example of **prostitution** to metaphorically instruct the people of their infidelity. Very graphic examples were used to illustrate the cheating ways of God's people. They even made the prostitutes look pretty good. God had made a pure commitment to Israel yet she had given her soul to others.

Through the parable of the eagles and the vine, a political and spiritual picture was drawn. This demonstrated the contrast between the political judgment on Judah and the messianic future with God's blessing. God would continue His covenant with the offspring of the adulterous generation.

Reflect on these thoughts:
- Nothing's worse than cheating on God.
- Love God with a pure and sincere heart.
- God judges all human behavior.
- Don't miss being a part of God's blessings.

Take this to the next level: If you said yes to God are you keeping your promise?

prostitution: say it, believe it, don't do it!

This is my perspective for today, Pastor Scott

Dr. Scott Payne

Day Two Hundred Forty-Four
The Pastor's Perspective: Your word for the day!

exilic – *(adjective)* **pertaining to being banished**
eg-**zil**-ik

Reading Plan: Ezekiel 18-20

The **exilic** experience was unavoidable for the sinful nation of God. Commanded by God, Ezekiel clearly stated those that sinned would die, and the righteous would live. The prophet posed a series of examples that declared the righteousness of God's judgments.

Ezekiel addressed the corruption of the political leaders of God's people. Their evil leadership resulted in God's harsh judgment.

Israel would not learn from the failures of their fathers. The Israelites would continue to rebel against God's truth, and their defiant ways would separate them from the Lord. Their profanity would rob them of God's protection.

Reflect on these thoughts:
- You don't want to be separated from God.
- Your actions will affect your relationship with God and others.
- God will judge leaders.
- Avoid the sins of those who have lived before you.

Take this to the next level: Do you feel alone, deserted and separated from God? He hasn't moved!

exilic: say it, believe it, avoid it!

This is my perspective for today, Pastor Scott

Day Two Hundred Forty-Five
The Pastor's Perspective: Your word for the day!

deportment – *(noun)* ***manner; demeanor***
dih-**pawrt**-m*uh* nt

Reading Plan: Ezekiel 21-22

The **deportment** of God's people in Jerusalem produced a failing grade. God announced through the prophet that He would judge with a sword. The sword would be used on the people and their leaders.

Israel was being judged because of their corrupt and evil ways. There was no way they could avoid paying the price for their abominations.

Reflect on these thoughts:
- Evil conduct produces bad consequences.
- God can judge with a surgical strike.
- Wickedness really gets God's attention.

Take this to the next level: If you claim to be a child of God, are you living like a child of God?

deportment: say it, believe it, pray it's pleasing to God!

This is my perspective for today, Pastor Scott

Dr. Scott Payne

Day Two Hundred Forty-Six
The Pastor's Perspective: Your word for the day!

derision – *(noun)* ***scorn; contempt***
dih-**rizh**-*uh* n

Reading Plan: Ezekiel 23-24

The unfaithfulness of the two sisters in chapter twenty-three portrayed both the broken relationship God had with Judah and the judgment to come. These women had defiled themselves by idol worship, disgraceful actions in God's sanctuary, profaning the Sabbath, and sacrificing their children to idols. They would face **derision** from others. God would put an end to their sinful ways, and then the people would know He was the Lord God.

In the next chapter Jerusalem fell to the Babylonians, Ezekiel lost his voice, and his wife died. As painful as these experiences were, Ezekiel remained faithful to God. This was a precursor to what the people were about to experience during the days of judgment.

Reflect on these thoughts:
- Sin is a very destructive habit.
- Sinful actions will be rejected by the righteous.
- Serving God may produce painful times, but God's results are what matters.

Take this to the next level: If your actions are drawing questions from your friends, maybe you should hear them out.

derision: say it, believe it, avoid it!

This is my perspective for today, Pastor Scott

Day Two Hundred Forty-Seven
The Pastor's Perspective: Your word for the day!

coalition – *(noun)* ***partnership; affiliation***
koh-*uh*-**lish**-*uh* n

Reading Plan: Ezekiel 25-27

The prophet was told to speak against a **coalition** of nations that had stood with Judah against Babylon. These nations would be judged for their cruel treatment of Judah. God was ready to show the world that He was the Lord God of all.

An extra amount of judgmental accountability was given to Tyre, mainly because of her prideful position based on her international commerce. The metaphor of a merchant ship that was struck with calamity served to declare their fate.

Reflect on these thoughts:
- Don't insult the House of the Lord.
- Never put down the people of God.
- Don't let your assets go to your head.

Take this to the next level: Is your life acknowledging the Lord God?

coalition: say it, believe it, beware of its effects!

This is my perspective for today, Pastor Scott

Dr. Scott Payne

Day Two Hundred Forty-Eight
The Pastor's Perspective: Your word for the day!

squandered – *(verb) **wasted; frittered away***
skwon-der

Reading Plan: Ezekiel 28-30

Tyre and her king experienced great prosperity which contributed to a prideful and arrogant people. God pronounced His judgment on the king of Tyre, because he had made himself out to be a god. Even though given all the assets to become a great king and a great city, they had failed. They had **squandered** their resources on themselves.

God opposed Sidon because of her wickedness and would judge them by the sword.

The prophet would speak out against Pharaoh and Egypt. Because Pharaoh declared he had created the Nile and had done evil in the sight of the Lord, judgment would come swiftly. God would put an end to their wealth and idols, and they would fall to Babylon.

Reflect on these thoughts:
- Use your resources to honor God.
- Building larger barns for yourself never works out very well.
- There's only one God. He will judge the false gods.

Take this to the next level: Are the sum total of your resources honoring God?

squandered: say it, believe it, avoid it!

This is my perspective for today, Pastor Scott

Day Two Hundred Forty-Nine
The Pastor's Perspective: Your word for the day!

permanence – *(noun)* ***durability; lastingness***
pur-m*uh*-n*uh* ns

Reading Plan: Ezekiel 31-33

Egypt's pride had led to the belief of her **permanence** in the world. The prophet was called by God to remind Egypt that Assyria had thought the same thing at one time, and then had been removed from the world stage. Egypt was about to experience the same fall from significance.

Ezekiel then turned his message to Israel. He reminded the people that God was judging those nations that had been an offense to Him and to them. Judgment was coming by the sword, and these nations would be no match for the mighty Lord God.

God spoke into Ezekiel's life reminding him that he was to be a watchman, and he should speak hope and comfort to the people.

Reflect on these thoughts:
- The sin of pride is destructive.
- Learn from the failures of others.
- Always keep an eye open for the enemy.

Take this to the next level: Remember there's only ONE that is supreme.

permanence: say it, believe it, avoid it!

This is my perspective for today, Pastor Scott

Dr. Scott Payne

Day Two Hundred Fifty
The Pastor's Perspective: Your word for the day!

animosity – *(noun)* ***hostility; loathing***
an-*uh*-**mos**-i-tee

Reading Plan: Ezekiel 34-36

The prophet spoke out against the wicked shepherds who fed themselves rather than the people. The sheep have been scattered, but God would find them, as a good shepherd looks for the sheep. God promised He would provide a new shepherd and restore the land and the people.

God judged the **animosity** Edom held against Judah. Mount Seir would become desolate. The judgment of God would serve to make His greatness known to all.

While God had judged the mountains of Israel earlier, He readied himself to restore their fruitfulness. They would once again become a blessing to the nation. By this the people would know that God is the Lord. God would also replace the old heart of stone the people had possessed with a new heart of flesh. God was ready to do for the people what they could not do for themselves.

Reflect on these thoughts:
- God appoints shepherds to feed His people.
- God will hold shepherds accountable.
- God doesn't need anyone to declare His glory for Him.
- Only God can do a spiritual heart transplant.

Take this to the next level: Are you worried about those who hold ill will against you? Let it go; love and serve God, and He will protect your path.

animosity: say it, believe it, avoid it!

This is my perspective for today, Pastor Scott

Day Two Hundred Fifty-One
The Pastor's Perspective: Your word for the day!

resuscitate – *(verb) revive; restore; rejuvenate*
ri-**suhs**-i-teyt

Reading Plan: Ezekiel 37-39

God gave Ezekiel a vision of a valley with dry bones. Ezekiel saw a valley filled with human bones, and God told him He would **resuscitate** those bones by recreating life. Ezekiel was to share this vision with the people of God who had become hopeless. God was announcing He was about to breathe life back in their hopeless bodies.

Gog would experience the judgment of God. Because Gog had come up against Israel they would now face the power of Almighty God. After judging Gog, God would turn to Israel and restore her fortune and future.

Reflect on these thoughts:
- If you find yourself in a dry place, ask God to breathe new life into your body.
- Only God can bring what is dead back to life.
- God will destroy the enemies of His people.
- God has wonderful plans in store for His people.

Take this to the next level: Are you depleted of life's resources? Call out to God for His life giving breath.

resuscitate: say it, believe it, call out for it!

This is my perspective for today, Pastor Scott

Dr. Scott Payne

Day Two Hundred Fifty-Two
The Pastor's Perspective: Your word for the day!

supremacy – *(noun) **sovereignty; superiority***
s*uh*-**prem**-*uh*-see

Reading Plan: Ezekiel 40-42

Ezekiel's vision of the temple moved the message from establishing hope for the nation to seeing the **supremacy** of God. The greatness of God would now be revealed among His people. The abominations the people had practiced in the temple that had brought judgment on them were now in the past. Ezekiel was given a vision of the new temple and the glory of God. The temple measurements seemed to point to the perfection and completeness of God's rebuilt house. There was a clear distinction made between the holy and the common.

Reflect on these thoughts:
- The ultimate authority in your life must be God.
- God is not first in your life if you are accommodating sin.
- God's presence makes a place or person holy.
- Good things are not always holy things.

Take this to the next level: Have you asked God to rebuild your life by the power of His holiness?

supremacy: say it, believe it, experience God!

This is my perspective for today, Pastor Scott

Day Two Hundred Fifty-Three
The Pastor's Perspective: Your word for the day!

remnant – *(noun) remainder; fragment*
rem-n*uh* nt

Reading Plan: Ezekiel 43-45

Just as God's glory had left the city and Temple before its destruction, His glory would return with the advent of His **remnant** coming home. Ezekiel caught a vision of the restored Temple filled with God's glory. Unfortunately, the people would not accept God's call to repentance, and the fulfillment of Ezekiel's vision would be delayed.

God revealed how He would reestablish the Temple's holy purpose. He would reconnect with the priestly line of Zadok, who had remained faithful, and call them back to their servant responsibilities as spelled out in Exodus and Leviticus. There was an expectation that God's leaders and people would return to a life of trustworthiness and honesty.

Reflect on these thoughts:
- Remain faithful to God in good and bad times.
- You are His temple; ask Him to fill you with His glory!
- Delayed obedience is disobedience.
- Do right by God and others.

Take this to the next level: Do you count yourself as part of God's faithful family? If not, do something about it now!

remnant: say it, believe it, live it!

This is my perspective for today, Pastor Scott

Dr. Scott Payne

Day Two Hundred Fifty-Four
The Pastor's Perspective: Your word for the day!

ingress – *(noun)* ***entrance; admission***
in-gres

Reading Plan: Ezekiel 46-48

The record of the Temple offerings called the people and their leaders back to the sacrificial requirements. The focus was on worship and leading the people back to a spiritual life that was driven by their love and obedience to God.

The vision of the water flowing from the Temple was a picture of the life and blessings God offered those who would trust and obey Him. God would take them deeper into the waters of faith and eventually to the river of greatest reward.

The tribal land assignments reflected God's provision for those who were a part of His family. The **ingress,** given to the Prince and the people, to the Temple and the land declared that God would be with His people.

Reflect on these thoughts:
- Worship requires a sacrificial response to God's grace.
- A growing spiritual life is the result of consistent worship of God.
- Walking with God always takes your faith deeper.
- There's plenty of room for more people in God's forever family.

Take this to the next level: Are you spending enough time focusing on your relationship with God?

ingress: say it, believe it, live it!

This is my perspective for today, Pastor Scott

Day Two Hundred Fifty-Five
The Pastor's Perspective: Your word for the day!

restore – *(verb)* ***reinstate; revive***
ri-**stawr**

Reading Plan: Joel

The prophet Joel was given a message to Judah and Jerusalem that the judgment of God was imminent on them and all nations. For Israel this judgment would begin with severe famine and culminate with a military assault on God's people. The driving message of Joel was to prepare for "the day of the Lord." Joel understood there was a great need for repentance and with repentance God would **restore** the people and their land. Not only would He **restore** the repentant nation, but He would also pour out His Spirit on all flesh. There would be an abundance of all things given to those who turned to God. "The day of the Lord" would usher in judgment for evil but forgiveness for those who returned to the Lord.

Reflect on these thoughts:
- God rules even when it seems like evil is winning.
- Only the repentant and righteous will find the favor of God.
- God's wrath can be avoided.
- "The day of the Lord" is unavoidable, but if you walk with God He will see you through to the other side. God will give you His Spirit to live by.

Take this to the next level: Are you ready to confess your failures and rebellion towards God and live for Him? Do it and there'll be no regrets!

restore: say it, believe it, experience it!

This is my perspective for today, Pastor Scott

Dr. Scott Payne

Day Two Hundred Fifty-Six
The Pastor's Perspective: Your word for the day!

malicious – *(adjective) **hateful; vengeful***
m*uh*-**lish**-*uh* s

Reading Plan: Daniel 1-3

The Babylonians took Judah into captivity, and King Nebuchadnezzar required many of the young Jewish boys be trained for service in the palace. Four of these Jewish boys became standouts because of their commitment to God: Belteshazzar, Shadrach, Meshach, and Abednego.

Nebuchadnezzar's dream team magicians and sorcerers could not interpret his dream and he was ready to kill them all. Then Daniel stepped up and provided to the king an account of the dream and its interpretation, giving God all the credit. Nebuchadnezzar celebrated Daniel and the God he served and he gave the young Jewish boy and his three friends positions of authority.

The enemies of God's boys became **malicious** in their accusations about their service. The offense Shadrach, Meshach, and Abednego gave King Nebuchadnezzar, with their refusal to worship his created statue, would cost them a trip into the furnace. Once again, God would watch over these boys while they were in the furnace; they emerged unharmed. Once again Nebuchadnezzar would be astounded by their God and promoted them in Babylon.

Reflect on these thoughts:
- Faithfulness to God reaps a great harvest of provision.
- Serving others, giving God the glory, may reap a harvest for others.
- No compromise to false gods gives the true God an opportunity to put His power on display.

Take this to the next level: Are you threatened by the opinions of others when your desire is to please God? Never turn your back on God!

malicious: say it, believe it, avoid it!

This is my perspective for today, Pastor Scott

Day Two Hundred Fifty-Seven
The Pastor's Perspective: Your word for the day!

decipher – *(verb) decode; translate*
dih-**sahy**-fer

Reading Plan: Daniel 4-6

Nebuchadnezzar had a second dream that his staff could not interpret. Daniel came before the king and was able to give the king the understanding he needed. The interpretation came true, and Nebuchadnezzar found himself totally humiliated because of his prideful spirit. After God's judgment period came to an end Nebuchadnezzar repented, and God restored his reign.

Belshazzar would assume leadership in Babylon. He held a feast and commanded the vessels of the Temple be used for drink wine. This offended God. The Lord would use the appearance of a mysterious finger that wrote on the plaster wall. When no one in the kingdom could interpret this event the queen remembered Daniel. Daniel was given the ability from God to **decipher** the writing on the wall. Belshazzar's arrogance would cost him his life, and the kingdom fell to the Medes.

Darius, ruler of the Medes, would appoint Daniel as one of his three presidents to oversee the kingdom. Jealousy among the other leaders motivated them to convince Darius to make a rule that only he, as king, could be petitioned for anything during the next 30 days. This would challenge Daniel's faithfulness to God. Daniel remained faithful to God, and Darius (regretting his declaration) was forced to throw Daniel into the lions' den. God would protect Daniel by closing the mouth of the lions!

Reflect on these thoughts:
- Never forget who's in charge. God rules!
- Return to the Lord, and He will show mercy. Confession works!
- Don't misuse the things of God. Avoid an unholy use of things!
- Count the cost before making a commitment. All choices have effects!
- Trusting God is always the best option. Let God lead!

Take this to the next level: Are you allowing God to make the difference in your life?

decipher: say it, believe it, listen to God!

This is my perspective for today, Pastor Scott

Dr. Scott Payne

Day Two Hundred Fifty-Eight
The Pastor's Perspective: Your word for the day!

cogitation – *(noun) pondering; contemplation*
koj-i-**tey**-sh*uh* n

Reading Plan: Daniel 7-9

Daniel's visions continued. He had a dream that would account for the nations' struggle for world supremacy. This struggle would culminate in the arrival of the Antichrist. The **cogitation** of Daniel did not always lead to a complete understanding of God's ways. Therefore, scholars have given understanding to some of the symbolic language of Daniel's dreams.

As many of the prophets of his day, Daniel prayed to God to heal the people. He realized they had been rebellious and extremely sinful before the Lord, and could only plead for God's mercy and grace. One accepted view of the time period Daniel spoke of in chapter nine would be to relate it to the seven years of tribulation in the future.

Reflect on these thoughts:
- God may use your dream life to communicate His plans or purposes.
- The battle with evil ultimately ends with victory in Jesus.
- Listen to the prophets (preachers, teachers, and spiritual leaders) of God.

Take this to the next level: Are you taking the time to listen and learn from God as He speaks into your life through all your experiences?

cogitation: say it, believe it, live it!

This is my perspective for today, Pastor Scott

Day Two Hundred Fifty-Nine
The Pastor's Perspective: Your word for the day!

chasten – *(verb)* ***discipline; punish***
chey-suh n

Reading Plan: Daniel 10-12

Daniel would fast and **chasten** himself before the Lord God in order to discover God's greatness and goodness. His prayers were answered in a final vision. God gave Daniel the insight into the final days of conflict between the nations before He totally intervened and brought about His peaceable reign.

Reflect on these thoughts:
- Only God can bring healing and hope to those in need.
- Wicked agents can impede the coming of God's messengers, but they can't stop God's delivery.
- The difficulties of this world serve to point us to God for help.
- God will break the arrogance of our pride that some might accept Him as Lord.

Take this to the next level: Make sure God is on the throne of your life.

chasten: say it, believe it, live it!

This is my perspective for today, Pastor Scott

Dr. Scott Payne

Day Two Hundred Sixty
The Pastor's Perspective: Your word for the day!

homecoming – *(noun)* ***return; arriving***
hohm-kuhm-ing

Reading Plan: Ezra 1-3

The priest, Ezra, recorded the **homecoming** of the Jews from Babylonian captivity. The Persian King Cyrus had defeated the Babylonians and released the Jews to return to Judah. The Jews were freed after seventy years in exile. Those Jews that chose to return were given permission to rebuild the Temple. Because genealogies were important to verifying one's relationship to Abraham, there was a recording of those who would go back to Jerusalem. God's people immediately began submitting their offerings and sacrifices as expressions of worship.

Reflect on these thoughts:
- God will use people outside His family to bless His people.
- God offers a fresh start to those who will love and obey Him.
- Family is important.
- Building a life of worship is more important than building walls.

Take this to the next level: If you find yourself too far away from God, come home!

homecoming: say it, believe it, celebrate it!

This is my perspective for today, Pastor Scott

Day Two Hundred Sixty-One
The Pastor's Perspective: Your word for the day!

tactics – *(noun) strategies; procedures; schemes*
tak-tiks

Reading Plan: Ezra 4-6; Psalms 137

The enemies of God's people used common **tactics** to plot against the successful rebuilding of Jerusalem and the Temple. They appealed to King Artaxerxes pointing out the potential threat the Jews would be if they were allowed to rebuild the city. The king ordered work at Jerusalem stopped.

During the reign of King Darius the construction in Jerusalem would restart. Once again the enemies of God's people would appeal to the king. King Darius looked into the matter and discovered King Cyrus had given the command for God's people to return and rebuild the Temple. He stood by that decision and even ruled that the enemies of Israel would provide for the construction needs. The Temple was completed!

Reflect on these thoughts:
- God's work will attract opposition.
- Don't allow those outside the faith to control the issues of faith.
- God always keeps His promises.
- May God's work and your worship continue in His Temple (YOU).

Take this to the next level: Don't be unequally connected to nonbelievers or let the opposition of the wicked deter your spiritual growth.

tactics: say it, believe it, recognize them!

This is my perspective for today, Pastor Scott

Dr. Scott Payne

Day Two Hundred Sixty-Two
The Pastor's Perspective: Your word for the day!

priorities – *(adjective)* ***higher rankings***
prahy-**awr**-i-tee

Reading Plan: Haggai

God brought the prophet Haggai on the scene to challenge the people's misplaced **priorities**. The pressures from outsiders, who wanted the work on the Temple to cease, discouraged Judah. They had stopped the work and focused their attention on their own needs. God's people had become more interested in their own houses than the house of God. They sought to satisfy their own desires rather than obey the voice of God. Once Haggai spoke God's message to them they immediately restarted the work on the Temple and found God's favor.

Reflect on these thoughts:
- Always review your priorities and make sure God is number one.
- Don't allow others to influence your agenda.
- Respond quickly to God's Word.
- When you do God's work He will supply the assets needed to accomplish the task.

Take this to the next level: Inventory your activities and make sure God is first.

priority: say it, believe it, live it for God!

This is my perspective for today, Pastor Scott

Day Two Hundred Sixty-Three
The Pastor's Perspective: Your word for the day!

invigorate – *(verb) energize; revitalize*
in-**vig**-*uh*-reyt

Reading Plan: Zechariah 1-4

Zechariah worked alongside Haggai prophesying God's plan to return the people back to Jerusalem and allow them to rebuild the Temple. Not only would they be freed from the Babylonian rule, their enemies would be defeated and crushed. God would reject the accusations against His people, and, instead, He expressed his love and support for them. The people had done nothing to deserve God's favor, but He was ready to **invigorate** His people in order that they would know He is God.

Reflect on these thoughts:
- Team up with other people who are connecting with God's Word and declare His truth.
- God will defeat your enemy that you might live in the glory of His presence.
- God blesses you when you glorify Him.

Take this to the next level: Turn to God, live by faith, and trust Him. Your life will be refreshed!

invigorate: say it, believe it, live it!

This is my perspective for today, Pastor Scott

Dr. Scott Payne

Day Two Hundred Sixty-Four
The Pastor's Perspective: Your word for the day!

imagery – *(noun)* ***mental picture(s); figurative likeness(es); symbolism***
im-ij-ree

Reading Plan: Zechariah 5-9

Zechariah's visions continued to portray spiritual **imagery**. The flying book was a symbol of God's judgment on the thieves and liars. The basket was a symbol of the sins of the world. The chariots depicted the releasing of God's Spirit. The branch was a foreshadowing of Jesus.

God was interested in a relationship with people, not the practice of religion. God was blessing His people, and it was getting the attention of the world. As the world witnessed what God was doing among His people, the appearance of the true coming King was realized, a humble King with unmatched power.

Reflect on these thoughts:
- No sin will be overlooked.
- Where the Spirit is there is freedom.
- Do life God's way not man's way.
- Don't let the humbleness of Jesus fool you, He is King.

Take this to the next level: Do you seek a spiritual understanding to what you see in the physical?

imagery: say it, believe it, live it!

This is my perspective for today, Pastor Scott

Day Two Hundred Sixty-Five
The Pastor's Perspective: Your word for the day!

slaughter – *(noun)* ***massacre; bloodbath***
slaw-ter

Reading Plan: Zechariah 10-14

Judah's leaders were seen as shepherds. They were given the assignment to care for God's people (the sheep), but their greed and lack of faithfulness to God placed the people in danger. Because of the failure of the shepherds to tend to the people a great **slaughter** was imminent. God promised He would replace the shepherds with One Shepherd that would provide for their safety and wellbeing.

Nations that opposed God's commandments were doomed, but Jerusalem would be spared. God would show His grace on His people, that they and the world would know He was the Lord. He would provide salvation for those who would trust in Him. God would remove the influence of idols and would bring the nations to a place of submission.

Reflect on these thoughts:
- Choose your leaders well.
- Listen to God's voice and follow His words.
- Jesus is the good shepherd, and His sheep know His voice.
- God rules, and His ways are always best.

Take this to the next level: Are you listening to the right voice for instruction and truth?

slaughter: say it, believe it, avoid it!

This is my perspective for today, Pastor Scott

Dr. Scott Payne

Day Two Hundred Sixty-Six
The Pastor's Perspective: Your word for the day!

genocide – *(noun) annihilation; mass extermination of a segment of society*
jen-*uh*-sahyd

Reading Plan: Esther 1-5

King Ahasuerus of Persia threw a great party for the nobles and princes. He reached out to his queen, Vashti, who rejected his call for attention and affection. Upon the recommendation of Memucan, King Ahasuerus sought to replace Vashti with another women who would become the new queen. In his search for a new queen Esther was found. The king loved her and had no clue she was a Jew.

King Ahasuerus appointed Haman to lead all the princes, and he became second in command to the king. Haman disliked the Jews and talked the king into a program of **genocide**. A decree was made that all Jews would be killed on a certain day. Once Esther found out about Haman's plan, she put her own plan into action that would save the Jews.

Reflect on these thoughts:
- God is always working both sides of an issue.
- You are where you are because God has a plan for you.
- Stay faithful to God and He will remain faithful to you.
- Dangerous times require difficult decisions.

Take this to the next level: Are you willing to let God use you to make a difference in your current circumstance?

genocide: say it, believe it, reject it!

This is my perspective for today, Pastor Scott

Day Two Hundred Sixty-Seven
The Pastor's Perspective: Your word for the day!

Purim – *(noun) celebration of Jewish deliverance in ancient Persia*
poo r-im

Reading Plan: Esther 6-10

Haman's plot to kill Mordecai and all the Jews was foiled. King Ahasuerus had Haman hung on the gallows that had been prepared by Haman himself for Mordecai. What a twist of fate. King Ahasuerus would reverse the letter of Haman condemning the Jews to death, and then allowed them to punish those that had intended them harm. The freedom the Jews received from the king became a festival known as **Purim**. Mordecai was elevated to a place of great authority and served King Ahasuerus well.

Reflect on these thoughts:
- Be sure your sins will find you out.
- Evil's ultimate reward is not good.
- People respond to leadership that is grounded in character not control.

Take this to the next level: Are you placing people in bondage for your purposes, or are you breaking their chains and setting them free?

Purim: say it, believe it, celebrate it!

This is my perspective for today, Pastor Scott

Dr. Scott Payne

Day Two Hundred Sixty-Eight
The Pastor's Perspective: Your word for the day!

iniquity – *(noun) sin; wickedness*
ih-**nik**-wi-tee

Reading Plan: Ezra 7-10

After receiving the approval from King Artaxerxes of Persia, Ezra and many of the exiles would return to Jerusalem. Ezra also sent a call out for the priests to return to Jerusalem in order to perform their duties in the Temple on behalf of the people.

When he arrived in Jerusalem, Ezra went into mourning because of the great **iniquity** of the people. He called God's people to repentance and challenged them to separate from their pagan relationship and obediently follow the Lord God. The people confessed their sins, and their relationship with God was restored.

Reflect on these thoughts:
- You must be committed to learn and share God's Word with others.
- God is the giver of all success you might experience.
- A humble spirit and a soul driven by confession will find God's blessings.
- Don't allow the culture to change you; instead you change the culture.

Take this to the next level: Are you embracing the ways of the world or the ways of God?

iniquity: say it, believe it, avoid it!

This is my perspective for today, Pastor Scott

Day Two Hundred Sixty-Nine
The Pastor's Perspective: Your word for the day!

opposition – *(noun)* ***disagreement; hostility***
op-*uh*-**zish**-*uh* n

Reading Plan: Nehemiah 1-5

Nehemiah was a cupbearer for the Persian King Artaxerxes. After hearing that Jerusalem was lying in waste, he asked the king if he could return home to repair the city. With the king's blessing he returned to Jerusalem and challenged the people to rebuild the walls of the city. They would face strong **opposition** from nearby governors, but Nehemiah had the people ready for battle as they continued building the walls. Nehemiah also relieved the financial pressures the poor were facing by instructing the rich to stop charging interest on loans to their needy countrymen.

Reflect on these thoughts:
- Ask and you shall receive.
- When serving God's purposes you will face opposition.
- You can overcome the attacks of the wicked while remaining faithful in your service.
- Be willing to help other Christians in time of need.

Take this to the next level: Are you allowing **criticism** to deter you from serving God's purposes?

opposition: say it, believe it, overcome it!

This is my perspective for today, Pastor Scott

Dr. Scott Payne

Day Two Hundred Seventy
The Pastor's Perspective: Your word for the day!

criticsim – *(noun) critique; judgment; disapproval*
krit-*uh*-siz-*uh* m

Reading Plan: Nehemiah 6-7

The harsh **criticism** from the opposition continued against Nehemiah and God's people. As the wall neared completion a new tactic was used - attack the character of Nehemiah. The enemy would even influence the priest, who in turn tried to trick Nehemiah into hiding, rather than trusting God. The priest's deception did not work; Nehemiah continued to trust God and completed the task. A review of the genealogy was conducted, and assignments to guard the wall were made. The people were safe and began to faithfully give to the Lord.

Reflect on these thoughts:
- The enemy is persistent.
- Overcome evil by trusting God and remaining faithful to Him.
- Complete the task or assignment.
- Giving is a God-like characteristic.

Take this to the next level: Is there any unfinished business that requires your attention?

criticism: say it, believe it, faith God through it!

This is my perspective for today, Pastor Scott

Day Two Hundred Seventy-One
The Pastor's Perspective: Your word for the day!

backslide – *(verb)* ***regress; relapse***
bak-slahyd

Reading Plan: Nehemiah 8-10

The people turned to the scribe Ezra to bring the law of Moses out and read it to them publicly. Ezra read from the book, and the people responded with a broken heart and a desire to repent. The spiritual leaders gave instruction on the law read to them, and the people were ready to obey God's Word. They understood the history of God's provision for the nation and were ready to return to the Lord. They cried out that they would not **backslide** as their forefathers had.

Reflect on these thoughts:
- Do you have a hunger for God's Word?
- Will you pray for understanding as you read His Word?
- Will you ask the Holy Spirit to be your instructor?
- Are you willing to faithfully obey what God tells you to do?

Take this to the next level: Live by God's Word not the words of others!

backslide: say it, believe it, avoid it!

This is my perspective for today, Pastor Scott

Dr. Scott Payne

Day Two Hundred Seventy-Two
The Pastor's Perspective: Your word for the day!

advent – *(noun)* ***arrival; appearing***
ad-vent

Reading Plan: Nehemiah 11-13; Psalm 126

Nehemiah recorded the **advent** of God's people to Jerusalem. Lots were cast to determine which families would repopulate Jerusalem. The rest of the people would live in the surrounding villages. The identity of the priests and Levites was followed by the service to dedicate the walls and Temple at Jerusalem. Nehemiah turned his final attention to issues that related to community and personal responsibility.

The psalmist reminded the people of past experiences that required God's mercy and encouraged them to seek God once again. The health of the nation and the people depended on God's faithfulness.

Reflect on these thoughts:
- God will bring His people home.
- Home is where God places you, and He will be with His people.
- Dedicate your dwelling place to the Lord.
- God will show mercy to those who seek it.

Take this to the next level: Come to God with a repentant heart, and He will accept you back home!

advent: say it, believe it, live it!

This is my perspective for today, Pastor Scott

Day Two Hundred Seventy-Three
The Pastor's Perspective: Your word for the day!

orthodoxy – *(noun)* ***belief; doctrine***
awr-thuh-dok-see

Reading Plan: Malachi

Malachi was speaking to a people who had a dead **orthodoxy**. They had become all too willing to compromise God's truth, and their worship had become totally offensive to God. They had defiled the altar of sacrifice with their detestable gifts. The prophet challenged the people to remember the laws of the Lord and obey them.

Reflect on these thoughts:
- Your ideas about God must be grounded in Scriptures.
- There can be no compromise with evil as a child of God.
- Your offerings must be worthy of a Holy God.
- God responds to obedience.

Take this to the next level: You can't serve two masters. Who is your master?

orthodoxy: say it, believe it, practice it!

This is my perspective for today, Pastor Scott

Dr. Scott Payne

Day Two Hundred Seventy-Four
The Pastor's Perspective: Your word for the day!

incarnate – *(adjective)* ***personified; embodied***
in-**kahr**-nit

Reading Plan: Luke 1; John 1

The gospel stories of Luke and John declared God to be **incarnate** in Jesus Christ. Both Luke and John experienced the powerful work of the Holy Spirit and announced His importance in the work of God the Father.

Luke began his gospel with the encounter that the priest Zechariah (Zacharias) had with the angel of God in the Temple. The angel proclaimed the pending birth of a baby boy to Zechariah and his wife Elizabeth. This little boy would grow up to become John the Baptist. Elizabeth was a relative of Mary, the mother of Jesus. John the Baptist would prepare the way for the coming Messiah, God **incarnate**.

John established a clear understanding of who Jesus Christ was. John spoke of the first encounter between John the Baptist and Jesus, the baptism of Jesus, and Jesus' calling of His first disciples. Jesus was God in the flesh!

Reflect on these thoughts:
- Don't be surprised by God's activity in your life.
- Where God is active, His Holy Spirit is active.
- You can expect miracles when God is at work.
- When God calls be ready to respond.

Take this to the next level: Are you looking for God to make a difference in your life?

incarnate: say it, believe it, know it!

This is my perspective for today, Pastor Scott

Day Two Hundred Seventy-Five
The Pastor's Perspective: Your word for the day!

validate – *(verb) **authenticate; verify; confirm***
val-i-deyt

Reading Plan: Matthew 1; Luke 2

Matthew would trace the genealogy of Jesus back to Abraham. This would **validate** the prophecy of Messiah coming through the lineage of Abraham and King David.

God told Joseph that Mary was pregnant by the Holy Spirit and would give birth to a son. After Jesus was born and circumcised, Joseph and Mary presented him at the Temple. Simeon and Anna recognized Him as Messiah. Twelve years later, Jesus and His parents would return again to the Temple in Jerusalem where He would astound the teachers with His understanding of the Word.

Reflect on these thoughts:
- God has always been among His creation accomplishing His purposes.
- God responds to your obedience.
- Others can recognize the work of God in your life.
- You can understand God's Word by listening to the Holy Spirit.

Take this to the next level: Are you paying attention to the miracles of God?

validate: say it, believe it, God will do it!

This is my perspective for today, Pastor Scott

Dr. Scott Payne

Day Two Hundred Seventy-Six
The Pastor's Perspective: Your word for the day!

Magi – *(plural noun)* **Wise Men who followed the star to find and worship Baby Jesus**
mey-jahy

Reading Plan: Matthew 2

The **Magi** arrived at Jerusalem seeking to worship Jesus. Upon hearing of the birth of King Jesus, Herod immediately perceived Jesus as a threat and therefore, wanted to kill Him.

The **Magi** found the young child and worshipped Him. After being warned in a dream, they would return to their home avoiding a report, to King Herod, as to Jesus' location. Herod was so angry that he had all boys two years and younger killed, but Jesus had already escaped to Egypt.

Reflect on these thoughts:
- Wise people will seek Jesus.
- If you know Jesus you will worship Him.
- Jesus is always a threat to those who want attention and power.
- What God declares will come to pass.

Take this to the next level: If you are truly wise nothing will deter you from finding Jesus!

Magi: say it, believe it, live it!

This is my perspective for today, Pastor Scott

Day Two Hundred Seventy-Seven
The Pastor's Perspective: Your word for the day!

forerunner – *(noun)* ***precursor; herald***
fawr-ruhn-er

Reading Plan: Matthew 3; Mark 1; Luke 3

John the Baptist was the **forerunner** of Jesus Christ (Messiah). John was preaching a message that called the people to repent from their sins and be water-baptized. He was preparing the way for the coming of Messiah who would baptize with the Holy Spirit and fire. After John recognized Jesus as Messiah and baptized Him, Jesus would call His first disciples to follow Him. Jesus would heal many and preached in the synagogues.

Reflect on these thoughts:
- In what way can you prepare the way for Jesus in the lives of others?
- Have you received the baptism of Jesus Christ?
- Can you think of some things Jesus has removed from your life?
- What does it mean to be a disciple of Jesus Christ?

Take this to the next level: Ask Jesus to heal your spiritual and physical needs, and then faithfully declare His Kingdom has come!

forerunner: say it, believe it, live it!

This is my perspective for today, Pastor Scott

Dr. Scott Payne

Day Two Hundred Seventy-Eight
The Pastor's Perspective: Your word for the day!

regenerate – *(verb) re-create; cause spiritual re-birth*
ri-**jen**-*uh*-reyt

Reading Plan: Matthew 4; Luke 4-5

The public work of Jesus started after His wilderness experience and the temptations He rejected from the Devil. He came to **regenerate** the souls of men. His teaching and healing pointed to the new life He could offer anyone who would join His forever family. After being rejected in his hometown of Nazareth, he moved into Galilee teaching and healing. He also added disciples that would forsake all to follow Him.

Reflect on these thoughts:
- The Devil's mission is to keep you from trusting and obeying God.
- Jesus is the only One who can give you new and abundant life.
- Many will reject God's message of forgiveness and hope.
- Jesus wants to be your Lord of all.

Take this to the next level: If Jesus has transformed your life, tell someone!

regenerate: say it, believe it, know it!

This is my perspective for today, Pastor Scott

Day Two Hundred Seventy-Nine
The Pastor's Perspective: Your word for the day!

fortuitous – *(adjective)* ***unplanned; unexpected; unforeseen***
fawr-**too**-it-t*uh* s

Reading Plan: John 2-4

There were no **fortuitous** events in the life of Jesus. He was very intentional in his activities.
His first recorded public miracle occurred at a wedding in Cana.

After His encounter with Nicodemus He made His way to Sychar in Samaria, where He met the woman at the well and stayed in the area for several days making disciples.

Then He returned to Cana where an official asked Him to heal his sick son. Jesus told him his son would be healed and live. As the official was returning home his servants met him and told him the boy was better. The official believed! This was the second miracle.

Reflect on these thoughts:
- Jesus is purposefully reaching out to people in need with life changing help.
- What Jesus offers is so much better than what the world offers.
- Jesus offers new life to anyone who will receive and obey His message.
- What Jesus says will come to pass.

Take this to the next level: Are you looking for Jesus to perform miracles in your life?

fortuitous: say it, believe it, Jesus is not it!

This is my perspective for today, Pastor Scott

Dr. Scott Payne

Day Two Hundred Eighty
The Pastor's Perspective: Your word for the day!

rebuked – *(verb)* ***reprimanded; censured***
re-**byook** d

Reading Plan: Matthew 8; Mark 2

The gospel of Matthew highlighted several of the miracles of Jesus. When His disciples feared the weather, Jesus **rebuked** the elements of nature. In another situation, He cast out the evil spirits that possessed a man.

Mark expanded on some of the miracle accounts of Jesus' life. Mark's story brought to light the extravagant love Jesus had for sinners. The world seemed to be caught up in religious legalism but Jesus was totally driven by love and relationships.

Reflect on these thoughts:
- There is always a God response to your faith.
- Miracles always point you to the Creator.
- God has power and authority over everything and everyone.
- Love the Lawgiver, and then you will understand the Law.

Take this to the next level: Jesus will deal with the evil in your life. Will you let Him?

rebuked: say it, believe it, accept it when needed!

This is my perspective for today, Pastor Scott

Day Two Hundred Eighty-One
The Pastor's Perspective: Your word for the day!

identified – *(verb)* ***acknowledged; recognized***
ahy-**den**-t*uh*-fahy

Reading Plan: John 5

Jesus healed the physical need of the lame man at the pool of Bethesda. Later Jesus would find him at the temple and encourage him to consider the spiritual healing that comes only through the forgiveness of sins.

Jewish leaders confronted Jesus for His Sabbath healing of the lame man. Jesus **identified** Himself as the Son of the Heavenly Father, which infuriated them. They called Him a blasphemer, but Jesus supported His claim with Old Testament scriptures. The Holy Word verified that Jesus and the Father were one!

Reflect on these thoughts:
- Never feel hopeless. Jesus heals!
- Forgiveness of sin is greater than physical healing. Jesus forgives!
- God's approval is all that matters. Jesus saves!
- All scripture points to Messiah. Jesus rules!

Take this to the next level: Which resurrection will you attend: one with the righteous or one with the unrighteous?

identified: say it, believe it, live it as a child of God!

This is my perspective for today, Pastor Scott

Dr. Scott Payne

Day Two Hundred Eighty-Two
The Pastor's Perspective: Your word for the day!

arbiter – *(noun) mediator; judge; go-between*
ahr-bi-ter

Reading Plan: Matthew 12; Mark 3; Luke 6

Jesus conducted several activities on the Sabbath; the disciples fed themselves from the cornfields, and Jesus healed a man's hand. Because these actions were done on the Sabbath, the religious leaders accused Jesus of serving the Devil. Jesus declared He was the **arbiter**. He explained that His authority honored the Father and not the Devil. He affirmed a house divided would not stand. He could not be working for both.

From a mountain retreat Jesus called twelve men to be His closest disciples. He gave them power to preach, heal and cast out devils.

Jesus used the arrival of His mother and some followers to teach about true family. Anyone who followed Him would be part of God's forever family.

Jesus shared one of His greatest teachings, the Beatitudes. He would challenge those who followed Him to love others and to express love to their enemies. Jesus gave great caution about judging others and encouraged people to evaluate the foundation on which they built their lives.

Reflect on these thoughts:
- The needs of people are more important than the laws of man.
- Jesus is the supreme authority.
- Jesus still gives power to those who serve with Him.
- Believe and obey Jesus, and you become family.
- Love is a pure expression of God.

Take this to the next level: On what foundation are you building your life?

arbiter: say it, believe it, let Jesus be yours!

This is my perspective for today, Pastor Scott

Day Two Hundred Eighty-Three
The Pastor's Perspective: Your word for the day!

phony – *(adjective)* ***insincere; bogus***
foh-nee

Reading Plan: Matthew 5-7

Those who followed Jesus as Messiah were to be different from other people. They were to be marked by a different attitude about serving and avoiding sin. Christians were to be driven by love.

Jesus taught how a true child of God should live. There was to be a difference between the **phony** piety of the religious and the sincerity of the genuine Christ follower. When experiencing God through the personal relationship with His Son, your life, values, and actions would take on the character of God. The Word of God would be loved and obeyed.

Reflect on these thoughts:
- You don't wait for the change; you thank God for the change that He is making in you now!
- God looks at your heart and motive, not your appearance.
- You might fool others, but you won't fool God.
- God wants you to be His example of love to others.

Take this to the next level: Are you fooling yourself or trying to fool others? Take an honesty checkup, and turn to God for help.

phony: say it, believe it, avoid it!

This is my perspective for today, Pastor Scott

Dr. Scott Payne

Day Two Hundred Eighty-Four
The Pastor's Perspective: Your word for the day!

contradicted – *(verb) **countered; opposed; denied***
kon-truh-**dikt**

Reading Plan: Matthew 9; Luke 7

Jesus' life **contradicted** the religious leaders of His day. His miracles and message were an offense to their self-imposed importance. Jesus taught God's kingdom needed more people to testify to others of His hope and forgiveness. Many people were humbled by their plight in life and saw Jesus as the only way for deliverance. He would compliment their faith, forgive their sins, and meet their physical needs.

Reflect on these thoughts:
- Are you looking for miracles or listening to the message?
- Will you change any area of your life if it is in disagreement with the values of Jesus?
- Is life something you can handle, or are you ready to confess you need a savior?

Take this to the next level: Every area of life is better with HIM than without HIM.

contradicted: say it, believe it, avoid it!

This is my perspective for today, Pastor Scott

Day Two Hundred Eighty-Five
The Pastor's Perspective: Your word for the day!

tribute – *(noun) accolade; acknowledgement*
trib-yoot

Reading Plan: Matthew 11

After Jesus confirmed to the disciples of John the Baptist that He was Messiah, He returned to instructing the crowd. Jesus gave **tribute** to John the Baptist saying he was the greatest man born of woman. Yet, Jesus stated that all born of the kingdom of heaven were greater.

John was preparing the way for Messiah, and neither man's message was well received by the religious leaders. Faith in Jesus would provide freedom to those who had been oppressed by religious legalism. Jesus would grant forgiveness and rest.

Reflect on these thoughts:
- Jesus declares He is the one and only Messiah.
- The greatness the world offers does not compare to the greatness given to the children of God.
- Every Christ-follower should prepare the way of Christ to a lost world.
- Only Jesus can restore your soul and provide the rest you need.

Take this to the next level: If your burdens are too heavy turn them over to Jesus!

tribute: say it, believe it, live life for God's glory!

This is my perspective for today, Pastor Scott

Dr. Scott Payne

Day Two Hundred Eighty-Six
The Pastor's Perspective: Your word for the day!

accidence – *(noun)* ***basis; fundamental components***
ak-si-d*uh* ns

Reading Plan: Luke 11

The disciples asked Jesus for the **accidence** of prayer. The Lord's Prayer might be better named Our Prayer! When asked how to pray, Jesus taught them.

Jesus gave clear instruction about the work of evil spirits. If a person did not fill their life with Godly things, then evil would multiply itself in that life.

Jesus warned those in influential positions that they would give an account for their actions. They would be held to the same standard they expected from the people. When Jesus called them out for their crooked and evil treatment of others, they began to plot against Him.

Reflect on these thoughts:
- Seek biblical principles to guide your life.
- Your heavenly Father wants you to make your requests known to Him.
- Your life is either lived in darkness or in light, for evil or for good.
- Good leaders must serve the people, not rule over them.

Take this to the next level: Are you seeking to live by the standards God has established for your life?

accidence: say it, believe it, live them!

This is my perspective for today, Pastor Scott

Day Two Hundred Eighty-Seven
The Pastor's Perspective: Your word for the day!

immixed – *(verb) intermingled; blended*
ih-**miks**

Reading Plan: Matthew 13; Luke 8

Jesus made it very clear that the gospel would be **immixed** with unacceptable and counterproductive elements. Jesus insured the gospel would find receptive places for the message to flourish. Several parables promoted the value of the gospel and what a true follower of Jesus would be willing to sacrifice for the eternal treasure.

The miracles of Jesus continued to validate His message of salvation to those who would accept His message of forgiveness of sin and hope for the future. Only He had the authority to overcome the threat that separated people from their Creator.

Reflect on these thoughts:
- Only God can judge evil and protect what is good.
- Your responsibility is to share the gospel seed; you are not responsible for the result.
- Life eternal is more valuable than life temporal.
- Jesus truly lived the life He offered.

Take this to the next level: Will you focus on what has true and eternal value?

immix: say it, believe it, Jesus will deal with it!

This is my perspective for today, Pastor Scott

Dr. Scott Payne

Day Two Hundred Eighty-Eight
The Pastor's Perspective: Your word for the day!

contagious – *(adjective)* ***catching; communicable; spreadable***
kuh n-**tey**-j*uh* s

Reading Plan: Mark 4-5

The gospel was **contagious** because the message of life that Jesus Christ shared was penetrating the lives of hopeless people. Jesus was using parables containing truth that could only be understood through faith in Him. The miracles Jesus performed would open up eyes and ears of faith that could receive His life-giving message.

Reflect on these thoughts:
- It's impossible to stop the spread of God's message to His creation.
- Jesus supplies the hope a hopeless person needs.
- Jesus provides His spirit to reveal the truth of His teaching.

Take this to the next level: If you have caught the life-changing truth from Jesus, are you sharing it?

contagious: say it, believe it, live it!

This is my perspective for today, Pastor Scott

Day Two Hundred Eighty-Nine
The Pastor's Perspective: Your word for the day!

martyrdom – *(noun)* ***death or suffering for a cause***
mahr-ter-d*uh* m

Reading Plan: Matthew 10

Jesus began His public ministry by calling twelve men to follow Him and share in His mission. They would have authority to deal with many of the afflictions of the people. He warned them that they would face rejection and persecution; they were being called to **martyrdom**. God would be with them and give them the words to say and the wisdom to flee evil places and people.

Reflect on these thoughts:
- Jesus is still calling people to follow Him.
- Jesus is still giving His followers authority over evil.
- Jesus is looking for people to live for His cause.

Take this to the next level: Are you allowing people or circumstances to discourage your Christian walk?

martyrdom: say it, believe it, embrace it!

This is my perspective for today, Pastor Scott

Dr. Scott Payne

Day Two Hundred Ninety
The Pastor's Perspective: Your word for the day!

transfiguration – *(noun)* ***supernatural transformation***
trans-fig-y*uh*-**rey**-sh*uh* n

Reading Plan: Matthew 14; Mark 6; Luke 9

Herod was tricked into having John the Baptist beheaded. When this was reported to Jesus, He retreated to a desolate place to reflect. The curious crowds followed Him, and He was moved with compassion for them. He would satisfy their hunger by blessing a boy's lunch and serving 5,000 men in addition to the women and children.

Jesus would call to Peter to join Him as He was walking on the water. Boldly, Peter left the boat he was in to meet Jesus on the water. But when the waters began to stir, he was afraid, took his eyes off Christ and began to sink. Jesus reached out and saved him.

Peter, John, and James witnessed the **transfiguration** of Jesus. These men were able to catch a glimpse of His marvelous glory. They were so taken by the experience that they wanted to withdraw from the world, build tents and stay on the mountaintop.

Jesus continued His teachings and miracles, but His own hometown would not receive Him. He clearly declared the demands that would be placed on His disciples and left no room for compromise.

Reflect on these thoughts:
- Evil still influences people to do horrific things.
- Jesus wants to do more than feed you physically; He wants to satisfy your soul.
- When your eyes are on Jesus you can accomplish the impossible.
- You must follow Jesus on His terms.

Take this to the next level: Are you willing to take a great step of faith?

transfiguration: say it, believe it, celebrate it!

This is my perspective for today, Pastor Scott

Day Two Hundred Ninety-One
The Pastor's Perspective: Your word for the day!

nutrition – *(noun)* ***nourishment; sustenance***
noo-**trish**-*uh* n

Reading Plan: John 6

Jesus offered **nutrition** for the soul. After experiencing the miracle of the feeding of thousands, the people sought Him out for more food. He cautioned them to not seek after perishable food, but to seek after food that endured throughout eternal life. Jesus declared He was the Bread of Life; His words would feed their spirit not their flesh.

Reflect on these thoughts:
- Profit for the soul is more important than profit for the body.
- Eternal life is the greatest gift Jesus offers.
- The Bible is true food for the soul.

Take this to the next level: Are you growing spiritually, and are you certain about your future?

nutrition: say it, believe it, discover it!

This is my perspective for today, Pastor Scott

Dr. Scott Payne

Day Two Hundred Ninety-Two
The Pastor's Perspective: Your word for the day!

deiform – *(adjective) Godlike; possessing divine characteristics*
dee-uh-fawrm

Reading Plan: Matthew 15; Mark 7

The religious leaders challenged Jesus, because He was allowing His disciples to break their laws. They did not see Jesus as **deiform,** and therefore, did not recognize His authority. Jesus taught the importance of what was in a person's heart and that the heart shaped the language and actions of a person.

The faith of a Canaanite woman would save the life of her daughter. She cried out to Jesus declaring He was the only One who could heal her child. He spoke of her faith and proclaimed her daughter was healed. Jesus continued healing many, and those healed glorified God.

Reflect on these thoughts:
- Jesus is the standard to live by.
- A heart that loves God is more important than acting religious.
- Faith always gets God's attention.

Take this to the next level: Are you letting Jesus direct your thoughts and actions?

deiform: say it, believe it, trust Him!

This is my perspective for today, Pastor Scott

Day Two Hundred Ninety-Three
The Pastor's Perspective: Your word for the day!

discern – *(verb) distinguish; differentiate; recognize*
dih-**surn**, -zurn

Reading Plan: Matthew 16; Mark 8

Jesus expected a spiritual person to **discern** the meaning of events in their lives. He challenged the Pharisees and Sadducees, when they tempted Him, to show a sign from heaven. Even when His disciples could not perceive the meaning of an experience, He questioned them about their spiritual understanding. But, unlike the Pharisees and Sadducees, their response to Jesus' question was truly spiritual. Peter turned to Jesus and declared Him to be the Christ, the Son of the living God. Jesus affirmed Peter by saying that only God could have revealed that to him. From that time forward Jesus began to prepare His followers for His death.

Reflect on these thoughts:
- The events of life can only be understood by God's truth revealed to His people.
- True discernment comes from God the Father.
- A believer might miss some things, but he won't miss Jesus.

Take this to the next level: Are you willing to stop trying to figure things out and instead ask God?

discern: say it, believe it, live it!

This is my perspective for today, Pastor Scott

Dr. Scott Payne

Day Two Hundred Ninety-Four
The Pastor's Perspective: Your word for the day!

lunatic – *(noun)* ***insane or crazy person; reckless or maniacal one***
loo-n*uh*-tik

Reading Plan: Matthew 17; Mark 9

When you think about it, everyone who rejects God is a **lunatic**. Satan works overtime to deceive people into thinking they don't need God, or that God is an empty thought created by man. The truth is Satan destroys, and God redeems. Satan tears down, and God builds up.

When a father came to Jesus with his demon-possessed son, the naysayers of God met their match. God relieved the boy of his possession and placed His power on display.

Jesus taught His followers to pay their taxes and respect the government. He and His disciples paid their tax burden and faithfully lived as good citizens.

Reflect on these thoughts:
- Which is more ridiculous; you are god, or there is a God?
- Will you allow God to restore the things in your life that are broken?
- Will you let God's power be released through your life?
- Do you trust God to meet your needs?

Take this to the next level: Is there anything keeping you from trusting God?

lunatic: say it, believe it, avoid it!

This is my perspective for today, Pastor Scott

Day Two Hundred Ninety-Five
The Pastor's Perspective: Your word for the day!

debtor – *(noun)* ***borrower***
det-er

Reading Plan: Matthew 18

The disciples were about to understand what true greatness in the kingdom of heaven looked like. It required childlike faith and obedience.

Jesus would give His followers a clear picture of how to relate to others. They were not to be an offense to one another. They were to remain humble and helpful, hold one another accountable, and forgive the **debtor** his debts, because God had forgiven them so much.

Reflect on these thoughts:
- A relationship with Jesus requires surrender and submission.
- Christians care for other Christians.
- A Christ follower will be accountable to other believers.
- Christians are forgiving people.

Take this to the next level: Are you willing to forgive much, because you have been forgiven much?

debtor: say it, believe it, release it!

This is my perspective for today, Pastor Scott

Dr. Scott Payne

Day Two Hundred Ninety-Six
The Pastor's Perspective: Your word for the day!

eternal – *(adjective)* ***unending; from everlasting to everlasting; forever***
ih-**tur**-nl

Reading Plan: John 7-8

Jesus had a divine appointment with the cross, and nothing would deter or alter that event. A frequent phrase was repeated by John, "His time had not yet come." There were many near-miss death experiences that John understood as God's protection, because the mission of Messiah was incomplete and the cross was waiting in the near future.

When the adulterous woman was brought before Him, the scribes and Pharisees sought to trick Jesus into condemning her. Instead He scornfully threw their unrighteous accusations back in their faces, turned to the woman and forgave her sin.

Jesus warned the people of coming judgment and that finding God's forgiveness by receiving Him, as true Messiah, was the only escape. Jesus could offer **eternal** life, because He was eternal. If they would look for truth they would find it in Him, because He was sent from God the Father.

Reflect on these thoughts:
- Do you believe Jesus died on the cross for your sins? Declare it!
- Do you believe in the sovereignty of God? Walk in it!
- Do you believe Jesus forgives sin? Accept it!
- Do you believe Jesus offers eternal life? Receive it!

Take this to the next level: Do the words of Jesus offend you or secure you?

eternal: say it, believe it, live it!

This is my perspective for today, Pastor Scott

Day Two Hundred Ninety-Seven
The Pastor's Perspective: Your word for the day!

skepticism – *(noun) apprehension; distrust; suspicion*
skep-t*uh*-siz-*uh* m

Reading Plan: John 9-10

Most of the time, Jesus was met with great **skepticism**. After witnessing the healing of the blind man, the Jews were reluctant to believe that a man, who had grown up in the area, could be the Son of God. "God with them" was not a reasonable answer for such a miracle. The religious leaders expressed their disbelief on the grounds of Jesus' claim to be from God, yet some could not help but entertain the idea. The healed blind man had nothing but confidence in his growing faith in Jesus.

Jesus would seize the opportunity to contrast the work of a thief to that of a good shepherd. God would only send a good shepherd (Jesus, God's Son), not a thief, to care for His sheep (His people).

Reflect on these thoughts:
- Doubt yourself, but don't doubt God.
- When your life is changed there's no going back.
- If you feel threatened by God, who is at fault?
- Do you recognize the voice of God?

Take this to the next level: Can you remember a time when Jesus healed your life?

skepticism: say it, believe it, avoid it!

This is my perspective for today, Pastor Scott

Dr. Scott Payne

Day Two Hundred Ninety-Eight
The Pastor's Perspective: Your word for the day!

harvest – *(noun)* ***the yield from seed that has been sown***
hahr-vist

Reading Plan: Luke 10

Jesus would send out seventy-two disciples as laborers to gather a **harvest**. He gave them instructions and power to accomplish the task. They returned with joy, but Jesus cautioned them to find their joy in their own salvation.

Jesus spoke a parable about a man who had been robbed and beaten. Those expected to help him passed him by, and instead, an unexpected Samaritan cared for the injured man. Jesus concluded those who truly loved God and had received eternal life should do likewise.

The encounter Jesus had at the home Martha and Mary became a teachable moment. The experience taught that time spent with Jesus, as in Mary's case, should be valued over things you do for Jesus, as in Martha's case.

Reflect on these thoughts:
- Those ready to receive God's Truth are more abundant than those willing to share the Truth.
- The secret to abundant living is the joy of your salvation.
- The things you do can be taken from you; your relationship with Jesus is eternal.
- Stay connected with your Savior and Lord.

Take this to the next level: Do you see people as needing a Savior?

harvest: say it, believe it, reap it!

This is my perspective for today, Pastor Scott

Day Two Hundred Ninety-Nine
The Pastor's Perspective: Your word for the day!

leaven – *(noun) an ingredient, such as yeast, that causes fermentation and is an altering influence; symbolic of sin*
lev-uh n

Reading Plan: Luke 12-13

Jesus compared the **leaven** used in dough to what sin does in the life of a person. Sin was deceptive and destructive, causing a person to trust in his own resources rather than God. Jesus taught the certainty of God's provisions for those that trusted Him.

God was seen as a master who could require an account from any of His creation at any time. This meant every person had to live ready to answer to God for how he was living his life. God was always looking for the person with a heart of repentance and faith.

Reflect on these thoughts:
- Avoid sin.
- Confess sin.
- Acknowledge God.
- Trust God.

Take this to the next level: Don't let sin deform you; let God transform you!

leaven: say it, believe it, avoid it!

This is my perspective for today, Pastor Scott

Dr. Scott Payne

Day Three Hundred
The Pastor's Perspective: Your word for the day!

Sabbath – *(noun)* **Lord's Day; rest day**
sab-*uh* th

Reading Plan: Luke 14-15

Keeping the **Sabbath** was a big deal to the religious leaders in the days of Jesus. They had gone far beyond the command and expectation of God for this holy day. Jesus used a visit for dinner at the house of a ruler to correct their perspective about this important day.

Jesus would challenge a lack of humility among those who were serving God's people. The parables of the wedding feast and the great banquet placed an emphasis on a lowly spirit and a loving response to God.

The parables, related to lost things, focused on the value given to what was important in one's life. Great sacrifice should be made for the things and the people you love.

Reflect on these thoughts:
- Jesus is the Lord of every day.
- People are more important than rules.
- Be honest about what you love and whom you love.

Take this to the next level: Are you listening and responding to God's invitations?

Sabbath: say it, believe it, live it God's way!

This is my perspective for today, Pastor Scott

Day Three Hundred One
The Pastor's Perspective: Your word for the day!

steward – *(noun)* ***overseer; managing agent***
stoo-erd, styoo-

Reading Plan: Luke 16-17

Jesus taught the personal responsibility that comes with being a good **steward** of things and relationships. All of life should be viewed as a gift from God, and that demands an account must be given as to how one manages life. Choices would either honor God or not. The story of the rich man and the beggar reflected the selfishness that can influence the stewardship of life and the drastic effects of being an unrighteous manager.

Jesus clarified that forgiveness and a thankful spirit were characteristics of a true child of God. Not only were these attributes vivid pictures of the Kingdom of God come to man, but they also represented a change of spirit only God could bring about. Jesus confirmed this Kingdom would eventually culminate in His certain return.

Reflect on these thoughts:
- Manage your affairs well every day; you never know when you'll give an account.
- Be ready to seize any opportunity to share your trust in God; it might make the difference in someone's eternity.
- Forgive because you have been forgiven.
- Experience the Kingdom of God, and you'll live in it for eternity.

Take this to the next level: Are you honoring God in all that you say and do?

steward: say it, believe it, live it!

This is my perspective for today, Pastor Scott

Dr. Scott Payne

Day Three Hundred Two
The Pastor's Perspective: Your word for the day!

glorify – *(verb)* ***exalt; worship***
glawr-*uh*-fahy, glohr-

Reading Plan: John 11

The death of Lazarus would **glorify** God and His Son Jesus Christ. The lack of knowledge and understanding about life is a product of man's separation from God. When a person connects to God through Jesus Christ as Savior and Lord, he walks in the Light (receives knowledge and understanding).

When arriving at Bethany Jesus related to those grieving over the death of Lazarus but quickly assured them that Lazarus would live! From the time Jesus raised Lazarus from the dead, the religious leaders began plans to kill Him.

Reflect on these thoughts:
- Does your life glorify God? Give Him some Glory!
- Do you find yourself walking in darkness? Trust Jesus!
- Are you in a season of grief? Let Jesus comfort you!

Take this to the next level: What are your plans for Jesus?

glorify: say it, believe it, live it!

This is my perspective for today, Pastor Scott

Day Three Hundred Three
The Pastor's Perspective: Your word for the day!

exalted – *(verb) lifted up; revered; praised*
ig-**zawl**-tid

1. raised or elevated, as in rank or character; of high station: *an exalted personage.*

Reading Plan: Luke 18

Jesus taught that everyone had a choice to live a life that **exalted** God or one's self. It was the widow and the beggar who **exalted** God. The rich man chose to **exalt** himself.

Reflect on these thoughts:
- Nobody heals like Jesus!
- When Jesus moves, He gets the glory.
- Denying God is way too costly.

Take this to the next level: Are you robbing God of anything for which He deserves the glory?

exalted: say it, believe it, give Him praise!

This is my perspective for today, Pastor Scott

Dr. Scott Payne

Day Three Hundred Four
The Pastor's Perspective: Your word for the day!

tempt – *(verb) **lure; attract; appeal to***
tempt

Reading Plan: Matthew 19, Mark 10

Many of the religious leaders tried to **tempt** Jesus with their interpretations of the Law and human situations. Jesus would answer their challenges by exposing the wickedness of their hearts.

A rather rich young man approached Jesus with the desire to have the life Jesus promised. When Jesus presented the opportunity to possess eternal life by giving up his possessions and following him, the man turned away with great sorrow.

The blind man, Bartimaeus, knew his only hope for healing was Jesus, and nothing would stop him from connecting with Christ. Jesus responded to the faith of Bartimaeus and healed him.

Reflect on these thoughts:
- Don't tempt God; He doesn't tempt you!
- You can't save your own soul.
- Jesus plus faith will make you whole!

Take this to the next level: If you sense temptation you know it's from Satan!

tempt: say it, believe it, avoid it!

This is my perspective for today, Pastor Scott

Day Three Hundred Five
The Pastor's Perspective: Your word for the day!

begrudged – *(verb) resented; felt bitter about a good thing in someone's life*
bih-**gruhj**

Reading Plan: Matthew 20-21

In the parable of the laborers in the vineyard some **begrudged** the payment scale used to compensate the workers. Jesus would teach that the master does what he wants with his money. The heavier part of the teaching was an introduction of The Kingdom principle that the last would be first, and the first would be last.

The triumphal entry of Jesus into Jerusalem continued the theme of Christ fulfilling prophecy. After His entry, He would cleanse the Temple and then be challenged by the religious leaders as to whose authority He had to conduct such actions. Jesus would turn their question on them, challenging their spiritual position and place of authority.

Reflect on these thoughts:
- Do you ever compare what you receive to what others may receive?
- Does God have the right to determine a person's return on investment?
- Does your life reflect a humble attitude?
- Do you allow the Holy Spirit to keep your life clean?

Take this to the next level: Live to serve!

begrudged: say it, believe it, avoid it!

This is my perspective for today, Pastor Scott

Dr. Scott Payne

Day Three Hundred Six
The Pastor's Perspective: Your word for the day!

stature – *(noun)* ***build; physique; also, level of accomplishment***
stach-er

Reading Plan: Luke 19

Zacchaeus was a man of short physical **stature,** but he became a man of great spiritual **stature**. He hosted Jesus at his house, and the whole family received eternal life.

Jesus told a parable that required the servants of a nobleman to manage their master's money. Several of the servants invested the money while one was afraid to invest. When the master returned he rewarded those who invested and harshly judged the one who refused to take a risk.

Reflect on these thoughts:
- God looks at the spiritual size of a person.
- Invite Jesus to your house and He will change lives.
- Invest your life for God's glory and there will be a reward.

Take this to the next level: Seek God and you will find His blessings.

stature: say it, believe it, live it!

This is my perspective for today, Pastor Scott

Day Three Hundred Seven
The Pastor's Perspective: Your word for the day!

anointed – *(verb) **blessed by applying oil or ointment as a symbol sacredness***
uh-**noint**

Reading Plan: Mark 11, John 12

Mary **anointed** the feet of Jesus and wiped his feet with her hair. This was not a waste of money on expensive oil, because this was a rare opportunity to acknowledge the Messiah. It was also a foreshadowing of a burial **anointing** of Jesus Christ.

Jesus explained that He must die because it was the will of the Father, and through His death many would find salvation. Jesus proclaimed that only through Him could a person connect with God the Father.

Reflect on these thoughts:
- Are you giving to Jesus while you have the opportunity?
- Do you give God your best or what you really don't care to keep?
- Are you willing to do the will of the Father instead of pursuing your own desires?

Take this to the next level: Do you truly love the Lord with ALL your heart, soul, and mind?

anointed: say it, believe it, do it!

This is my perspective for today, Pastor Scott

Dr. Scott Payne

Day Three Hundred Eight
The Pastor's Perspective: Your word for the day!

commandment – *(noun)* ***directive; order***
k*uh*-**mand**-m*uh* nt

Reading Plan: Matthew 22; Mark 12

Jesus told a parable of a king who sent out invitations for his son's wedding feast. The king sent servants to ensure those invited were coming, but the servants were killed. The king executed judgment for the death of his servants and sent invitations to the highways for others to attend. There was one who attended the event that neglected to dress appropriately. He was cast out of the feast.

When Jesus was challenged about the taxes Rome imposed, He called for a coin. Looking at the image on the coin, Jesus taught His disciples to give Caesar what he required, and to give God what He required.

The Pharisees approached Jesus and asked Him to state the greatest **commandment**. There was no follow-up to His concise and clear answer.

Reflect on these thoughts:
- God has sent an invitation to the world to attend His Son's feast.
- More people will refuse the invitation to join the feast of Jesus than accept it.
- The supreme act of obedience in your life is to love God!

Take this to the next level: Let God define your relationships and direct your possessions.

commandment: say it, believe it, obey Him!

This is my perspective for today, Pastor Scott

Day Three Hundred Nine
The Pastor's Perspective: Your word for the day!

pretense – *(noun) fabrication; faking*
pri-**tens**, **pree**-tens

Reading Plan: Matthew 23; Luke 20-21

Jesus was calling out the **pretense** of the religious leaders. They had the outward appearance of godliness, but their hearts were corrupt and evil. The scribes and Pharisees were true hypocrites. They failed to live what they taught.

The religious leaders were spiritually bankrupt. They could not answer the simplest questions associated with the Scriptures. Jesus' counsel was to avoid their practices.

Jesus would prepare His followers for His return. He gave a picture of what the final days before His return would look like (signs of the times). His followers could trust the presence of His Holy Spirit in those final days to guide them.

Reflect on these thoughts:
- You can't fool God. God knows your heart!
- You must practice what you preach. God knows your inconsistencies!
- You should examine the spiritual life of those from whom you learn. God understands your desires!
- You can trust God to lead you in all truth. God knows what you need!

Take this to the next level: Confess anything that is not a true desire of your heart and ask God to shape your life.

pretense: say it, believe it, avoid it!

This is my perspective for today, Pastor Scott

Dr. Scott Payne

Day Three Hundred Ten
The Pastor's Perspective: Your word for the day!

abomination – *(noun) outrage; abhorrence; detestation*
uh-bom-*uh*-**ney**-sh*uh* n

Reading Plan: Mark 13

Jesus assured His disciples their lives would change. He warned that times would get worse before getting better. But in the end, life would be victorious for those who loved and followed Him. Jesus gave them the signs of the times that would usher in His return. They would witness the **abomination** of desolation spoken of by the prophet Daniel and the uprisings of false prophets and messiahs. Then they would know His return would be soon.

Reflect on these thoughts:
- Times will change as the end grows near.
- When life is over, God and His followers will be the winners.
- Before the end of time comes there will be an abominable act committed in the Temple in Jerusalem.
- Never do anything that is an abomination to God.

Take this to the next level: Are you ready for the second coming of Jesus?

abomination: say it, believe it, avoid it!

This is my perspective for today, Pastor Scott

Day Three Hundred Eleven
The Pastor's Perspective: Your word for the day!

imminent – *(adjective)* ***looming; forthcoming; immediate***
im-*uh*-n*uh*-nt

Reading Plan: Matthew 24

Jesus told His disciples He would die, three days later be resurrected, and then return to God the Father. He encouraged them, that in spite of difficulties they would face after His going, they were to live with hope - a divine hope that would rest in His promise to come back. They should expect His **imminent** return and live a life ready for His return, because He would come back at a time they least expected.

Reflect on these thoughts:
- Do you believe Jesus died for your sin? Declare it!
- Do you believe He will return to end the conflict between right and wrong? Trust it!
- Do you believe He's coming back for you? Celebrate it!

Take this to the next level: Live in a continual state of readiness. He's coming soon!

imminent: say it, believe it, look for it!

This is my perspective for today, Pastor Scott

Dr. Scott Payne

Day Three Hundred Twelve
The Pastor's Perspective: Your word for the day!

foolish – *(adjective)* ***senseless; unwise;***
foo-lish

Reading Plan: Matthew 25

This could be called the chapter of **foolish** behavior; there were the foolish virgins, the foolish servant, and the foolish people. The five virgins didn't prepare for the possibility of needing more oil. The foolish servant refused to invest what he was a steward of. The foolish people failed to meet the needs of the hurting.

Reflect on these thoughts:
- You are responsible for preparing for the return of Christ.
- You will give an account for how you invested your life!
- You are to serve Christ by serving others.

Take this to the next level: Ask God to give you clear judgment about how you are living your life.

foolish: say it, believe it, avoid it!

This is my perspective for today, Pastor Scott

Day Three Hundred Thirteen
The Pastor's Perspective: Your word for the day!

stealthy – *(adjective)* ***sneaky; secretive***
stel-thee

Reading Plan: Matthew 26; Mark 14

The **stealthy** plot of the chief priests and elders was to have Jesus arrested and killed. Little did they realize Jesus had already made preparation for His crucifixion? He had already informed His disciples of His pending death and resurrection.

Judas struck a deal with the Jewish leaders to identify Christ to them. As Jesus was departing the Garden of Gethsemane, Judas identified Jesus with a kiss. The betrayal put in motion God's perfect plan to offer salvation to those who would trust in Christ as the Son of God.

Reflect on these thoughts:
- No one can get ahead of God and His plans.
- Jesus always completes His mission.
- Betrayal can be overcome by God's power.

Take this to the next level: Honesty with God covers a multitude of failures.

stealthy: say it, believe it, avoid it!

This is my perspective for today, Pastor Scott

Dr. Scott Payne

Day Three Hundred Fourteen
The Pastor's Perspective: Your word for the day!

pusillanimous – *(adjective) fearful; cowardly*
pyoo-suh-**lan**-uh-muhs

Reading Plan: Luke 22; John 13

Peter followed Jesus from a distance after His arrest and found himself warming by a fire with the enemy of Christ. The **pusillanimous** behavior of Peter caused him to betray his Lord. Just after the rooster crowed, Peter remembered Jesus had foretold of his betrayal.

Jesus would demonstrate the humility He expected His disciples to live by, when He washed their feet. Peter was reluctant to allow his Lord to wash his feet, but Jesus made it very clear that it was not an option. Peter was ready to receive a complete washing after Jesus had rebuked him. The disciples learned by example how they were to serve and love one another.

Reflect on these thoughts:
- Watch the company you keep.
- Failure is a result of bad choices.
- Humility is a mark of a Christ-follower.
- If you love Jesus you love to serve!

Take this to the next level: The flesh is weak, but the Spirit in you is strong.

pusillanimous: say it, believe it, avoid it!

This is my perspective for today, Pastor Scott

Day Three Hundred Fifteen
The Pastor's Perspective: Your word for the day!

Paraclete – *(noun)* **Holy Spirit; Helper;**
par-*uh*-kleet

Reading Plan: John 14-17

Jesus expected those that followed Him to keep His commandments. That would be the mark of their genuine love and devotion for Him. In preparation for the time when He would return to the Father, Jesus promised them He would send the **Paraclete.** This Spirit of Truth would be the Comforter and Teacher who would bring to remembrance what He had taught them. The **Paraclete** would give them peace in the midst of turbulent times, guidance in the time of need and conviction in the hours of temptation.

The followers of Christ were to be productive by sharing the miraculous message of Jesus with others. They were to live in the world but no longer be of the world. Consequently, they would be hated, ridiculed and persecuted by the world. But praise God, they would not be alone. Jesus had overcome the world!

Reflect on these thoughts:
- A genuine follower of Christ will love His Word.
- A true believer has a spiritual partner, the Holy Spirit.
- An authentic disciple of Jesus bears fruit.
- A pure Christian will experience persecution.

Take this to the next level: Are you acknowledging and surrendering to the Holy Spirit in your life?

Paraclete: say it, believe it, live it!

This is my perspective for today, Pastor Scott

Dr. Scott Payne

Day Three Hundred Sixteen
The Pastor's Perspective: Your word for the day!

crucify – *(verb)* ***to kill by hanging someone on a cross***
kroo-s*uh*-fahy

Reading Plan: Matthew 27; Mark 15

During the trial of Jesus no fault could be found. He was by all legal judgment an innocent man, guiltless of any crime. Pilate decided to free one person during the feast; he gave the Jewish mob a choice, the criminal Barabbas or Jesus the Son of God. They wanted Barabbas released. Pilate asked them what he should do with Jesus, and they shouted, "**crucify** Him!" Reluctantly, Pilate gave them what they wanted. The Roman soldiers would mock and beat Jesus before His death. After His death, His burial tomb was sealed, and a guard posted in order to avoid theft of the body.

Reflect on these thoughts:
- Jesus is the perfect Son of God.
- There's no middle ground with Jesus, you are either for Him or against Him.
- God can't be killed.
- The purposes of God can't be stopped.

Take this to the next level: Have you let Jesus take your death sentence, so you can live?

crucify: say it, believe it, live it!

This is my perspective for today, Pastor Scott

Day Three Hundred Seventeen
The Pastor's Perspective: Your word for the day!

mission – *(noun)* ***undertaking; work***
mish-*uh* n

Reading Plan: Luke 23; John 18-19

Jesus was close to accomplishing His **mission** here on earth. The only tasks left to complete it would involve a mock trial and a brutal crucifixion. There was no "Plan B" for Jesus. He had committed His life to doing the will of His Father, and His resolve was sealed. Mission accomplished! The sin debt was paid for those who trusted in the message of Jesus Christ. They would receive life, abundant and eternal.

Reflect on these thoughts:
- Stay committed to the end.
- Commitment requires sacrifice.
- God's way is the perfect way.
- You also can experience life, abundant and eternal by trusting in Jesus.
- Experience and share the "good news!"

Take this to the next level: Does God have a mission for you?

mission: say it, believe it, celebrate its completion!

This is my perspective for today, Pastor Scott

Dr. Scott Payne

Day Three Hundred Eighteen
The Pastor's Perspective: Your word for the day!

sepulcher – *(noun)* ***tomb; resting place***
sep-*uh* l-ker

Reading Plan: Matthew 28; Mark 16

On Sunday morning several of the women went to the **sepulcher** of Jesus to anoint His body with spices. When they arrived at the site, an angel of the Lord greeted them. Announcing the resurrection of Jesus, the angel prompted the women to go and tell the disciples that He was alive! Jesus would then appear to His disciples and commission them to spread the gospel.

Reflect on these thoughts:
- You won't find Jesus among the dead.
- Jesus will reveal Himself to those who truly seek a relationship with Him.
- You can't keep the truth to yourself; you will share it!

Take this to the next level: Only the One who conquered death can offer eternal life.

sepulcher: say it, believe it, declare it empty!

This is my perspective for today, Pastor Scott

Day Three Hundred Nineteen
The Pastor's Perspective: Your word for the day!

rabbi – *(noun)* ***chief clergyman in Judaism; biblical teacher and scholar***
rab-ahy

Reading Plan: Luke 24; John 20-21

After His resurrection Jesus would continue His role as **rabbi** to His people. He enlightened and encouraged those at His tomb, imparted truth to the two men walking the Emmaus road, informed the disciples closed up in a room, and taught and challenged those He had breakfast with before His ascension. Holy Spirit was coming to continue the God-relationship Jesus had provided.

Reflect on these thoughts:
- Jesus is the greatest teacher because He is the TRUTH.
- Jesus spends time with His disciples.
- Jesus went back to His Father but did not leave us alone!
- Jesus will always value the relationship with His people.

Take this to the next level: Jesus promised to continue as **rabbi** to those who trust Him, through the work of Holy Spirit.

rabbi: say it, believe it, obey Him!

This is my perspective for today, Pastor Scott

Dr. Scott Payne

Day Three Hundred Twenty
The Pastor's Perspective: Your word for the day!

perplexed – *(adjective)* ***confounded; confused***
per-plekst

Reading Plan: Acts 1-3

The disciples were **perplexed** after Jesus returned to His Father. They stayed in Jerusalem with a cloud of uncertainty filling their minds. The Apostles fasted and prayed, and chose Matthias to take the place of Judas as one of the twelve.

The Holy Spirit filled the place where the disciples were meeting and they were filled with wonder. Peter preached the gospel, and called the people to receive Jesus as Savior and His Holy Spirit as their great gift from the Father. Many lives were transformed and the disciples began their ministry of healing and teaching.

Reflect on these thoughts:
- Follow Jesus' directions even when you may not understand them.
- There's always something you can do even while you're waiting.
- The Holy Spirit is an essential part of your transformation.

Take this to the next level: Are you sharing the life transforming power of God's saving grace?

perplexed: say it, believe it, trust Him!

This is my perspective for today, Pastor Scott

Day Three Hundred Twenty-One
The Pastor's Perspective: Your word for the day!

fulmination – *(noun)* ***tirade; denunciation***
fuhl-m*uh*-**ney**-sh*uh* n

Reading Plan: Acts 4-6

The religious leaders felt threatened by the teaching of the apostles. The only answer was a **fulmination** of these followers of Jesus Christ. This action by the opposition backfired! Instead of diminishing the influence of these early Christians, it actually served to increase the acceptance of their message. The believers of Jesus became more emboldened.

The news of the deaths of Ananias and Sapphira spread throughout the Christian community. This husband and wife team chose to deceive other believers about the gift they were making to the church. God revealed their deception to the spiritual leadership, and when challenged with their lie, the couple fell dead.

The first servants (deacons) were selected to assume responsibilities within the church family. Stephen was a true standout among those chosen and was quickly arrested by the leaders of the synagogue. His wisdom and spirit intimated them.

Reflect on these thoughts:
- If you feel threatened by Truth then you're wrong.
- You'll never be successful trying to defeat God's purposes.
- There's never a reason to lie to God or others about your contributions.
- If you're walking with the Lord will be enough evidence for the world to see that you are a Christ follower.

Take this to the next level: Are you being accused of being a Christian?

fulmination: say it, believe it, you'll face it!

This is my perspective for today, Pastor Scott

Dr. Scott Payne

Day Three Hundred Twenty-Two
The Pastor's Perspective: Your word for the day!

serf – *(noun)* ***slave; captive worker***
surf

Reading Plan: Acts 7-8

In Stephen's address to the Sanhedrin, he recalled how the people of God had been **serfs** to false gods. He pointed out the rebellious nature of God's people, and how, through very poor decisions, they had rejected the words of the prophets and found themselves in bondage. But God loved them and had always called up a leader to deliver them from enslavement. Now Jesus had come to be their true Savior. The Sanhedrin was angered by Stephen's message and stoned him to death.

Philip came on the scene as a strong voice for the gospel. He was preaching and healing in the name of Jesus. He had an encounter with Simon the sorcerer. Simon thought the power of God could be purchased, but Philip rebuked him, and Simon ended up confessing his lack of understanding about spiritual matters. Philip's next encounter was with the Ethiopian official who was ready to be freed from his sinful bondage. He received Philip's message about Jesus and was baptized.

Reflect on these thoughts:
- Religious leaders can be void of spiritual life.
- The message of Jesus is not always received.
- Spiritual power comes as a gift from God; it's not something you can purchase.
- A changed life will be characterized by an obedient life.

Take this to the next level: Have you been freed from your false gods, and are you celebrating your adoption into God's forever family?

serf: say it, believe it, avoid it!

This is my perspective for today, Pastor Scott

Day Three Hundred Twenty-Three
The Pastor's Perspective: Your word for the day!

conversion – *(noun) **transformation; metamorphosis***
k*uh* n-**vur**-zh*uh* n, -sh*uh* n

Reading Plan: Acts 9-10

Conversion became a central theme in the New Testament after the ascension of Jesus and His return to the Father. Paul went from being a persecutor of Christians to being a Christian convert. Peter went from rejecting anyone outside the Jewish community to converting Gentiles to faith in Jesus Christ. These giant men of the faith moved from self-reliance to God-reliance through life-changing **conversions** that reaped eternal benefits.

Reflect on these thoughts:
- Jesus shares a message that offers an exchange: your sin for His righteousness.
- Only God can set a criminal free.
- Man's opinions are no match for God's ways.
- Only God can give a person a clean heart.

Take this to the next level: Are you willing to allow God complete control of your life?

conversion: say it, believe it, experience it!

This is my perspective for today, Pastor Scott

Dr. Scott Payne

Day Three Hundred Twenty-Four
The Pastor's Perspective: Your word for the day!

oppugnant – *(adjective)* ***hostile; contentious***
uh-**puhg**-n*uh* nt

Reading Plan: Acts 11-12

The Jews felt that Christianity was an **oppugnant** position to those who served God. James was killed because of his faith in Jesus Christ as Messiah. His death pleased the Jews, and Herod proceeded with plans to martyr Peter next. The Holy Spirit rescued Peter from prison before Herod could kill him, partly because of the prayers of God's people. The anger and arrogance of Herod would cost him his life.

Reflect on these thoughts:
- Listen for God to declare who's on His side.
- Standing faithfully with Jesus may cost you.
- God responds to the prayers of His people.
- God will judge a prideful spirit.

Take this to the next level: Are you opposing the work of God?

oppugnant: say it, believe it, avoid it!

This is my perspective for today, Pastor Scott

Day Three Hundred Twenty-Five
The Pastor's Perspective: Your word for the day!

villainy – *(noun)* ***evil; treachery***
vil-*uh*-nee

Reading Plan: Acts 13-14

A behavior of **villainy** characterized the opponents of Christianity. Wherever Paul and his companions went to share the message of Jesus, the antagonists followed. This did not deter Paul and others from teaching truth and finding people who would receive the gospel. Even when stoned and left for dead, Paul continued his mission of sharing Jesus Christ as true Messiah.

Reflect on these thoughts:
- Christians will always attract opponents.
- Evil is driven to destroy truth and what is good.
- Never let opposition keep you from obedience to the Lord.
- God gives sustaining and rewarding power to those who trust Him.

Take this to the next level: Do you give up too easily when times are challenging?

villainy: say it, believe it, avoid it!

This is my perspective for today, Pastor Scott

Dr. Scott Payne

Day Three Hundred Twenty-Six
The Pastor's Perspective: Your word for the day!

credible – *(adjective)* ***valid; plausible***
kred-*uh*-b*uh* l

Reading Plan: James

James encouraged the early Christians to live by faith, trust God through difficult and trying times, and live consistent lives as children of God's Kingdom. Some of the key thoughts James addressed were: handling trials and temptations, practicing pure religion, the relationship between faith and works, the proper use of the tongue, seeking true wisdom, and living for God instead of living for the world. A **credible** Christ-follower should be a humble and prayerful person.

Reflect on these thoughts:
- You must live by faith.
- Your actions must be consistent with the faith you express.
- You should speak to and treat others with understanding and love.

Take this to the next level: Is your faith demonstrated by good deeds done for God and others?

credible: say it, believe it, live it!

This is my perspective for today, Pastor Scott

Day Three Hundred Twenty-Seven
The Pastor's Perspective: Your word for the day!

bias – *(noun) **partiality; favoritism***
bahy-*uh* s

Reading Plan: Acts 15-16

There were obvious times of **bias** in the early propagation of the gospel. In this passage there were three experiences of bias: (1) Paul and Barnabas went to Jerusalem in order to report about the Gentiles who received the message and Spirit of Jesus. The Jews believed the Gentiles had to be circumcised in order to be saved. The witness from Paul and Barnabas gave evidence that the Gentiles had become believers and therefore did not need to be circumcised. (2) Paul would part ways from Barnabas because of a misunderstanding related to John Mark. (3) The Philippian jailer would experience a real change of heart about Paul and Silas and the gospel message.

Reflect on these thoughts:
- Watch out for preconceived thoughts about people or principles.
- People are more important than opinions.
- God's power can overcome any prejudice.

Take this to the next level: Are you seeing through God's eyes or yours?

bias: say it, believe it, avoid it!

This is my perspective for today, Pastor Scott

Dr. Scott Payne

Day Three Hundred Twenty-Eight
The Pastor's Perspective: Your word for the day!

nullify – *(verb) invalidate; abolish*
nuhl-*uh*-fahy

Reading Plan: Galatians 1-3

Paul wrote to the believers at Galatia questioning their lack of faithfulness to the gospel they once declared to be truth. He assured them that the gospel he had shared with them was from God, and they should not listen to false teachers and preachers.

The gospel freed those who believed in Jesus to live by faith and not as slaves to the law. Jesus did not **nullify** the law; rather He fulfilled it.

Reflect on these thoughts:
- Stay faithful to the truth of God's Word.
- Don't fall for the lies of false teachers.
- Faith in Jesus sets you free to love God's ways.
- Jesus fulfilled all the law on your behalf!

Take this to the next level: Are you allowing Jesus to keep you in a right relationship with God?

nullify: say it, believe it, you can avoid it!

This is my perspective for today, Pastor Scott

Day Three Hundred Twenty-Nine
The Pastor's Perspective: Your word for the day!

adoption – *(noun)* ***taking on, as belonging to one or owning***
uh-**dop**-sh*uh* n

Reading Plan: Galatians 4-6

Paul used the picture of **adoption** to describe the relationship between God and those who trusted in Jesus Christ as Messiah, Savior, and Lord. Through faith in Jesus, Christians became sons of the true Father. As **adopted** children of God they had received His Spirit in order to overcome the evil desires of the flesh. One of the greatest marks of the Christian faith was love for each other. Paul closed his letter by reminding believers to remember they were new creations and must stay true to the gospel.

Reflect on these thoughts:
- Accept God's invitation to become a part of His forever family.
- As a child of God you have a wonderful and eternal future.
- Love must be a significant trait of the child of God.
- The child of God will remain true to the gospel of Jesus.

Take this to the next level: Are you a member of God's family?

adoption: say it, believe it, accept it and live it!

This is my perspective for today, Pastor Scott

Dr. Scott Payne

Day Three Hundred Thirty
The Pastor's Perspective: Your word for the day!

superstition – *(noun)* ***belief without basis; irrational notion***
soo-per-**stish**-*uh* n

Reading Plan: Acts 17

Paul and Silas continued to travel to different regions preaching the gospel and calling people to trust in Jesus Christ as Messiah. Paul eventually parted for Athens without Silas. Once he arrived in Athens he was called to give his message to a group of philosophers. **Superstition** had caused the devout thinkers of Athens to construct an altar to "the unknown god." Paul spoke to them of how the living God had sent Jesus to reveal Himself to His creation. Many believed the words Paul shared and committed to become a disciple of Christ.

Reflect on these thoughts:
- People will not always accept God's message.
- Always appreciate the partners God provides you during your life's journey.
- There's no reason to feel threatened by false gods.
- Faithfully share Jesus, and some will receive the gospel.

Take this to the next level: Do you believe what people think or what God convicts you to know?

Superstition: say it, believe it, avoid it!

This is my perspective for today, Pastor Scott

Day Three Hundred Thirty-One
The Pastor's Perspective: Your word for the day!

postulated – *(verb)* ***presuppose; guess***
pos-ch*uh*-leyt

Reading Plan: 1 & 2 Thessalonians

Many have **postulated** as to why Paul wrote 1 & 2 Thessalonians. The two letters were probably written close together and would have been well received by the church at Thessalonica.

It is widely held that 1 Thessalonians chiefly addressed the second coming of Jesus. Those who were Christians would be delivered from God's wrath, but those who had denied Jesus would face His judgment. Paul encouraged followers of Jesus to make it their highest priority to please God, which required the acknowledgement of the Holy Spirit and His power.

Jesus' return continues a driving theme of 2 Thessalonians. Paul exhorted the believers to avoid the false teachers who wanted to draw them away from the Truth. Christians were to stand firm and avoid idleness.

Reflect on these thoughts:
- God takes all the guesswork out of life.
- Live like Jesus will return today.
- Ask God to fill you with His Holy Spirit.
- Stand firm and serve with a joyful heart.

Take this to the next level: Are you focused on the victory of His return?

postulated: say it, believe it, just trust the Word!

This is my perspective for today, Pastor Scott

Dr. Scott Payne

Day Three Hundred Thirty-Two
The Pastor's Perspective: Your word for the day!

exorcise - *(verb) purge; often used to describe the religious, ritualistic attempted expulsion of evil spirits*
ek-sawr-sahyz, -ser-

Reading Plan: Acts 18-19

While in Corinth Paul found a husband and wife that were tentmakers by trade. He stayed with them while he preached in the city. Paul's message quickly became a threat to many Jews who did not accept Jesus as Messiah. He departed for Antioch.

In Ephesus a Jew named Apollos began instructing people in the Lord. Priscilla and Aquila heard some of his incorrect teaching, and explained the gospel to him more accurately. Apollos ministered in Ephesus and Corinth, and his faith grew.

Paul was in Ephesus preaching Jesus. He found some disciples who had not heard of the Holy Spirit. Paul taught them the difference in the baptism of John and that of the Lord Jesus. Without the Holy Spirit at work in a person salvation was impossible. They received the full gospel message and the Holy Spirit.

The Jewish high priest's seven sons tried to **exorcise** demons, but the demonic spirits overpowered them. People learned that the Holy Spirit was a gift from God and not something to be treated lightly. The gospel Paul preached became a threat to the silversmiths and those who followed the goddess Artemis. When challenged by the false worshippers the message of God overcame the opposition.

Reflect on these thoughts:
- You will find friends in the marketplace.
- When opposition occurs God will open ways to serve Him and others.
- You are always learning and growing in your faith.
- The Holy Spirit gives life and grows life!

Take this to the next level: Are you living a personal relationship with God through His Holy Spirit?

exorcise: say it, believe it, it can't be about you!

This is my perspective for today, Pastor Scott

Day Three Hundred Thirty-Three
The Pastor's Perspective: Your word for the day!

spectacle – *(noun) **display; exhibition***
spek-t*uh*-k*uh* l

Reading Plan: 1 Corinthians 1-4

Apparently there were divisions in the church at Corinth caused by pride. Credit for increase within the church was being given to people, rather than Jesus Christ. Paul made it clear that people could plant and sow, but only God could give any increase. The declaration and work of the church should be to give God glory through His Son Jesus Christ. The members of the church were to be a **spectacle**, counted a fool by the world but wise in Christ.

Reflect on these thoughts:
- There's only One great among us, Jesus Christ!
- Serve faithfully but give God the glory!
- Don't hesitate to be an example of Jesus to the world.

Take this to the next level: Is there enough evidence in your life to convict you of being a Christian?

spectacle: say it, believe it, be it!

This is my perspective for today, Pastor Scott

Dr. Scott Payne

Day Three Hundred Thirty-Four
The Pastor's Perspective: Your word for the day!

defile – *(verb) dishonor; besmirch*
dih-**fahyl**

Reading Plan: 1 Corinthians 5-8

The early church had to avoid anything that would **defile** her. Marriage and sexual issues seemed to create questionable behavior.

Paul encouraged Christians to settle their differences without turning to the world for help. When conflicts were experienced among believers they were to settle the disputes within the Christian family.

Actions that caused other Christians to stumble must be identified and avoided. Paul spoke directly about food offered to idols: avoid it if it causes weakness in another Christ-follower.

Reflect on these thoughts:
- God's Word is clear about the things He wants you to avoid.
- God takes marriage seriously, and so should you.
- You can't avoid conflict, but you can deal with it properly.
- Spiritually maturing other believers is a high priority.

Take this to the next level: Ask God to reveal anything that might harm you or His church!

defile: say it, believe it, avoid it!

This is my perspective for today, Pastor Scott

Day Three Hundred Thirty-Five
The Pastor's Perspective: Your word for the day!

Apostle – *(noun)* **One of the original, official disciples of Christ; (apostle, with a small "a" includes any number of additional disciples)** *uh-***pos***-uh* l

Reading Plan: 1 Corinthians 9-11

Paul gave a clear defense to his claim to be an **Apostle**. He drew the parallel of reaping the benefits of his labors with those in whom he had spiritually invested.

Christians needed to avoid idolatry. They were not to eat in the temple of pagan gods. They were to flee sexual immorality, abstain from grumbling, and rebuke the pride of life.

The celebration of the Lord's Supper was an experience every believer was to take seriously. The bread and the cup represented the body and blood of Christ. The supper was never to be taken in an unworthy manner.

Reflect on these thoughts:
- Invest in the lives of others.
- Avoid wickedness.
- The Lord's Supper is spiritual food for the believer.

Take this to the next level: Are you preaching the gospel to the world needing to hear the truth?

Apostle: say it, believe it, live as they did!

This is my perspective for today, Pastor Scott

Dr. Scott Payne

Day Three Hundred Thirty-Six
The Pastor's Perspective: Your word for the day!

diversity – *(noun)* ***unlikeness; dissimilarity***
dih-**vur**-si-tee, dahy

Reading Plan: 1 Corinthians 12-14

Paul taught that Christianity functioned as a body. This meant that **diversity** would be essential for good health. The church would be similar to a body in that it would consist of many different working parts.

Love would be the heartbeat of the body. The body would function at its best when the members valued prophecy. Speaking in tongues was a gift to the church, primarily, as a witness to non-believers. Order within public worship was required.

Reflect on these thoughts:
- You are a part of the church. Where is your local membership?
- You must do your part within the church. What is your service in the church?
- You are to love other believers. How are you expressing your love for others?
- You must worship with other believers on a regular basis. When do you gather?

Take this to the next level: How are you contributing to the health of your church?

diversity: say it, believe it, live it!

This is my perspective for today, Pastor Scott

Day Three Hundred Thirty-Seven
The Pastor's Perspective: Your word for the day!

resurrection – *(noun)* ***reappearance; being raised from the dead***
rez-*uh*-**rek**-sh*uh* n

Reading Plan: 1 Corinthians 15-16

Paul called out a false teaching that was slipping into the church; some were saying that there would be no **resurrection** of the body. His appeal was based on the gospel; Jesus Christ was born of a virgin, lived a perfect life, died for the sins of those that would trust Him, and was resurrected from the dead three days later. Because of His resurrection those who trusted the gospel would also be resurrected.

Reflect on these thoughts:
- If there's no resurrection then there's no justification to believe Jesus.
- Jesus forgives sin and guarantees life will continue after physical death.
- As you are born physically, you must also be born spiritually.
- Jesus backs up His claim to give eternal life to those who trust in Him.

Take this to the next level: Are you trusting in Jesus for life abundant and eternal?

resurrection: say it, believe it, live it!

This is my perspective for today, Pastor Scott

Dr. Scott Payne

Day Three Hundred Thirty-Eight
The Pastor's Perspective: Your word for the day!

consolation – *(noun)* ***relief; comfort***
kon-s*uh*-**ley**-sh*uh* n

Reading Plan: 2 Corinthians 1-4

Christians would face challenging and difficult circumstances in their lives, but Paul taught that those experiences would strengthen the person and encourage others. Because of the struggles Christians would face, it would be important to support and pray for one another. Their **consolation** would come through God's presence and the influence of others.

The Spirit of God wrote His truth on the hearts of those who trusted Him. The early believers discovered their sufficiency in Christ alone! If sin brought judgment, how much more would righteousness bring blessing? The Spirit of the Lord removed the veil from the heart and allowed Christians to see the truth that set them free.

Satan bound the mind of those in the world, but God revealed His truth to those who trusted Jesus. Christians would not invest in the things of the world, rather in things that had eternal value.

Reflect on these thoughts:
- Don't let difficulties discourage you.
- When you come through hard times you can help others who will face hard times.
- Receive and live by the presence of Holy Spirit in your heart.
- Lay up treasures in Heaven.

Take this to the next level: Are you serving God by seeking to help others?

consolation: say it, believe it, receive it!

This is my perspective for today, Pastor Scott

Day Three Hundred Thirty-Nine
The Pastor's Perspective: Your word for the day!

altruism – *(noun)* ***unselfishness; benevolence***
al-troo-iz-*uh* m

Reading Plan: 2 Corinthians 5-9

It was important for followers of Christ to have a proper life perspective; life's focus was to be shaped by Heaven not earth. Believers realized they would face the judgment of Christ. Their sins would be forgiven, and their service to others would be recognized and rewarded.

Paul recognized the incredible giving spirit within the family of faith. **Altruism** characterized the early Christian church. Believers were to live in a sense of preparedness to support those who served or had need.

Reflect on these thoughts:
- You must be prepared for eternity.
- Your eternal home will be determined by your relationship to Jesus.
- Your response to God's favor in your life is to be a giver.
- You should be looking for opportunities to support those who love and serve the Lord.

Take this to the next level: Do you enjoy giving?

altruism: say it, believe it, live it!

This is my perspective for today, Pastor Scott

Dr. Scott Payne

Day Three Hundred Forty
The Pastor's Perspective: Your word for the day!

disguise – *(noun) façade; deceptive appearance*
dis-**gahyz**, dih-**skahyz**

Reading Plan: 2 Corinthians 10-13

Paul was very concerned with the **disguise** used by false apostles in the church. They were making much of themselves rather than Christ. The gospel was under assault by the corrupt message of these evil leaders. Paul gave a final warning to the church that he would deal with the troublemakers during his next visit.

Reflect on these thoughts:
- Don't deceive yourself or others with lies.
- Glory always goes to God not man.
- You will answer for the damage you do to the body of Christ.

Take this to the next level: Are your motives shaped by God or driven by your own interests?

disguise: say it, believe it, avoid it!

This is my perspective for today, Pastor Scott

Day Three Hundred Forty-One
The Pastor's Perspective: Your word for the day!

obdurate – *(adjective)* ***stubbornly unrepentant***
ob-doo-rit, -dyoo-

Reading Plan: Romans 1-3

There was some confusion among the early Christians as to their relationship to the Law. Paul made it very clear that a person was saved by grace through a personal relationship with Jesus Christ as Messiah, and that one's life became a righteous example. The righteous would live by faith in Jesus.

God's judgment would fall fairly on those who practiced unrighteousness. Some in the church community became known for their **obdurate** attitudes towards sinful actions. They thought they could practice evil believing it provided God greater opportunity to show His grace. That was the wrong attitude. Christians needed to live to glorify God through faithful actions.

Reflect on these thoughts:
- Believers are to live obedient lives by faith.
- A righteous God will judge sin.
- Becoming a part of God's family means you live like a child of God.
- Trust what Jesus did on the cross and then live following in His mission.

Take this to the next level: Are you practicing works of the law or works of faith?

obdurate: say it, believe it, avoid it!

This is my perspective for today, Pastor Scott

Dr. Scott Payne

Day Three Hundred Forty-Two
The Pastor's Perspective: Your word for the day!

justification – *(noun)* ***declaration of righteousness***
juhs-t*uh*-fi-**key**-sh*uh* n

Reading Plan: Romans 4-7

Christians discovered **justification** before God by faith in Jesus Christ rather than the Law. If the Law pointed out the sinfulness of man then Jesus pointed to the freedom faith brought to the soul of man. A person who received Jesus and His gospel died to the old sinful nature and was given a new life that would glorify the Lord.

The believer faced a daily struggle between the flesh and the Spirit. The conflict could only be handled successfully with a complete surrender to the Holy Spirit. Just as sin had once ruled one's life, now the born again believer would be ruled by the righteousness of Christ through the indwelling of His Spirit.

Reflect on these thoughts:
- Trust in Jesus and Him alone for your salvation.
- You are in a right relationship with God by the righteousness of Christ Jesus.
- You're no match for Satan but the Spirit of God can overcome the evil one.

Take this to the next level: Are you trying to please God with your works or your faith?

justification: say it, believe it, accept it!

This is my perspective for today, Pastor Scott

Day Three Hundred Forty-Three
The Pastor's Perspective: Your word for the day!

carnal – *(adjective)* ***worldly; sensual***
kahr-nl

Reading Plan: Romans 8-10

The early believers were to know the difference between living a **carnal** life versus a spiritual life. When a person received Jesus Christ as Messiah and Savior they were to die to their fleshly desires, and live the abundant life given by the indwelling of the Holy Spirit. The Holy Spirit also became the great advocate for the believer, interceding before the Heavenly Father.

Jews and Gentiles alike were to come to the Father by faith in Jesus Christ. Jesus fulfilled the law on behalf of anyone who would believe and confess Him as Savior and Lord. This was the message that Christians were to share with the whole world.

Reflect on these thoughts:
- His Spirit, not sin, controls Christians.
- The Holy Spirit is God's guarantee of abundant and eternal life.
- You are the object of God's love.
- Salvation is available to anyone who is willing to receive and confess Jesus.

Take this to the next level: Are you sharing the Good News?

carnal: say it, believe it, avoid it!

This is my perspective for today, Pastor Scott

Dr. Scott Payne

Day Three Hundred Forty-Four
The Pastor's Perspective: Your word for the day!

dissimulation – *(noun)* ***insincerity; dishonesty***
rez-*uh*-rek-sh*uh* n

Reading Plan: Romans 11-13

All Jews in the Old Testament were not saved; salvation came only to those that remained faithful to God. God's invitation of salvation was offered first to the Jew and then to the Gentile. God would reject anyone, including the Jew, if they did not trust in Him as the true God.

Each person of faith was to present himself or herself as a living sacrifice before God. Love would be a critical identifying mark of the Christian family. Love was to be without **dissimulation** among the members. This love would overcome the sinful temptations within the individual and the larger Christian family.

Reflect on these thoughts:
- A faith relationship with God is essential.
- Salvation is a gift from God to anyone who will surrender to Him.
- Everyone who trusts Jesus has a place in God's forever family.
- Love grows from serving the Spirit not the flesh.

Take this to the next level: Are you a fully committed follower of Jesus Christ?

dissimulation: say it, believe it, avoid it!

This is my perspective for today, Pastor Scott

Day Three Hundred Forty-Five
The Pastor's Perspective: Your word for the day!

edification – *(noun)* ***uplifting enlightenment or teaching; the building up of another***
ed-*uh*-fi-**key**-sh*uh* n

Reading Plan: Romans 14-16

Unity was a critical issue for the early Christian community. Believers were to avoid judging one another and do nothing to cause one another to stumble. The **edification** of believers was essential to the health of the church.

Paul wanted the believers in Rome to understand and value his call to share the gospel with Jews and Gentiles. This was an expectation he had for all believers; Gentiles would support Jews, and Jews would support Gentiles. He symbolized this spirit by expressing personal greeting to many of his co-workers in this endeavor.

Reflect on these thoughts:
- Always consider your witness before engaging in any activity.
- Be on the lookout for opportunities to help other believers.
- To be like Jesus live by the power of His Holy Spirit.
- Look for ways to encourage and thank other Christians.

Take this to the next level: Are you building up or tearing down the purposes of Christ?

edification: say it, believe it, live it!

This is my perspective for today, Pastor Scott

Dr. Scott Payne

Day Three Hundred Forty-Six
The Pastor's Perspective: Your word for the day!

constrained – *(adjective)* ***pressured; compelled***
k*uh* n-**streynd**

Reading Plan: Acts 20-23

Paul was a man **constrained** by the Holy Spirit to complete his God given mission. Nothing could deter him from accomplishing his faith walk to share the gospel to the Jews and Gentiles. The journey would bring great hardship on Paul, but God's provisions and protection would sustain him.

Reflect on these thoughts:
- Go where God leads, and He will guide you all the way.
- The Spirit will always be a threat to the flesh.
- God will use the most unlikely people and circumstances to accomplish His will.
- The plans of man are no match to the purposes of God.

Take this to the next level: Are you aware of God's spiritual covering over your life?

constrained: say it, believe it, live it!

This is my perspective for today, Pastor Scott

Day Three Hundred Forty-Seven
The Pastor's Perspective: Your word for the day!

witness – *(noun) testimony or one who gives a testimony of something observed, heard, or personally experienced*
wit-nis

Reading Plan: Acts 24-26

Paul was a threat to the Jews because he proclaimed Jesus as Messiah. His **witness** was having a great effect on the people but offended the popular position of the religious leaders. In their attempt to silence Paul, they had appealed to Rome to justify their decision to kill him. Roman leaders could find no reason for such action, and Paul's appeal to Caesar would send him to Rome.

Reflect on these thoughts:
- If God has changed your life then tell someone.
- Your **witness** is simply your story about what God has done and is doing in your life.
- You can always appeal to a higher authority.
- God is with people of faith.

Take this to the next level: Are you a credible **witness** for the gospel message of Jesus Christ?

witness: say it, believe it, live it!

This is my perspective for today, Pastor Scott

Dr. Scott Payne

Day Three Hundred Forty-Eight
The Pastor's Perspective: Your word for the day!

custody – *(noun)* ***responsibility for; charge of someone or something;*** **kuhs**-t*uh*-dee

Reading Plan: Acts 27-28

The Roman guards felt like they had been given **custody** of Paul, but he was really in God's hands. God had told Paul he would go to Rome, and He would protect Paul all the way. Paul refused to let the circumstances he faced during the journey to Rome discourage him. He trusted God's promise and would overcome the adversities by exercising his faith in the One behind the promise. After arriving in Rome he would continue his mission to share the good news, the gospel of Jesus Christ.

Reflect on these thoughts:
- God's promise is better than man's plans.
- God has your back when you're walking out His purpose.
- When you listen to God you look at your life differently.
- God finishes what He starts.

Take this to the next level: Are you allowing God to raise you above your circumstances?

custody: say it, believe it, live it God's way!

This is my perspective for today, Pastor Scott

Day Three Hundred Forty-Nine
The Pastor's Perspective: Your word for the day!

deceit – *(noun) **dishonesty; fraud***
dih-**seet**

Reading Plan: Colossians, Philemon

Paul wrote to the church at Colossae warning them about the **deceit** being used by certain teachers within the group. He exhorted them to avoid becoming disqualified by ungodly actions. The believers were to follow the faithful teachings Paul had given them and mature their faith to reflect Christ's character.

Paul wrote commending the slave Onesimus to his once master Philemon. Onesimus had fled to Rome and apparently taken something of importance from Philemon when he escaped. Once in Rome he became a Christian and served the imprisoned Paul. Because of his transformation and servant's heart, Paul sent him back to Philemon with a letter encouraging his forgiveness and acceptance.

Reflect on these thoughts:
- Check all teaching to the Word of God.
- People should see Christ in you.
- Failure does not have to be final.
- As a Christian you should take responsibility for the way you live.

Take this to the next level: Do you value your relationship with God's Word and people?

deceit: say it, believe it, avoid it!

This is my perspective for today, Pastor Scott

Dr. Scott Payne

Day Three Hundred Fifty
The Pastor's Perspective: Your word for the day!

grieve – *(verb)* ***sadden or distress someone***
greev

Reading Plan: Ephesians

The work of the Holy Spirit was very active sealing the gospel of salvation in the lives of the first local Christians. The Gentile converts were to understand this truth and thankfully celebrate their acceptance into God's forever family. Paul warned believers not to **grieve** the Holy Spirit. Prayers were to be offered up on a daily basis for strength that only the Holy Spirit could give. Paul encouraged the church to be driven by unity and love, respecting diversity and personal responsibility.

Reflect on these thoughts:
- You should acknowledge and celebrate the gift of the Holy Spirit.
- God's grace comes to you through faith not works of the Law.
- Unity and love is discovered through a personal relationship with Jesus Christ.
- Christianity functions within the context of submission to other believers.
- The battles believers face are spiritual not physical.

Take this to the next level: Does self or Spirit fuel your life?

grieve: say it, believe it, avoid it!

This is my perspective for today, Pastor Scott

Day Three Hundred Fifty-One
The Pastor's Perspective: Your word for the day!

rivalry – *(noun)* **contention; conflict**
rahy-v*uh* l-ree

Reading Plan: Philippians

Paul counseled the early Christians to avoid a spirit of pride and **rivalry**. Believers were to live out the character of Jesus, which was best demonstrated through humility and love. To live like Jesus meant to honor and give glory to God the Father.

It was important for Christians to keep their focus on godly living. They were to think about, put into practice, and constantly encourage righteous living.

Reflect on these thoughts:
- Make sure your walk is worthy of your Lord.
- Don't make life all about you.
- Do the will of the Father.
- Your highest priority is to bring God glory.

Take this to the next level: How are you encouraging other Christians to mature in their faith?

rivalry: say it, believe it, avoid it!

This is my perspective for today, Pastor Scott

Dr. Scott Payne

Day Three Hundred Fifty-Two
The Pastor's Perspective: Your word for the day!

mediator – *(noun) go-between; peacemaker*
mee-dee-ey-ter

Reading Plan: I Timothy

The instruction to Timothy was to teach and protect sound doctrine within the church. God's people would face false teachers, and it was the responsibility of faithful leaders to uphold the Truth to the believers. Paul emphasized a central doctrine that was to be proclaimed, one **mediator** between God and man, the man Jesus Christ. Paul also encouraged the church to select sound leaders. There were clear expectations given for those servant leaders.

Reflect on these thoughts:
- Christians must receive the instruction of the scriptures and live by them.
- Always test what is taught against the whole Word of God.
- Jesus is the only way to connect with God.
- The best leaders are faithful to the Word and have a servant's heart.

Take this to the next level: Do you approach God through Jesus Christ as Savior and Lord?

mediator: say it, believe it, trust Him!

This is my perspective for today, Pastor Scott

Day Three Hundred Fifty-Three
The Pastor's Perspective: Your word for the day!

subvert – *(verb) sabotage; corrupt; overthrow*
s*uh* b-**vurt**

Reading Plan: Titus

Paul exhorted Christians to live worthy of their calling. This meant righteous living within the church and outside the church in the non-believing community. They had been saved by faith to serve.

Titus was given clear instruction to stop those that would **subvert** the church or individual believers through their false teachings. Titus would recognize these wicked teachers because their works would not match their profession of Christ.

Through their righteous deeds the early believers would become great witnesses for the gospel of Jesus Christ, and the world would take note of their Christian character.

Reflect on these thoughts:
- Your behavior should be consistent with your claim to be a Christian.
- Good works are natural expressions for godly people.
- May your life be an attractive reflection of God's glory.

Take this to the next level: What are you doing to ensure you stay well connected to Christ?

subvert: say it, believe it, avoid it!

This is my perspective for today, Pastor Scott

Dr. Scott Payne

Day Three Hundred Fifty-Four
The Pastor's Perspective: Your word for the day!

imperishable – *(adjective)* ***everlasting; permanent***
im-per-i-sh*uh*-b*uh* l

Reading Plan: I Peter

Peter wanted to encourage believers facing persecution with a reminder of the **imperishable** gift they had received by accepting the gospel of Jesus Christ. The gift was both present and future for those who trusted Jesus as Messiah. God's power would guide them through the sufferings of this life and His power would provide for them eternal life to come. They would not be disappointed. They were to reflect God's glory before all people by living holy lives.

Reflect on these thoughts:
- Those who suffer will be rewarded.
- Keep your daily life perspective in check by remembering God's promise of eternal life.
- Christ's death and resurrection is God's guarantee of what awaits His children of faith.
- Keep Christ first at home and in the community.

Take this to the next level: Do you live like you're a member of God's forever family?

imperishable: say it, believe it, live it!

This is my perspective for today, Pastor Scott

Day Three Hundred Fifty-Five
The Pastor's Perspective: Your word for the day!

guarantor *(noun)* ***insurer; backer that guarantees***
gar-*uh* n-tawr, ter

Reading Plan: Hebrews 1-6

Jesus was superior to the angels, prophets, and Moses because He was fully God. He became the **guarantor** of the complete covenant relationship God offered man. All those who came before Him set the stage for God's pure purpose in salvation to be realized. Jesus became the perfect High Priest for His people because he suffered like them; therefore, with understanding, He could present their requests to the Father. In addition, He overcame the temptation to sin in order to defeat death.

Reflect on these thoughts:
- Jesus is the ultimate revelation of God to you.
- Jesus is the perfect sacrifice for your sins.
- You can depend on Jesus as your true High Priest.

Take this to the next level: Do you trust Jesus as your only connection to the Father?

guarantor: say it, believe it, celebrate it!

This is my perspective for today, Pastor Scott

Dr. Scott Payne

Day Three Hundred Fifty-Six
The Pastor's Perspective: Your word for the day!

indemnify – *(verb)* ***repay; make payment to insure or guarantee against future loss***
in-**dem**-n*uh*-fahy

Reading Plan: Hebrews 7-10

Jesus became the High Priest like no other. Former high priests were men of flesh called out to service in their role by their birthright. Jesus was the Son of God who came to the earth to open a new door of access to God that no man could open. Not even the Law could do what Christ Jesus did. Jesus would **indemnify** God for the sin debt of those who trusted Him as Messiah. The priests that preceded Jesus could offer the blood of animals to symbolize forgiveness, but Jesus would offer His sinless blood to atone for sin. Those who confessed Jesus and received His guarantee of eternal life would have total connection to the Father.

Reflect on these thoughts:
- God's judgment is inevitable; let Jesus pay your sin debt.
- Faith in Jesus produces the perseverance needed to be victorious.
- Jesus gives access to the Father to all who trust Him as Savior and Lord.

Take this to the next level: Have you asked Jesus to pay your sin debt?

indemnify: say it, believe it, receive it!

This is my perspective for today, Pastor Scott

Day Three Hundred Fifty-Seven
The Pastor's Perspective: Your word for the day!

wanion – *(noun)* ***curse***
won-*yuh* n

Reading Plan: Hebrews 11-13

The writer of Hebrews continued the theme of faith by listing a group of Old Testament hall of famers. These men and women kept faith in God even though they never saw the fulfillment of God's promise to send Messiah. The writer declared that his readers were without excuse, because they knew the founder and perfecter of their faith, Jesus Christ.

Christians could endure times of testing believing God would strengthen and purify them. Difficulties would become defining moments separating the children of God from the children of the world. God was the righteous judge who could be trusted and worshipped by the person committed to serve Him. The **wanion** of the unrighteous was as certain as the absolution of the righteous.

Believers were to honor and follow their faithful leaders. They were also directed to live holy lives, avoiding the sins that would hinder their spiritual sight and wisdom.

Reflect on these thoughts:
- Faith sees life through God-given eyesight.
- Faith produces a God-given endurance.
- God can be trusted.
- Jesus came first as Savior-Servant; He will come again as Supreme-King.

Take this to the next level: Are you living by faith or by sight?

wanion: say it, believe it, avoid it!

This is my perspective for today, Pastor Scott

Dr. Scott Payne

Day Three Hundred Fifty-Eight
The Pastor's Perspective: Your word for the day!

allure – *(verb)* ***entice; captivate***
*uh-***loo r**

Reading Plan: 2 Timothy

Suffering was a path many early Christians had to walk, and Paul was no exception. He reminded Timothy that God could get glory even through trying times. Believers had the assurance that their faithful, unwavering commitment to God would be rewarded.

Paul warned Timothy and the early Christians to be watchful for the tactics used by Satan to harm the believer. One of Satan's destructive ploys was to **allure** people with temporary pleasures that led to broken fellowship with God or even physical death.

Reflect on these thoughts:
- Be bold in your faith remembering God is with you.
- You are always teaching someone something; make sure it's Truth.
- The closer you walk with God the more obvious sin becomes.
- Know the Truth and the Truth will set you free!

Take this to the next level: Are you fleeing the Devil and seeking the Lord?

allure: say it, believe it, avoid it!

This is my perspective for today, Pastor Scott

Day Three Hundred Fifty-Nine
The Pastor's Perspective: Your word for the day!

consanguinity – *(noun)* ***kinship; close relationship***
kon-sang-**gwin**-i-tee

Reading Plan: 2 Peter, Jude

Peter emphasized the **consanguinity** with Jesus and the Holy Spirit that was required in order to avoid the lure of false prophets and teachers. Those who twisted the gospel for their gain would reap a disastrous end. God's people who remained faithful to the Word and the leadership of the Holy Spirit would reap a harvest of joy.

Jude continued the theme of faithfulness to the Truth and the avoidance of false teachers. Believers were to defend and live by the truth of sound doctrine.

Reflect on these thoughts:
- Celebrate God in you by living in the power of His Holy Spirit.
- Only God can reveal His Truth.
- Overcome opposition by trusting God's Word and presence.
- God will judge the wicked.

Take this to the next level: Are you staying close to God and His Truth?

consanguinity: say it, believe it, live it!

This is my perspective for today, Pastor Scott

Dr. Scott Payne

Day Three Hundred Sixty
The Pastor's Perspective: Your word for the day!

gnosticism – *(noun) religions with doctrines centered around extreme works and search for mysterious knowledge*
nos-t*uh*-siz-*uh* m

Reading Plan: 1 John

One of John's main concerns was to combat the false doctrine of salvation that had been promoted by **gnosticism**. The Christian teaching was that salvation came through the repentance of sin and faith in the death and resurrection of Jesus Christ to guarantee new life. The early Christians were to focus on the essentials of their faith: sound doctrine, spiritual maturity, and a passionate commitment to Christ and the faith family. The Holy Spirit would give the believer everything needed for victorious living.

Reflect on these thoughts:
- Jesus is God.
- Christians are sinners saved by grace.
- Christians love righteousness and hate sin.
- Denying Jesus is saying no to God.
- To know Jesus is to know Truth, receive forgiveness of sin, have an advocate with God, and receive power over Satan.

Take this to the next level: Are you living by faith grounded in a personal relationship with Jesus Christ?

gnosticism: say it, don't believe it, avoid it!

This is my perspective for today, Pastor Scott

Day Three Hundred Sixty-One
The Pastor's Perspective: Your word for the day!

purveyor – *(noun)* ***providers; transmitters***
per-**vey**-erz

Reading Plan: 2, 3 John

John took written action to combat the **purveyors** of falsehoods that seemed to be acceptable in the early church. He encouraged the Christian community to guard against teachings and individuals that were spreading deceit. Believers were to validate their lives with actions that were consistent with God's Word.

Reflect on these thoughts:
- It is the nature of Christians to love and obey God's Word.
- It's never too difficult to find false teachers and false doctrine.
- Christians should support those that are in full-time ministry.
- Christian discipline is necessary for church health.

Take this to the next level: Are you doing all you can to avoid those who live and teach deceptively?

purveyor: say it, believe it, avoid it!

This is my perspective for today, Pastor Scott

Dr. Scott Payne

Day Three Hundred Sixty-Two
The Pastor's Perspective: Your word for the day!

cosmic – *(adjective)* ***beyond the earth; universal;***
koz-mik

Reading Plan: Revelation 1-5

John began Revelation by addressing seven churches in Asia (now western Turkey). God had made it known to John that five of these churches were not prepared for the return of Jesus Christ. They had become too focused on the material world instead of on the **cosmic** conflict between good and evil, the demonic versus the spiritual.

John's vision into Heaven saw continuous worship being experienced. The Lamb became the center of attention as He received a sealed scroll.

Reflect on these thoughts:
- Jesus has already defeated Satan through His death and resurrection.
- The Holy Spirit is with His church and knows the demonic forces Christians must battle.
- Christians must allow the Holy Spirit to define life.
- Jesus is in control, and you can trust His plan.

Take this to the next level: Do you recognize life's spiritual realm and the victory Jesus offers you?

cosmic: say it, believe it, acknowledge it!

This is my perspective for today, Pastor Scott

Day Three Hundred Sixty-Three
The Pastor's Perspective: Your word for the day!

tribulation – *(noun) **extreme misery; severe distress and suffering***
trib-y*uh*-**ley**-sh*uh* n

Reading Plan: Revelation 6-11

Human history would climax with a final period of **tribulation**. John's vision revealed seven seals related to the scroll given to the Lamb. Each seal was opened introducing a new era of suffering. After the final seal was opened, John heard the sound of seven separate trumpets. Each trumpet announced a judgment against the world, precipitated by the prayers of the saints, all God's people in Heaven.

Reflect on these thoughts:
- Suffering will strengthen a saint but destroy a sinner.
- There's no way God's final judgment can be avoided.
- Trusting in God will get you through times of suffering.
- Those who witness for God live resurrected lives.

Take this to the next level: Are you prepared to stand firm in your faithful witness of God?

tribulation: say it, believe it, faith Him through it!

This is my perspective for today, Pastor Scott

Dr. Scott Payne

Day Three Hundred Sixty-Four
The Pastor's Perspective: Your word for the day!

enmity – *(noun) **loathing; hostility***
en-mi-tee

Reading Plan: Revelation 12-18

The **enmity** between God and Satan was entering its final days. Satan was determined to destroy as many lives as possible before his demise. God would begin a final series of judgments against Satan and those who carried his mark. Even during an intense season of God releasing His wrath, the nonbelievers cursed Him. The stage was now set for the final conflict and Satan's ultimate defeat.

Reflect on these thoughts:
- Don't be deceived by the false claims and destructive ways of Satan.
- Pay attention to what is eternal, not what is temporal.
- Flee what is evil.
- God wins!

Take this to the next level: Have you declared whose side you are on? Choose well!

enmity: say it, believe it, avoid it!

This is my perspective for today, Pastor Scott

Day Three Hundred Sixty-Five
The Pastor's Perspective: Your word for the day!

adoration – *(noun) **devotion; worship***
ad-*uh*-**rey**-sh*uh* n

Reading Plan: Revelation 19-22

John saw a time when everyone would know that only God is or has ever been worthy of our **adoration**. The Bible began and would end with all of creation praising God. What was the difference from beginning to end? The sin, rebellion and death that soon entered in Genesis ended in Revelation when John saw evil totally destroyed and eliminated. God prepared a new earth of perfection for His people to dwell and live eternally with Him.

Reflect on these thoughts:
- Jesus guarantees the ultimate victory over evil.
- Jesus first came to offer forgiveness. He'll come again to judge.
- Faith in Jesus places your name in the Book of Life.
- Come quickly Lord Jesus!

Take this to the next level: Are you ready to worship Him for eternity?

adoration: say it, believe it, give it to Jesus!

This is my perspective for today, Pastor Scott

FINAL THOUGHTS

So, the question really is, "Are you ready to worship Him for eternity?" After reading the Bible with me for a year, you should be more certain than ever before, that God loves you … He wants to be your God, and He wants you to be His people.

If you read the Scriptures with me, you have seen God from the beginning to the end of the age. You understand that God the Father, God the Son (Jesus), and God the Holy Spirit is one God, functioning in complete unity to redeem mankind. When the Son, who was "with God and was God" (John 1:1) "became flesh" (John 1:14) and came into this world to "seek and to save that which was lost" (Luke 19:10), man was no longer without hope. When this same Jesus died on the cross and took the sins of the world … my sin and your sin … on Himself to take our punishment and pay the penalty for our sins, hope was restored to the world. When the resurrection power of God, raised Jesus, death was overcome, and now you and I can live eternally, with God, our Creator and Sustainer of life.

To receive this gift of eternal life, which cannot be earned and is not deserved, you must repent … turn away from the sin in your life (Acts 3:19) and confess with your mouth that Jesus Christ is Lord and believe in your heart that He was raised from the dead, then you will be saved (Romans 10:9). Don't trust me! Trust the God breathed, inerrant Word that you have just read! If you need help understanding how this can apply to you, or if you just have some questions, please write to me at: drscottpayne@gmail.com. I want to hear from you, and I will respond to your email as quickly as possible.

If you have already received Salvation, I hope that reading through the Bible with me has brought you closer to God and will continue to change your life and cause you to love Him more every day, as you continue to know Him more and live your life for Him.

So, wherever you are on your Spiritual Journey, I have to ask you one last time to ...

Take this to the next level: Are you ready to worship Him for eternity? What will you do today to give Him the worship He is worthy of? What about tomorrow and every day going forward?

God the Father, God the Son, God the Holy Spirit: Love Him, Worship Him, Praise Him, Trust Him ... today, tomorrow and forever.

This is my perspective for ETERNITY, Pastor Scott

ABOUT THE AUTHOR

First and foremost, Dr. Scott Payne, or Pastor Scott, as he prefers to be called, is a Christian who loves the Lord and loves God's Word. His understanding of the Bible grows deeper and richer as he reads, studies, teaches, discusses the Scriptures, and most importantly, depends on the Holy Spirit to give him spiritual insight.

Pastor Scott and his wife, Billie, live in the Metro Memphis, Tennessee, area, where he is the pastor of The Church at Schilling Farms in Collierville, Tennessee. They have three children, Jason and his wife, Toni; Amanda and her husband, Todd; and Allison and her husband, Bobby. They also have nine grandchildren.

After obtaining his undergraduate degree and his master's degree, Pastor Scott received his doctorate of theology from Andersonville Baptist Theological Seminary. His ministry spans forty years, and he has been the senior pastor of his current church since 1990, when he founded it. He is the kind of pastor everyone wants! He is an excellent preacher, teacher, shepherd, evangelist, missionary, writer, leader, and follower of God's leading. He is an encourager, a worker, and a friend who is quick to give grace, ready to help, and has a heart of empathy, all of which the Lord uses to draw people closer to Himself.